PRAISE FOR *TRUST & BETRAYAL IN THE WORKPLACE*

"*Trust & Betrayal*'s principles are easily understood and transmitted into action steps. Not just a help in the workplace, the book provides an excellent road map for all life's relationships. In this new edition I especially appreciated the 'Stories from the Field'; they bring to life the model, the tools, and the underlying principles that make everything work."

> —Dale Hinman, senior manager, Global Staffing, the Boeing Company

"The power of *Trust & Betrayal in the Workplace* lies in the Reinas' effective formula for restoring and building trust in employees. The core characteristics of transformative trust can become guideposts for any individual or group."

> —Major General Martha Rainville, adjutant general, Vermont National Guard

"Samuel Clemens observed that everyone talks about the weather, but no one does anything about it. The same might be said for trust. Well, Samuel, the Reinas have done something about it! They have given us the insights and tools to take on one of the most important constructs in personal and business relationships. The Reinas' work will provide you with the means to build trust immediately and over the longer term. This is a must-read!"

> —Richard Hossack, Ph.D., president, Mercer Delta Consulting Limited, Toronto, Ontario, Canada

"Dennis and Michelle Reina have nailed it! *Trust & Betrayal in the Workplace* is *the* book on trust and workplace relationships. The Reinas clearly map out a heart-and-soul, practical approach to trust building—essential to developing leadership credibility, employee engagement, team collaboration, and organizational performance. A must-read for leaders hoping to retain talent and for employees wanting more fulfilling work."

> —Sharon Jordan-Evans, coauthor of *Love 'Em or Lose 'Em: Getting Good People to Stay* and *Love It, Don't Leave It: 26 Ways to Get What You Want at Work*

"The essence of organizational life flows from the relationships of people who work together. Michelle and Dennis Reina have created a handbook for leaders and followers alike that teaches us the techniques we need to attain and sustain these relationships. This book is *the* key to achieving a goal we all seek: a productive and joyful work life."

> —Nancy Formella, MSN, RN, CNAA, senior nurse executive, Dartmouth-Hitchcock Medical Center, Lebanon, New Hampshire

"This book highlights the importance of relationships and how trust can be harnessed to improve business outcomes and the working environment. This is essential reading for leaders and those who aspire to lead, as well as anyone who wants to understand how to build professional relationships. Thoroughly recommended!"

—Martin L. North, general manager, Fujitsu Consulting, Fujitsu, Australia

"An organization will never possess an environment of trust until the leadership possesses an understanding of the value a trust environment brings. The material contained in this book offers both a clear understanding of the value of trust and insights into methodologies for developing a high-trust environment."

—Darrell E. Thomsen Jr., chaplain, United States Military Academy, West Point

"Dennis and Michelle Reina provide a useful jump-start in their thorough analysis of trust and how to build it. Their book can help teams succeed, as people learn to create positive, productive, pain-free relationships."

—Rosabeth Moss Kanter, Harvard Business School, and author of *World Class* and *Rosabeth Moss Kanter on the Frontiers of Management*

"*Trust & Betrayal in the Workplace* has provided us with a practical pathway to organizational transformation. It contains tools that we have used in all of our relationships, internally and externally, to the organization. We consider the book a 'must read' for new leaders and mature executives alike."

—Lori J. Brown, vice president, Children's Hospital and Health System of Milwaukee

"Business leaders are constantly wrestling with and are often stymied by trust issues—that is, gossip, hoarding information, failure to take action, hidden agendas, people not delivering as promised. The Reinas show us how to respond to these complex situations in an effective way, one that cultivates workplaces where people *want* to produce!"

—Patricia S. Seemann, CEO, Sphere Advisors, Switzerland

"The Reinas remind us that it isn't love that makes the world go 'round—it's trust. We mustn't neglect it or take it for granted, for once it's lost, trust is almost impossible to rebuild and repair."

—B. J. Gallagher, coauthor of *A Peacock in the Land of Penguins* and *What Would Buddha Do at Work?*

"Dennis and Michelle Reina provide a simple formula to build effective relationships in our organizations. The book helps us focus on trust within ourselves and others, so we can significantly change our business world into an ethical, efficient, and productive environment. Their passion for the subject inspired us to use the Reina Trust & Betrayal Model to transform our organization."

—Barry Rassin, CEO and chairman, Doctors Hospital Health System, Nassau, Bahamas

"We are thrilled to use *Trust & Betrayal in the Workplace* in our Executive Leadership programs! Dennis and Michelle help our executives better understand the dynamics of trust and betrayal. They learn behaviors to develop and sustain trusting relationships."

   —Deirdre Dixon, program director, the TECO Center for Leadership, University of Tampa

"I just finished reading *Trust & Betrayal in the Workplace,* and I must tell you it's a great book! I've been using the Reinas' approach since I arrived at the Library of Congress, and it has made a huge difference in our office's credibility and productivity."

   —Col. Karen D. Lloyd, U.S. Army, *retired*, Washington, D.C.

"Wow, Reinas! I adore your easy and practical style. *Trust & Betrayal in the Workplace* demonstrates Emotional Intelligence in action. What every leader needs to know and develop in others."

   —Katrina Burrus, Ph.D., president, MKB Conseil and Coaching, Switzerland

"*Trust & Betrayal in the Workplace* is a road map to healing individuals, teams, and organizations. This book supports individuals to 'Know Thyself,' enables teams to create healthy and supportive relationships, and informs organizations of ways to avoid the pitfalls of betrayal. An essential asset to all leaders desiring increased effectiveness and productivity in the workplace."

   —Angela Airall, organizational effectiveness consultant, New Jersey

"All too often, organizations focus on the short term and, in the process, lose the essence of their greatness, their people, and their relationships. This book is the first to tackle the hard stuff of relationships—building trust."

   —Sharon Reynolds, program manager, Strategic Planning and Marketing, Fujitsu Australia and New Zealand

"*Trust & Betrayal* is an unusual mix of conceptual insights and real-world advice. Michelle and Dennis Reina bring us fascinating breakthroughs in understanding how trust is built and destroyed, as well as a very practical measurement model that provides vital information for improving corporate performance."

   —Philippe Masson, author of *Manager Humaniste,* France

"Most leaders acknowledge the need for trust to exist in their organizations, and the consequences when trust is broken. Yet few of us know what to do to rebuild and maintain trust. In *Trust & Betrayal in the Workplace,* the Reinas reveal how we all break trust without intending to, and then they show us how we can rebuild trust. They help make trust and leadership into a science, but happily not rocket science!"

   —Jonathan Winter, founder, the Ci Group, England

"Trust is the glue that holds relationships together. The Reinas give us valuable insights on how it can be built and preserved for the good of all parties."

—Price Pritchett, Ph.D., chairman, Pritchett & Associates

"Thank you for the road map to a place called *trust*. May we never lose our way."

—Sissy Franks, vice president, Health Care Education Association, and director, Outpatient Center and Education

"*Trust & Betrayal in the Workplace* is a timely reminder that business is built on relationships, not just profit-and-loss statements. The principles and accompanying descriptions resonated loudly and the exercises at the end of each chapter provoke further thought and discussion. A valuable handbook to help negotiate organizational change."

—Frances Bowron, project director, Australia

"The Reinas have shown us that trust is more than just a word, but the nexus that holds corporations together. This glorious homily demands the attention of all human resource professionals and executives at every level within any organization."

—Neil S. Reyer, vice president, Corporate Dining Services, Chase Manhattan Bank

"If mutual trust is present, a relationship can weather even the most violent upheavals and offensives; if trust is absent, a relationship will break beneath the stress of change. *Trust & Betrayal in the Workplace* shows how to develop trust and how to maintain its predominance within your company."

—Tom Corbin, assistant treasurer and director of business services, Middlebury College, Vermont

Trust & Betrayal in the Workplace

Second Edition

Trust & Betrayal in the Workplace

Building Effective Relationships in Your Organization

Dennis S. Reina, Ph.D. & Michelle L. Reina, Ph.D.

BK

BERRETT-KOEHLER PUBLISHERS, INC.
San Francisco

Copyright © 2006 by Dennis S. Reina, Ph.D. and Michelle L. Reina, Ph.D.

Berrett-Koehler Publishers, Inc.
235 Montgomery Street, Suite 650
San Francisco, CA 94104-2916
Tel: (415) 288-0260   Fax: (415) 362-2512   www.bkconnection.com

Ordering Information

Quantity sales. Special discounts are available on quantity purchases by corporations, associations, and others. For details, contact the "Special Sales Department" at the Berrett-Koehler address above.

Individual sales. Berrett-Koehler publications are available through most bookstores. They can also be ordered directly from Berrett-Koehler: Tel: (800) 929-2929;
Fax: (802) 864-7626; www.bkconnection.com

Orders for college textbook/course adoption use. Please contact Berrett-Koehler: Tel: (800) 929-2929; Fax: (802) 864-7626.

Orders by U.S. trade bookstores and wholesalers. Please contact Ingram Publisher Services, Tel: (800) 509-4887; Fax: (800) 838-1149; E-mail: customer.service@ingrampublisherservices.com; or visit www.ingrampublisherservices.com/Ordering for details about electronic ordering.
Berrett-Koehler and the BK logo are registered trademarks of Berrett-Koehler Publishers, Inc.

Printed in the United States of America

Berrett-Koehler books are printed on long-lasting acid-free paper. When it is available, we choose paper that has been manufactured by environmentally responsible processes. These may include using trees grown in sustainable forests, incorporating recycled paper, minimizing chlorine in bleaching, or recycling the energy produced at the paper mill.

Library of Congress Cataloging-in-Publication Data

Reina, Dennis S., 1950–
    Trust and betrayal in the workplace : building effective
relationships in your organization / Michelle and Dennis Reina.
      p. cm.
    Rev. ed. of: Trust and betrayal in the workplace. 1999
    Includes bibliographic references and index.
    ISBN-10:1-57675-377-8; ISBN-13:978-1-57675-377-4
    1. Organizational behavior.   2. Trust.   3. Interpersonal
relations.   4. Organizational effectiveness.   5. Work environment.
6. Psychology, Industrial.   I. Reina, Dennis, 1950– .   II. Title.
III. Title: Trust and betrayal in the workplace.

    HD58.7.R4388   2006
    158.7—dc22
                             2005052414

Second Edition
10 09 08 07   10 9 8 7 6 5 4 3 2

Cover design: permastudio
Interior design and production: Jonathan Peck, Dovetail Publishing Services

For our children, Patrick and William,

And our godchildren, Timothy and Julia,

Who open our hearts,

Feed our spirits,

Teach us about relationships,

And nurture our capacity for trust

CONTENTS

PREFACE

This book is about trust: the power when it exists, the problems when it doesn't, the pain when it is betrayed and the opportunities for its renewal. Our purpose in writing this book is to help people at all levels of any organization create, support, and, if necessary, rebuild trust in themselves and with others.

This book is about creating more productive, engaging, and rewarding work environments for all, arising from work relationships built on trust, infused with spirit—relationships that inspire leaders and employees alike. The principles, practices, tools, and techniques offered in *Trust & Betrayal in the Workplace* apply to anyone, in any kind of relationship, at any level of responsibility, and in any kind of setting.

Today, more than ever, there is a need for trust in the workplace. Our processes are growing in complexity, the global market poses increased demands on people, and collaboration is needed like never before. Organizations and people face increasing challenges, some associated with growth and expansion, others with downsizing or restructuring. Change and transition have become commonplace in all organizations. The universal element that never changes is the need for relationships. Why? Because of one simple truth: Business is conducted through relationships and trust is the foundation of effective relationships.

Countless numbers of people in the workplace today are in pain, and many organizations are hurting. After years of constant change— years of downsizing, restructuring, and reengineering, or of mergers and growth—trust among people at every level of organizations is at an all-time low. You may have personally felt the pain of a breach of trust or even a betrayal during the course of your working career. People with whom you work may have misread your intentions when you honestly felt you were acting in the best interests of the organization. You may have been accused of not "walking your talk" or been disappointed when you felt others fell similarly short.

Unmet expectations, disappointments, broken trust, and betrayals aren't restricted to big events like restructurings and downsizings. They crop up every day on the job. Leaders are beginning to realize that people's trust and commitment to the organization affect their performance. We use the term *leaders* in a broad sense, referring to all individuals who demonstrate leadership behaviors at all levels of responsibility.

Trust takes time to develop; it is easy to lose and hard to regain. It is a fragile yet indispensable element in any relationship. By first trusting in themselves, it is possible for leaders to develop caring, genuine relationships and build trust with their people and for employees to develop effective relationships with one another.

WHO SHOULD READ THIS BOOK

This book is designed to help anyone who has the desire to cultivate trusting relationships with the people with whom they work. You may feel that your organization has a fairly healthy level of trust and you want to further build upon it, because you know it will give your organization a competitive edge. You may see signs that tell you trust is vulnerable. The "grape vine" may be in overdrive, relationships may be breaking down, people may not be following through on their commitments, climate survey results may be less than desirable, and people may be leaving the company. Your instincts may be telling you that "something is just not quite right."

Our focus is on leaders, managers, and the people they serve, who value relationships and want to understand what trust means, how it is built, how it is broken and how it may be rebuilt in order to create effective relationships. For many, building trust—and more importantly rebuilding it—may seem like an overwhelming task. We find that whereas leaders want it, they are just not sure how to go about fostering it. Here we help you, those you serve, and those you turn to for support, such as human resource and organizational development professionals.

We explore behaviors that build trusting relationships, behaviors that contribute to betrayal, and the actions you can take to lead the process of rebuilding and sustaining trust. *Trust & Betrayal in the Workplace* will help you understand and appreciate the complex dynamics of trust and betrayal. Your understanding of trust will be improved—as will your awareness of betrayal and its consequences. This book serves as a comprehensive reference and practical guide to building trust and honoring relationships between individuals, within teams, and throughout organizations, in good times and in challenging times.

OVERVIEW OF THE BOOK

Understanding the complexity of trust and betrayal is challenging work, as we have learned from firsthand life experience, years of research and work in numerous organizations! The topic of trust is emotionally charged and means different things to different people. The Reina Trust & Betrayal Model provides an understandable framework for this book. We take the abstract and make it concrete; we take the intangible and make it tangible.

We use the model to raise your awareness of the dynamics of trust and betrayal and provide you with a shared understanding and a common language. The model helps you discuss trust-related issues and take action on them in a thoughtful manner to create and maintain healthy levels of trust in your organization. The model is built layer by layer, with figures illustrating the important components that contribute to trust between people, within teams, and throughout organizations.

The book has five parts. Part I, Chapter 1, discusses the need for trust in the workplace. We address its importance: the business need and the human need for trust. The price people and organizations pay when it is low and the payoff when it is high.

In Part II, we introduce the Trust and Betrayal Model, a practical and proven framework for understanding the dynamics of trust and betrayal in workplace relationships. We devote the three chapters in Part II to discussing the three specific types of trust in our model—*the trust of character:* contractual trust, *the trust of disclosure:* communication trust, and *trust of capability:* competence trust. We explore the specific behaviors that build each type of trust and bring life to them through examples and vignettes.

Part III takes us to where trust begins with Chapter 5 exploring our readiness and willingness to trust in ourselves and others, our capacity for trust. Chapter 6 takes us on a deeper exploration of *how* we trust through the lens of the four Capacity for Trust Attributes.

With trust comes betrayal. Part IV discusses the word "betrayal" and why it is important that we understand it. We look at what causes trust to break down or be betrayed, and what can be done when that happens. Chapter 7, How Trust is Broken, discusses the big things as well as the subtle, day-to-day occurrences that cause people to feel betrayed and the subsequent consequences to individuals, relationships and performance. Chapter 8, How Trust Is Rebuilt, provides steps to rebuild trust and to heal the disappointment or pain of betrayal. Chapter 9, Transformative Trust, examines the four characteristics that create transformative trust: conviction, courage, compassion, and community. We show you how they work, their value, and how you can achieve transformative trust within your team or organization.

Part V is about trust building in the field. Chapter 10 discusses rebuilding trust within teams. Chapter 11 talks about rebuilding trust within organizations. Chapter 12 pulls the book together through peoples' lived experiences. We tell stories of how people in organizations have used the Trust & Betrayal Model and the principles discussed throughout the book. We provide examples and vignettes that use their voices to tell their true stories.

At the end of each chapter "Trust Building in Action" provides reflective questions to help integrate your understanding of the material discussed. We also give application exercises to help you use the material in your work and relationships. Trust Tips and Trust Notes remind you of key points in each chapter.

DEVELOPMENT OF THIS BOOK

Collectively, we have worked and conducted research with people within organizations for thirty years to understand trust. We originally wrote the first edition of *Trust & Betrayal in the Workplace* to share what we have learned and to make a contribution to the development of trust in workplace relationships. That purpose holds true today more than ever.

Since the publication of the first edition, we have seen the power of trust, the pain of betrayal, the transformation that comes with healing, and the gift of renewal. We have had the privilege of working with leaders who value relationships and who are committed to building and rebuilding trust. We have also been privileged to work with leaders who were initially resistant to our work because they thought it was "too touchy-feely" who, nonetheless, remained open to learning about trust because they thought it was the right thing to do.

This book took root many years ago during our respective doctoral studies. We each studied elements of trust in our dissertations. We learned much about trust and how central it is in relationships and organizations. However, what was not clear is what trust meant and how it was created. We set out on a quest to answer that question. We began interviewing leaders to explore what trust meant to them and the behaviors they felt built it. We learned that it was not possible for people to talk about trust without talking about betrayal. Our quest expanded. To this day, we continue to learn about trust, betrayal, healing, and renewal.

We have conducted research and consulted with over 100 organizations in 19 industries. These have included manufacturing, aerospace, chemical, petroleum, pharmaceuticals, telecommunications, computer and electronics, engineering, utilities industries, accounting, law, finance, hotel and resort management, food service, health care, and higher education. Federal and state government agencies are also among our clients. We have worked with organizations in pain, organizations who are strong and want to be stronger, and with leaders who value relationships and want to honor them. We have interviewed hundreds of organizational leaders, managers, supervisors, human resource and organizational development professionals, and rank-and-file workers in a multitude of functions. We have conducted focus groups with thousands. They all have one significant thing in common: the indiividual and organizational need for trust.

People have opened their hearts to us and shared their experiences. Many expressed relief at being able at last to share thoughts, concerns, and feelings about the types of trusting relationships they desired, but had not felt safe discussing. The stories and quotes in the book come from the actual experiences lived by people and shared with us in our research, consulting, workshops and coaching. The names and locations of individuals and organizations have been changed to maintain anonymity and to protect their trust in us.

As a product of our research, we developed the Reina Trust & Betrayal Model, which is the foundation for this book and our trust building approach. We have designed trust-building processes to support strategic initiatives such as engagement, risk-taking, innovation, collaboration, resilience, speed-to-market, change and transition, and knowledge management. We bring ourselves in service to them and in so doing, continue to learn about trust. What we have learned is shared with you here.

Measuring trust is difficult. Leaders committed to sustaining or transforming their organizations need tools to monitor those efforts. To support that need, we have developed valid and reliable instruments that measure trust at the organizational, team, individual leadership, and consumer levels. These tools help organizations see where they have healthy levels of trust and where they have work to do.

All organizations strive for effectiveness. Yet many are challenged to bring people together to develop all of the components necessary for that effectiveness. Our commitment to the knowledge that trust is one of the most very basic components of organizational effectiveness has led us to develop Trust Building On-Line Community. It provides an on-line forum that overcomes the barriers of time and distance, bringing people together in dialogue to build trust. They have shared their stories with us and with one another and have come away with real insights into building and sustaining trust.

Our interest in trust is passionate. Our professional lives are devoted to supporting the cultivation of trust in relationships all over the world. We believe that all human beings deserve to trust in themselves and to feel safe to trust in others. We wrote this book and continue our work to that end.

Dennis S. Reina
Michelle L. Reina

Stowe, Vermont
July 2005

ACKNOWLEDGMENTS

The writing of this book has truly been a privileged experience. The process has provided us with an opportunity to learn to listen to our inner voice and speak from our minds and hearts in an integrated fashion. Because we have been working with and writing about a topic, *trust,* so dear to us, we wanted to be true to ourselves and those we have worked with in what we wrote and how we wrote it. We have been blessed to be surrounded by a circle of loving people who have trusted in us, trusted in the contribution this book will make to others, and remained supportive.

We thank Steve Piersanti for his thoughtful guidance, and the staff at Berrett-Koehler for their trust in us and what this book would bring.

We particularly thank Kristen Frantz of Berrett-Koehler, who has been a longtime champion, adviser, and friend.

Richard Weaver provided thoughtful guidance throughout the entire development of this book and helped conduct research for it. Dick, once again, you were there when we needed you most! Our friendship continues to be "transformative," and we are grateful for all we share.

Chris Francovich, longtime team member and friend of our company, Chagnon & Reina Associates, Inc., brought his heart and soul to supporting this book, from interviewing people helping with story scenarios to reading countless drafts.

Colleague Rick Tette provided invaluable research assistance. He tirelessly interviewed people who engaged with our work so that we could share their stories with you.

Christopher Dilts, trusted partner and collaborator, designed and developed groundbreaking technology that supported the research for this book and engaged people in trust building around the world.

Jeffrey Douglass brought insight to the idea of capacity for trust to help make a tough topic more readable.

Patti Christensen and James Nelson-Lucas told us, "You need to bring these stories to life." Then they showed us how! Thank you both.

Sharon Reynolds, a precious gem from Australia, supported us with anecdotes and vignettes of trust and betrayal overseas.

Denise Renter, Leslie Yerkes, Carol White, Jesse Mendoza, Angela Airall, and Jeffrey Aresty share our commitment to trust building. Numerous people certified in our Trust & Betrayal Model and trust-measuring instruments shared their trust building experiences with us to bring further life to the book. Thank you for your partnership, support, and conviction. Together we make a difference.

Stacey Hood, Kathy Leith, and Norma Farnsworth, members of the Chagnon & Reina Associates team, have been especially valuable. Stacey is the creative gem who brought our model to life through the use of graphics and design. Kathy and Norma provide infrastructure support that allows us to focus. Thank you.

We have worked with thousands of people in more than a hundred organizations. From them we have learned the power of trust and the hope for future relationships in organizations. We thank them for embracing our work and using it to build trust in their relationships. We continue to learn from them.

We are blessed with special relationships with kindred spirits with whom we have worked. Several took precious time to share how they have benefited from the trust work so that others may benefit as well. They told us what was important to include in this book, and we have included it! Thank you, Judi Della Barba, Lori Brown, Joyce Cofield, Lisa Daily, Beth Elliott, Steve Jordan, Maureen Johannssen, Ben Katcoff, Tim Klunk, Klon Kitchen, Brynne Lanning, Ted Mayer, Rosemary McGahey, Chris Ng, Cindy Petitt, Mary Beth Petersen, Mary Santiago, Maury Stout, Crystal Tanvas, and Darrell Thomsen. We are grateful for our work together. We bring ourselves in service to you and are served in return! Thank you for your trust in us.

Our families have provided a steady stream of encouragement and faith in us and what we might bring to others. They have graciously stood by us every step of the way.

Our godchildren, Timothy and Julia, remind us how precious relationships are and how important it is to nurture them with play and creativity.

Our sons, Patrick and William, have cheered us on for years. We are deeply proud of the young men they have become and the trustworthy way they lead their lives.

Finally, we would like to thank the process of life for bringing us together and for providing us with the opportunity to make a contribution to the development of trust in relationships. Together we continue.

PART

I

WHY TRUST

The relationship between trust and betrayal in the workplace is complex. That is why people have difficulty understanding trust, much less being able to deal with the dynamics associated with it. In Part I, we define trust and betrayal and introduce the Reina Trust & Betrayal Model to help you understand and manage trust in your workplace.

THE NEED FOR TRUST
IN THE WORKPLACE

Jamie was the vice president of global leadership development for a Fortune 50 corporation. She was charged with overseeing the implementation of the company's new performance management system, overhauling their approach to change management, and developing and rolling out a leadership development training program, among a host of other initiatives. This all had to be executed throughout the company, worldwide, in record time to support aggressive strategic deliverables.

Jamie had a 150-person global unit of highly committed, talented people with heart, soul, and deep pride for the work they do. After all, they were the unit that facilitated initiatives throughout the company that made a difference in people's lives. However, the unit was paying the price of three restructurings in two years, the loss of 35 percent of its people, and significant budget cuts. Roles and responsibilities were unclear, decision-making boundaries were blurred, and expectations were not understood. Anxiety was high. People no longer understood the direction of the unit or the direction of the company; they did not know

*what the future held for them, and they did not have a place to go to
talk about it.*

*This lack of clarity and alignment created confusion and distrac-
tions. The trust people once had in one another eroded, and relationships collapsed. Channels of communication and collaboration, already
challenged by having to accommodate people working all over the
world, gradually broke down. People were at each other's throats, fight-
ing for resources, hoarding information, and working at cross-purposes
with one another. The quality of the work declined, and the time line to
delivery was drastically off course. The group's reputation within the
organization was compromised.*

Does this scenario sound familiar? In it do you see yourself or others
with whom you have worked? Whether Jamie and her people realized it
or not, high levels of trust had previously enabled them to have highly
effective relationships that made them successful. Now, lower trust undermined relationships and compromised the unit's overall ability to perform.

Situations like Jamie's happen all the time. When they arise, we
often feel helpless and hopeless, and hold the perception that there is
nothing we can do. Yet we *can* do something about it! This book is about
trust—the power when it exists, the pain when it is betrayed, and the
steps you can take to rebuild it when it is lost.

To rebuild trust, Jamie and her people need to understand just how
important trust is to every aspect of their relationships with one another.
They need to learn the behaviors that build trust and how practicing those
behaviors contributes to their performance and the company's operations.
They need to learn what breaks trust and what they can do to rebuild and
maintain it. Let us begin!

THE NEED FOR TRUST

Today more than ever there is the need for trust—a business need and a
human need. The business landscape is constantly changing. Mergers and
acquisitions; restructuring; strategic initiatives that require collaboration,
employee engagement, risk taking, creativity, and innovation with shrink-

ing resources; and asking people to do more with less have become a way of life in industries across the globe. To take their organizations to the next level—whether it be increased speed to market, enhanced patient care, greater customer satisfaction, improved cost containment, cutting-edge technology, reduced union grievances, or expanded community out-reach—businesses need their employees to embrace and adapt to change and to show up fully engaged and committed. In short, businesses need people to work in relationship with one another to produce results.

Business is conducted through relationships, and trust is the founda-tion of effective relationships. People need their relationships with cowork-ers to be trusting ones if they're to get their job done. They need to be able to depend on each other to do his or her part, to believe that what cowork-ers are saying is the truth, to have confidence that they have what it takes to deliver, to receive honest feedback on the quality of their work and coach-ing from one another to learn new skills. Trusting relationships are what make the difference between people's feeling good about what they do and simply going through the motions. Trust is inspiring and energy producing.

People today have a need for connection with their coworkers, and trust makes that connection possible. People have a need to understand others and to be understood in return; to use their skills, talents, and full range of capability; to challenge and be challenged; to share information and receive information; and to count on others and be counted on.

When trust is present, people are excited about what they do. They collaborate freely, channels of communication open up, the sharing of ideas becomes the norm, and people are not afraid to make mistakes. They take pride in the organization they work for, are committed to the people they work with, and bring themselves more fully to their jobs. In trusting environments, people are able to focus on their jobs; they are more productive and want to come to work.

BUILDING TRUST

The good news is that leaders increasingly understand the need for trust. They realize that the cost of not having it is too great to be ignored. Yet trust is highly complex; it means different things to different people and is emotionally provocative. It takes time to develop and can be broken in an instant. The mere word *trust* stirs something in all of us, either warm feelings associated with positive experiences or sad or angry feelings associated with the loss of trust

Often people assume that it is *only* the organizations with morale and performance problems that engage in trust building. Although organizations with problems do engage in trust building as a viable solution, it is *not only* problems that draw organizations to this effort. Many organizations that enjoy strong performance and satisfied people commit to further building trust. They do so because they see trust as their competitive advantage and because their leaders value relationships. They want to make their organization's performance stronger, and they know that further building trust in relationships is the key to doing so. It is people working in relationship with one another that ultimately delivers results.

BREAKING TRUST—BETRAYAL

A three-star general of one of our country's largest federal government agencies, was uncomfortable with the word betrayal *and indicated that it did not belong in the workplace, particularly, his workplace.*

The CEO of a personal care products company asked us not to use the word betrayal *in a keynote speech we were to deliver to his worldwide leadership team.*

The VP of operations for one of the country's largest health care systems asked us to help her understand betrayal. She knew that the nurses, doctors, technicians, and administrators of a recently acquired community hospital she oversaw were feeling betrayed following the merger. Her employees described the acquisition as being "swallowed up" by the larger conglomerate and as losing the work life they once knew.

Your reaction to the word *betrayal* may be similar to one of these. Upon picking up this book, you may have been drawn to read further as a result of your interest in betrayal and in how we treat it. Or you may have thought twice about reading the book and may even have contemplated putting it back down.

It is important to understand betrayal because it is a natural part of relationships. It is going to happen, even in the most well-intended work environments and relationships. We can turn to our relationships in our personal lives to gain greater insight: How often do we feel betrayed by a loved one, a dear friend, a member of our church or community?

Betrayal stirs emotion in all of us. It represents disappointment, letdown, loss, and pain. People often associate betrayal with the "big stuff"— the things that happen that catch broad attention and get intense media coverage. There was a time, many years ago, when we too assumed that what broke the delicate fiber of trust in relationships were large acts that had significant impact. However, our research and work over the last fifteen years have taught us differently.

What gradually erodes trust and creates a climate of betrayal in our workplaces today are small, subtle acts that accumulate over time. When we don't do what we say we will do, when we gossip about others behind their backs, when we renege on decisions we agreed to, when we hide our agenda and work it behind the scenes, and when we spin the truth rather than tell it, we break trust and damage our relationships.

Betrayal is an intentional or unintentional breach of trust or the perception of a breach of trust. An intentional betrayal is a self-serving action done with the purpose of hurting, damaging, or harming another person. An unintentional betrayal is the by-product of another person's self-serving action that results in people being hurt, damaged, or harmed.

Betrayal shakes our identity, it causes us to wonder "who am I," it erodes our confidence, and causes us to question what we have to contribute. We become distracted and lose our ability to focus on getting the job done. Imagine for a moment the impact on performance when people show up for work distracted, unable to concentrate, and questioning their sense of belonging and capability.

What do we do when we feel betrayed? Do we shut down? Do we seek to get back? After all, we were hurt; it is only natural that we want to hurt in return. Do we withdraw our spirit and energy from our work and simply go through the motions, declaring, "They will get only the minimum from me"? Or do we seek to work through our pain and allow the experience to be a teacher that strengthens us and our relationships with others?

We have all been betrayed, and we have all betrayed others. When we learn that we have betrayed another, intentionally or unintentionally, how do we respond? Do we defend, rationalize, and justify our behavior? Do we excuse it—"I was busy and didn't mean it"? Do we imply that our act was not a big deal and that perhaps the other is overreacting? Or do we assume responsibility for our behavior that harmed another and reflect on what was going on inside of us to behave in such a way?

Clearly we have a choice. When we have been betrayed, we may choose to remain bitter, resentful, hurt, and angry. We may choose to feel victimized. When we have betrayed another, we may choose to deny the impact of our behavior. We may choose to view the other person as over-reacting and making a big deal out of nothing.

Or we can choose to reframe the experience of being betrayed or betraying another as an opportunity to learn more about ourselves and to deepen our relationships with others. The Trust & Betrayal Model will provide a framework in which to exercise those choices.

THE PAYOFF OF REBUILDING TRUST

Sandra, a customer service manager of a telecommunications firm, thought she was operating with the best interests of the company in mind. Yet at a meeting of her management team the day before, Sandra's boss did not support her. In fact, he belittled her with his unfounded remarks. Sandra was upset, but said nothing to her boss in her defense. After the meeting, she quickly left the room feeling quite defeated.

The next day Sandra took a risk. She knew she could be fired for speaking up. Yet she also knew she had to do something and do it soon! After a sleepless night worrying, Sandra walked into her boss's office and asked if they could talk. She told her boss her side of the story: that she felt misunderstood and betrayed by her boss's comments and actions the day before and that her boss's comments were not justified. The two of them talked the situation through. The boss admitted the mistake he made, and Sandra took responsibility for her part. Both talked about what they would do to prevent misunderstanding in the future. Sandra and her boss were able to restore trust and confidence in each other, and in their relationship.

In working through the issues and restoring trust in her relationship with her boss, Sandra was able to refocus on accomplishing the tasks of her job, instead of worrying about whether she had one. She did not have to waste her energy wondering about how her boss felt—she *knew*, because she asked him. She more fully understood her boss and was confident that they could work things through. What a relief to know that he too was human, that he made mistakes and would own them. She would never have known that if she had not taken responsibility for her feelings and concerns by speaking up.

Taking the time to build and maintain trust in the workplace allows employees to focus their energies on what they are there to do and want to do. As a result, suggestions for product and process improvements proliferate, and productivity increases as employees develop a sense of pride and ownership in their jobs and meaning in their work.

Trust-inspiring work environments are liberating. When employees feel good about the people they are working with and the company they are working for, they enjoy coming to work and generally work harder at their jobs, giving more of themselves—accepting challenges, stepping into the unknown, and seeing change as an opportunity rather than a threat.

We have heard from hundreds and hundreds of people that although they would not want to live their past betrayals again, they are grateful for the experience because of how it contributed to the people they are today and the insights they gained about themselves, relationships, and life.

LEADERSHIP TRUSTWORTHINESS

At the core of trust building is increasing our awareness of ourselves and our behaviors with others. Through our heightened awareness, we are in a stronger position to choose to practice behaviors that build trust. By practicing these behaviors consistently, leaders earn their trustworthiness.

Trust is reciprocal: you have to give it to get it, and it is built step-by-step over time. A common mistake leaders make is to assume that their position, role, or title earns them their trustworthiness. Nothing could be further from the truth. The only thing that earns a leader trustworthiness is the way they behave. And to be trusted by others, leaders must first be willing to trust them. Trust begets trust.

Leaders earn trustworthiness by practicing such behaviors as honoring their agreements; behaving consistently, even during challenging times; investing in their people by providing feedback and opportunities to learn new skills; acknowledging employees' capabilities by including them in decisions, even the big ones; by maintaining open channels of communication; and yes, by holding people accountable.

Trustworthy leaders are safe—safe to talk to, to share problems with, and to share fears and concerns with. They are safe to be human with. As a result, people are safe to challenge the system and perform beyond expectations. Employees feel more freedom to express their creative ideas. They are more willing to take risks, admit mistakes, and learn from those mistakes.

Trustworthy leaders are kept well informed. They know where their people and their work stand because their people tell them. There is no need to keep secrets and dance around the real story.

UNDERSTANDING TRUST AND BETRAYAL

Trust in the workplace is difficult for many people to understand because of its complexity and the emotions it stirs. However, its importance can not be overstated. Building trust is the *necessary* thing to do for business performance and the right thing to do for relationships. Without trust an organization will not meet or exceed its potential, and workplace relationships will not thrive.

Betrayal is a natural part of relationships and cannot be ignored. Betrayal breaks trust and the spirit of relationships. When betrayal is worked through appropriately, however, it will strengthen an organization and create opportunities for lasting transformation.

The Reina Trust & Betrayal Model is a practical framework for building trust. We take the complex nature of trust and make it simple. We take what means different things to different people and develop a shared understanding. We illustrate three specific types of trust, the Trust of Character (contractual trust), the Trust of Disclosure (communication trust), and the Trust of Capability (competence trust). We discuss specific trust-building behaviors, develop your awareness of what breaks trust, and describe the steps to rebuild it and the characteristics necessary to sustain healthy levels of trust. This model serves as the framework for the remainder of the book. We provide trust-building examples, tools, tips, and exercises for you to use with yourself and others. Although the focus of this book is trust, betrayal, and healing in workplace relationships, you can use the Trust & Betrayal Model and its underlying principles in relationships in all facets of your life.

TRUST BUILDING IN ACTION

Reflecting on Your Experience

1. How has trust in yourself and your relationships with others helped you accomplish your personal and professional goals?
2. How has broken trust or betrayal in yourself and your relationships with others hindered you in accomplishing your personal and professional goals?

Application Exercise

Think about and discuss the following questions with your team members as they relate to the team's or the organization's goals.

1. What are your team's key goals? What business needs must be met in order to achieve these goals? What do people need from one another to achieve these goals? How would trust building help meet business and human needs?
2. What key strategic initiatives are at play in your organization? What business needs must be met in order for these initiatives to be successful? What human needs must be met in order for these initiatives to be successful? How would trust building help meet business and human needs?

Trust Note

Today more than ever, there is the need for trust—a business need and a human need. When trust is present, people are excited about what they do; they collaborate freely, channels of communication open up, sharing ideas becomes the norm, and people are not afraid to make mistakes. They take pride in the organization they work for, are committed to the people they work with, and are more productive in their jobs.

Trust Tip

Business is conducted through relationships, and trust is the foundation of effective relationships. People need trust in their relationships with coworkers to get the job done. Trust building makes organizations work!

PART II

What Trust Means and How to Build It: Transactional Trust

Transactional trust is a mutual exchange; it is

reciprocal and is created incrementally over time.

In other words, you've got to give trust to get it. There

are three types of transactional trust: contractual trust,

communication trust, and competence trust. Each type

is associated with specific behaviors that build and

sustain relationships in the workplace.

Transactional Trust

Transactional Trust is:

➤ Reciprocal ("Got to give it to get it")
➤ Created incrementally (step by step)

Three Types of Transactional Trust

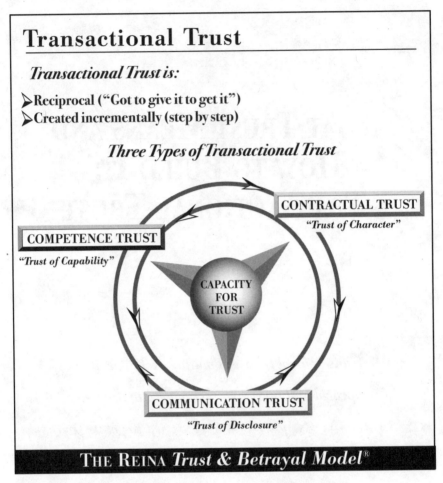

Figure 1 Transactional Trust

2

THE TRUST OF CHARACTER: CONTRACTUAL TRUST

"I'm really frustrated! Phil said he was going to get that report to me by 10 A.M., and here it is 3 P.M. and I still don't have it! It's my neck on the chopping block if I don't get that finished project to the boss by the end of the day!"

Have you ever been disappointed by people because they didn't do what they said they would, didn't do what they had promised?

"The boss wants it done yesterday!" Mary said in exasperation. "We've got to get this product to market in two weeks, yet there are major problems with it that will take longer to get ironed out."

Have you ever been frustrated because a leader made an unreasonable request of you, and you were not given an opportunity to negotiate that expectation? Did you end up with no time to do the job right in the first place, having to sacrifice the quality of the project for the sake of expediency? Did the company have to spend five times as much energy and money fixing the mistakes because the project was rushed?

"Sam is always late!" the team leader said in frustration. "He knows our team meetings are at nine o'clock every Wednesday morning, yet he consistently keeps us waiting to get started. Who does he think he is, anyway? Does he think his time is more valuable than ours? That he's more important than we are?"

Have you ever felt irritated because you schedule meetings, notifying people well in advance; get to meetings on time in spite of your busy schedule; yet find yourself waiting for the same people who are consistently late?

WHAT IS CONTRACTUAL TRUST?

Whether the situation involves an employee-to-employee or employee-to-supervisor relationship, unmet expectations, disappointments, broken promises, and frustrations happen every day on the job. They result in decreased risk taking and creativity, increased employee absenteeism and turnover, unhealthy and unproductive workplaces, and decreased *contractual trust*.

As we will discuss further in this chapter, contractual trust involves managing expectations, establishing boundaries, delegating appropriately, encouraging mutually serving intentions, keeping agreements, and being congruent in our behavior. How we practice these behaviors demonstrates the quality of our character as perceived by ourselves and others. Therefore, in our model we refer to Contractual Trust as *"Trust of Character"* (see Figure 1A).

Contractual trust implies that there is a mutual understanding that the people in the relationship will do what they say they will do. Contractual trust deals with keeping agreements, honoring intentions, and behaving consistently.

Contractual trust forms the basis of most interactions in the workplace. Employees have a strong need for confidence in the intentions of their boss and one another, and they need their leaders to be consistent

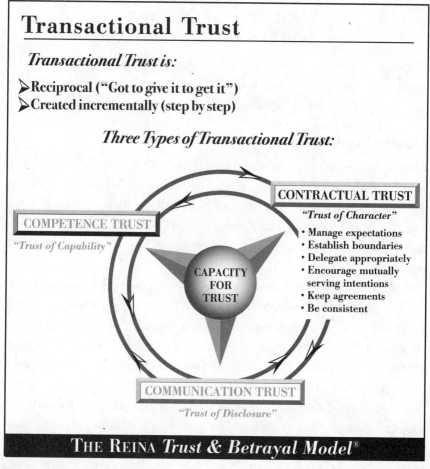

Figure 1A Contractual Trust

and reliable. Likewise, leaders need to have confidence in the intentions of their people, and they need employees to be consistent and reliable in meeting business objectives. The greater a leader's span of responsibility in the organization, the more the leader must rely on others to meet the objectives and the more imperative it is that the leader effectively model the behaviors that foster contractual trust.

Behaviors That Contribute
to Contractual Trust

Committed action, not empty words, builds contractual trust in relationships between individuals, on teams, and in organizations. Six specific behaviors are crucial to building contractual trust. Let's look at each.

Manage Expectations

Contractual trust relies on our managing expectations: our expectations of others, their expectations of us, and our expectations of ourselves. There are two kinds of expectations when dealing with others: *explicit* and *implicit*. Both kinds have their place, are appropriate and useful in everyday workplace relationships, and contribute to the development of contractual trust.

People often experience their leaders' expectations as unrealistic. In today's organizations, people feel they are being asked to do increasingly more with less. They understand what is expected of them, but do not receive the necessary clarity, direction, resources, or support to meet expectations successfully. This leaves employees feeling overwhelmed, underresourced, and ultimately resentful.

Is there a difference in the level of trust generated by one-sided or dictated expectations as opposed to mutually negotiated expectations? Contractual trust grows when expectations are mutually agreed on. Conversely, dictated expectations do not have the benefit of contributions from the person(s) expected to produce or deliver, and may undermine trust or even create betrayal. A leader can be trusted when making benevolent one-sided contracts with her employees if her expectations are reasonable. A leader whose expectations are unreasonable creates mistrust; people working with such leaders feel set up to fail. In law, contracts made under duress are not enforceable. Unfortunately, such contracts are enforced daily in many workplaces. Failure to fulfill unreasonable contracts costs organizations significant money and time. That doesn't even count the losses that come from the more subtle events resulting from the loss of contractual trust.

Leaders sitting down and discussing goals with employees and ensuring understanding of the steps, resources, and relational support needed to achieve those goals are critical to the success of any deliverable. Identifying the challenges and necessary assistance is important. When we strive for greater clarity we are managing our relationships and meeting business needs.

A leader's expectations of people greatly influence their performance. Leaders can empower people by setting realistic expectations and trusting in people's competence. If expectations of employees are set high and they are given proper support, they will be motivated to meet and even exceed the original expectations. And by setting expectations high, a leader demonstrates trust in people's abilities. It is in essence saying, "I trust you to do this work." However, if a leader's expectations are too high and employees are not given appropriate support, they will be demotivated and may even be demoralized by the unrealistic expectations.

Employees' expectations of leaders also affect contractual trust. Employees respect leaders who take their expectations into account when making decisions. Expectations reflect needs we have, relational and business needs. When employees' relational needs are met, trust grows between coworkers and leaders and among coworkers and employee engagement and collaboration grows. When employees' business needs are met their performance is enhanced and productivity grows.

At times, expectations are not met because they have not been identified or understood, or because they are unreasonable or inadequately supported. A lack of clarity regarding expectations causes misperceptions and misconstrued intentions. When people's expectations are not met, they may feel a range of emotions. They may feel disappointed, discounted, taken advantage of, angry, or hurt. The result may be distrust and feelings of betrayal.

Explicit expectations   How clear are we in communicating our expectations of others to them? How much do we understand what the people we work with need and expect from us? When expectations are unclear, leaders and employees have difficulty aligning toward achieving the organization's goals.

Explicit expectations are clearly stated and understood requirements. Trust comes out of the understanding of responsibility—that is, an understanding of what is expected of an individual and what the individual may expect in return. When people have a clear understanding of what is expected of them and they meet those expectations, trust grows and relationships prosper. When expectations are unclear and go unfulfilled, trust erodes and relationships decline.

Zack is too ambiguous in his expectations of his direct reports. When his employees don't deliver what he expects of them, he gets frustrated and angry at them. He attacks the individuals, not their performance. His behavior further pushes his employees away and destroys any trust that may exist between them.

Healthy working relationships require clear expectations, whether they are in regard to starting a project, forming a task force, developing a unit, or working on any number of initiatives. It is difficult for people to meet expectations that have not been made clear to them. When people don't find out what is expected of them until they run into a wall, go down the wrong road, or fail to get a promotion or pay raise, it's too late. In these kinds of situations, people may experience a range of emotions from disappointment to betrayal. Clarity around expectations affects relationships and productivity, determining what can get accomplished. Performance is significantly enhanced when leaders are candid and explicit about their expectations, because employees need to know what is expected of them and "need to understand, up front, the rules for engagement," as a telecommunications company division manager pointed out.

Contractual trust between leaders and employees serves as a relational foundation of understanding. With such a basis in trust, people are given more freedom to do their jobs and are able to manage that freedom appropriately. Obviously, the flip side of that coin is responsibility. As employees are given more freedom, leaders expect them to take on commensurate responsibility. Likewise, trust erodes when employees are given a task or a project but not given the corresponding authority to carry out the assignment. When employees are given the necessary resources and authority to fulfill expectations, they get the message that they are trusted, and they perform.

Implicit expectations   Have you ever taken a risk, tried something new in an attempt to solve a problem at work, thinking you were being resourceful and creative, only to get reprimanded for going "outside the bounds"? Were the rules of engagement implicitly understood by every-one else, but, being new to the organization, you had not yet learned them?

Implicit expectations are unwritten and unspoken rules, requirements, agreements, or understandings between people. Cultural norms of the orga-nization influence implicit expectations: "That's the way we do things around here." Previous experiences also contribute to implicit expectations: "The person who held that position before always did it this way."

Unfortunately, implicit expectations are often difficult to notice until we feel the consequences of not having met them. For example, if a new hire takes liberties that he was accustomed to at his old job without check-ing to see if they are appropriate in his new work environment, he may be setting himself up for a downfall. Furthermore, the more responsibility one holds in an organization, the greater the implicit expectations are.

Managing relationships up, down, and across the organization is important to success. When expectations are worked out specifically and in detail, contractual trust begins to develop. However, during times of change, expectations become increasingly difficult to manage. They can shift and become vague. The level of contractual trust may begin to decline, and relationships may be jeopardized. To help gain clarity around expectations, leaders will benefit from reflecting on the implicit contracts they have with the people with whom they work. Leaders should consider the degree to which the contracts are mutually under-stood and beneficial. They may need to clarify implicit expectations and make them explicit.

By and large, people want to meet the expectations others have of them, or would like the opportunity to negotiate if they feel the expecta-tions are unreasonable. People look to their leaders to take the time to clarify expectations. Leaders look to their people to fulfill those expecta-tions. People want to be successful and want the organization they work for to thrive. People seek work environments where expectations are shared, discussed, and mutual. In these work environments, relationships are valued and contractual trust flourishes.

Establish Boundaries

Are roles and responsibilities clearly defined? Are the parameters and direction of the project clearly mapped out?

Establishing and maintaining clear boundaries provide a framework for accountability in an organization and thus play a strong role in developing contractual trust. Boundaries refer to the roles and responsibilities of individuals, and the purpose, policies, and procedures of teams, departments, and units.

Clearly defined roles and responsibilities describe who does what and with whom. As stated by an employee we have worked with, establishing clear boundaries means "cultivating an atmosphere in which employees are not left hanging without enough information to complete tasks they are assigned within given parameters." Policies and procedures establish how things should or should not be done. The purpose and mission of an organization identify its "reason for being," and thus function as a kind of boundary for the people of the organization.

Boundaries help define the relationships between individuals, teams, and units, and within the organization. Although some may contend that boundaries separate people, boundaries actually aid in connecting people by serving as points of contact or terms of engagement. Today there is a greater need than ever for teams and people to work across functional lines and to collaborate. Clear boundaries help identify the points of exchange that foster collaboration.

Delegate Appropriately

"We've getting tons of work thrown on us at once. During peak times the workload can be too much. And we have no say in the matter."

"Many times we're not allowed to make decisions or be involved in fixing challenging problems. I think if we met and discussed the problems as a unit, we could come up with solutions, and it would help us [employees] feel more a part of making the unit better."

When people are given the responsibility to do a task or function but not the necessary authority and resources nor a voice on how it is managed, it is difficult to accomplish the goal; trust breaks down between the leader and his or her employees.

In contrast, when leaders delegate appropriately—in other words, give employees not only the responsibility but also the necessary authority, resources, and voice—they invest trust in their employees to do their jobs. Delegation demonstrates trust in people's abilities. It further defines people's roles and the boundaries of their responsibilities. To develop contractual trust in delegating, leaders must ensure that individual objectives are clear, explicit, visible, and mutually understood. Leaders and employees need to define and mutually agree on checkpoints and follow-up procedures. This approach helps everyone know the status of a project. It further helps develop people's readiness to trust in themselves and the organizations in which they serve.

Because trust is a reciprocal process, it is critical, as one project account manager explained, "to create a two-way feedback loop with employees to ensure mutual understanding." When people operate under an assumption of shared understanding rather than an explicit understanding, they set themselves up for some form of disappointment, frustration, or betrayal. Although it may be an unintentional betrayal, it is a betrayal nevertheless. The level of trust diminishes. "When we delegate a project to employees without giving them the authority, feedback mechanisms, or support to do the job well, we set ourselves and the employees up for failure, and put deliverables at risk," said the senior partner in an international accounting firm.

Linda, a project manager in an engineering firm, was overseeing a major project in which Ted played a role. The project was promised on time and on budget to the client. Linda reviewed the parameters three times with Ted and was confident that he understood them. However, Ted's part of the project came in over budget and behind schedule. When Linda questioned Ted regarding his performance, Ted's response was that "other things came up." Linda was furious with Ted and felt betrayed. She had given her word to the client, and now her word meant nothing.

Linda realized, however, that she had to own her part in the per-formance breakdown. She had not delegated appropriately; she had failed to establish periodic feedback mechanisms and regular progress checkpoints with Ted to ensure on-time, on-budget deliverables. Linda went back to Ted and reassigned him the project, this time setting up clear feedback mechanisms and support for Ted to be successful. "I gave him another chance. I had a heart-to-heart talk with him. I reviewed the expectations, clarified his questions. I checked for his understanding by having him repeat back his understanding of the expectations. Then I asked for his agreement to the new expectations, with incremental goals with deliverables at regular intervals. In validating the agreement, I shared the burden of project success with him."

Linda continued to clarify expectations and manage Ted's perfor-mance with incremental goals and deliverables each time she gave Ted a project. Over the next six months, Linda's consistent and firm behavior with Ted began to pay off. Within a year, Ted was one of the most reli-able project engineers in the group.

Encourage Mutually Serving Intentions

People can build contractual trust in their teams and organizations when they encourage mutually serving intentions. That is, when they think and act with others in mind. For example, as exemplified in the following com-ments by a head nurse in an intensive care unit.

> *"Each person is striving to do his or her job in the best way possi-ble so as to benefit others and make the other person's job easier. For example: the receptionists' promptness in having all the nec-essary paperwork completed benefits the nurses in their effort to complete their work in preparing information for the doctor and having the patient ready in a timely fashion . . . which in turn enables the doctor to work more efficiently and professionally to*

meet the needs of the patient. Happy patients reflect back to mak-
ing the receptionists' job more rewarding and less frustrating.
Working as a team during some very difficult times that occurred
in our unit has united everyone."

Mutually serving intentions exist when individuals support each other and operate with a sense of shared interests. "We may be going through some tough times, but if we pull together, we can all get through this." When there is a shared interest in helping one another serve customers or produce products, people develop a sense of community. When they support each other's intentions and are aligned in their purposes, contractual trust is reinforced and peoples' trust in others is enhanced.

Trust is facilitated when people are interested in each other's welfare. Trust is hindered or broken down when people are self-serving, driven by hidden agendas, and uninterested in other's well-being. It is hard to experience mutually serving intentions when we do not have a shared sense of why we are here and what we are to collectively produce. As one frustrated team member shared, "Some employees aren't team players. They only care about what will make them look good, even if it is at the expense of others."

Building trust is reciprocal. We have to give it to get it. Yet many people are unable to understand this and are reluctant to risk being the first one to give trust, for fear of revealing themselves and thus putting themselves in a vulnerable position.

Our perceptions of another's intentions influence our tendency to trust or be suspicious. What we perceive or attribute to another's intentions will affect our relationship with them. An attorney admitted, "I perceive that Jeff tries to manipulate me for his own advantage. As a result, I don't deal with him unless I have to!"

Unfortunately, if trust is low in a situation, most people perceive danger and tend to go into protective mode. In this hypervigilant state they personalize everything and assess risks in dealing with everyone, tending to cast themselves as the intended recipients of other people's harmful actions. This obviously makes getting the work of the organization done much harder.

Operating with a sense of mutually serving intentions makes it much easier to focus on and fulfill agreements with others. It builds contractual trust. Yet there are times when our behavior is not mutually serving and produces results we did not intend. For instance, we may have inadvertently left someone out of a decision-making loop, failed to include all pertinent parties in the circulation of a report, or left someone off the invitation list to an off-site planning meeting. Such actions, though not intentional, cause others to feel hurt, disappointed, and perhaps angry and are not mutually serving.

Although the outcome is not what we initially intended, we still need to assume responsibility for what occurred because our behavior was not mutually serving. People are especially frustrated and disappointed when leaders refuse to accept responsibility for unintentional acts. Hearing "but that was not my intention" strikes them as a lame defense. They consider that response an abdication or shirking of responsibility or a diversion of blame. People understand that the outcome may not have been intentional; nevertheless, they still look to their leaders to be responsible.

Denying responsibility or blaming others or the surrounding circumstances may allow one to deceptively save face in an awkward situation, but only temporarily. It certainly is not mutually serving and does not build contractual trust and is often experienced as a betrayal. Contractually, employees look to their leaders to talk straight with them and to admit and accept their role in performance outcomes. Every employee deserves nothing less.

Be Consistent

Leaders can create contractual trust when they act consistently toward their employees. As demonstrated in the following comments by a manufacturing team leader.

> "A leader's consistency in how he or she evaluates each employee's performance determines how fair the leader is perceived to be."

> "Leaders need to be consistent in their dealings with all staff— they must try not to play favorites."

Consistency is crucial to trust. A leader's consistency creates boundaries for employees, giving them parameters within which they can operate; employees know where they stand with a consistent leader. Further, consistency helps them remain connected to the leader when all else is changing. When leaders are not consistent in their expectations, unfair in evaluating employees' performance, or incongruent or untrue to their word, or when they play favorites, it is abundantly clear to employees. Leaders' behaviors are observable and have consequences; employees make evaluative conclusions about them. "How can I trust him when I don't know what he is going to do?" "How can I know whether I'm going to get equal or fair treatment or an honest performance evaluation?" employees ask. Likewise, a leader may have an employee who is totally unpredictable. "He's a loose cannon. He shoots from the hip. I never know what he's going to say." Inconsistent behavior makes it hard for people to know what they can expect or where to place their trust.

In our rapidly changing business climate, leaders must face the challenge of maintaining consistency in their treatment of employees while also being flexible enough to meet shifting business conditions. The direction leaders set for their company eighteen months ago may no longer be appropriate because of evolving market conditions. Adapting one's strategy to meet the demands of the changing business landscape does not mean that one is inconsistent in one's behavior, which should be based on principles and values, not expediency. Inconsistency in behavior may be perceived as dishonest, unfair, or self-serving and will undermine trust, especially when employees don't understand the rationale behind changes.

"Here we go again," Carlos said sarcastically to Susanna, his colleague on the XYZ project, as he read the latest email memo from their boss. "Why doesn't he just make up his mind and stop changing priorities every quarter? We can't ever seem to complete the projects we're working on before the boss shifts to a new 'top priority.'"

"Yeah, but at least you can count on him to listen to your concerns and brainstorm solutions with the team," Susanna retorted. "You know the whole industry is changing so fast, and he doesn't have control over the marketplace. He's just trying to keep up with the changing demands—just like we are! You can trust that he'll work with us."

Consistency in leaders' behavior toward their employees becomes particularly important during times of change. It isn't easy—leaders need to work hard at being consistent for themselves and for others. Consistency is a form of being true to oneself. People's perceptions become their reality; when there are gaps between what leaders say they are doing and what they are perceived to be doing, employees become distrustful. One senior manager of a utilities plant put it bluntly: "More trust is lost or gained by whether a leader is true to his word."

When times are good and things are going well, we may not notice how important consistency and the resulting trust are, but when times are bad, they are absolutely vital. Trust among employees and leaders is what will get an organization through the tough times.

Keep Agreements

Do we do what we say we are going to do?

> *"When we were bought out by Company X, everyone had expectations and reservations. I don't think the management of Company X was totally up-front with us. They wanted to get everyone on board, and as time has gone on they keep changing the rules."*

Do we keep our agreements, or renegotiate them if we cannot?

> *"When I make commitments to something, I commit to giving 100 percent to meet those goals. I feel guilty if I have made an agreement I can no longer carry out. I try to work out an agreement with the other party if I cannot follow through with my end. I try to give more than what is expected of me."*

Keeping agreements speaks to an individual's and an organization's reliability in carrying out their commitments. The first example illustrates the cost of not keeping agreements. The employees of the newly acquired unit have low contractual trust in the new management because they see the management as constantly changing the rules.

The second example demonstrates the positive payoff of keeping agreements. When we keep agreements with ourselves, we feel good, we know we can be counted on, we feel trustworthy. When we keep agreements with others, we empower our relationships; we build and nurture the trust between ourselves and others. "If I repeatedly meet my agreements, I enhance the readiness for trust between us," said a financial analyst. "There is an emotional payback you get from keeping your word and following through on your agreements—you feel better."

When we break agreements with ourselves—for example, if we fail to meet deadlines, even if they were a bit unrealistic—we disempower ourselves. We lose trust in ourselves. If we repeatedly fail to meet our agreements, we decrease our readiness to trust ourselves and our sense of trustworthiness.

When we break agreements with others, we disempower the relationship and compromise the trust between us. If we repeatedly fail to honor our agreements, we decrease our trustworthiness. The comments of a frustrated financial services manager reprimanding her employee illustrates this point: "Sally, if you can't do it, tell me. If you say you are going to come through and don't deliver, I am not able to meet my commitments. You lose credibility with me, and I lose credibility with my customers."

When we don't have a say in unrealistic agreements that we are expected to meet and that we can't renegotiate, we are set up to fail. "I feel as though this project deadline was shoved down our throats," exclaimed a frustrated employee. In these situations, we are unable to keep the agreement with ourselves and with others—a double disempowerment. However, by renegotiating broken agreements with more realistic expectations, we can renew and possibly strengthen the relationship. "This is a real opportunity to make or break your credibility," an international consultant pointed out. When you are rebuilding broken trust, it is not easy work and requires a great deal of commitment. Yet we as leaders need to persist in our commitments, regardless of the pitfalls. Know that you will make mistakes and when you do, some employees will be very unforgiving and critical and say, "I told you so. I knew you wouldn't keep your word." This comes with the territory of leadership.

Trust becomes more solidified when our actions match our words and we follow through on our intentions. Words help articulate our expectations, but actions demonstrate our trustworthiness. The most difficult challenge for a leader is to behave consistently, on a daily basis, in a way that reflects the organization's vision and values. As important as it is, walking the talk is not as easy as it sounds.

So we must be careful of what we promise. Leaders get into trouble when they want to make a good impression and promise the world, only to fall drastically short on their promises, lose credibility, and damage their reputations. If we fail to keep our promises, it is harder for us to regain people's trust. Unfortunately, people will forget the promises you kept and remember the promises you didn't keep.

Trust erodes when we fail to act consistently or follow through on our promises. Through their actions, leaders demonstrate their commitment and belief in people and the organization. By fulfilling their responsibilities and commitments and delivering what they promised, leaders produce business results and build their employee's trust.

In developing contractual trust with employees, it is important that the appropriate parties acknowledge that they have entered into a contract, that expectations have been set. Some leaders establish written contracts with their employees, often in the form of a written summary. And even some employees and teams have written contracts with one another! These are not used as weapons to hold over someone's head. On the contrary, they are used to develop trust: to make implicit expectations explicit and to establish clear boundaries. They are further used as a vehicle to track progress and to identify areas where additional support and resources may be needed. They provide a foundation for success.

Once the contract is established, whether it is in writing or verbally understood, both parties have a responsibility to themselves and others to keep agreements, monitor activities, measure performance, continually review commitments, and renegotiate when necessary. Relationships are work. Developing trust takes time, energy, and intention.

TRUST BUILDING IN ACTION

Reflecting on Your Experience

1. Where in your personal and work life do you experience high levels of contractual trust?

2. Of the six behaviors that contribute to contractual trust, choose one or two that you feel represent opportunities for you to build more trust in your relationships with others.

   - Manage expectations

   - Establish boundaries

   - Delegate appropriately

   - Encourage mutually serving intentions

   - Be consistent

   - Keep agreements

Application Exercises

The following questions are intended to facilitate dialogue as a team. Reflect on the following behaviors that create contractual trust. Share those thoughts with your teammates. Observe how you practice each of these behaviors and its impact on contractual trust.

1. *Manage expectations.* Are there expectations I have of my employees, peers, or boss that are not clear and explicit? If so, what implicit (unwritten, unspoken) expectations or working contracts should be made explicit?

2. *Establish boundaries.* Are there boundaries that I need to establish with my employees, peers, or boss? Are we aligned on goals, roles, and procedures? What is each person's level of commitment to the goals, roles, and procedures?

3. *Delegate appropriately.* When delegating a project or a job to an employee or peer, do I make sure the objectives are clearly under-

stood? Do I describe tangible, measurable results of performance that are to be achieved by specified due dates?

4. *Encourage mutually serving intentions.* In my interactions with my employees, peers, or boss, are my intentions self-serving or mutually serving? Do I operate with hidden agendas? What disagreements or misunderstandings do I need to reconcile or resolve with others?

5. *Keep agreements.* Do I keep my agreements? If I am unable to keep an agreement, do I renegotiate with the affected individuals promptly? What agreements do I need to renegotiate?

6. *Be consistent.* Am I generally consistent in my behavior in relating to others? Are my actions congruent with my words? Do I walk my talk? In what actions am I incongruent with my words? In my interactions with others, do I operate with integrity?

Trust Note

Contractual trust implies that there is a mutual understanding in the relationship that people will do what they say they will do, Whether it be producing a report, delivering a product, providing a service, managing priorities, attending a meeting on time, or simply returning an email or a phone call when they promised.

Trust Tip

The business of relationships starts with contractual trust—keeping our agreements, walking our talk, and doing what we say we will do.

3

THE TRUST OF DISCLOSURE: COMMUNICATION TRUST

"I'm really disappointed and disturbed!" Laurie stated. "As a supervisor of this unit, I am always looking out for my people and trying to do the right thing for the company. I can't believe my employees perceived my actions as self-serving!"

Have you ever felt the pain of being misunderstood? Have people misread your intentions as self-serving, yet you were honestly acting in the best interests of the organization? Have you been in situations where people's negative perceptions were far from the truth, yet they operated on those erroneous assumptions without checking their accuracy?

"All I did was inform the boss about what was happening out in the field—information he needed to know—and he blew up at me!" Bob said in exasperation. "I'm never going to stick my neck out again!"

Have you ever been shot as the messenger communicating bad news, yet you had nothing to do with creating that bad news? Perhaps you were trying to avert major problems, maybe even a disaster for the company, yet your good intentions were neither acknowledged nor appreciated and were in fact punished.

"I'm so grateful that Ethan came directly to me with his questions and concerns about my motivations. What a wonderful experience! He came to me rather than going to everyone else, the typical occurrence in this office. He gave me the opportunity to explain my actions and my needs. We now have a stronger understanding of one another, and our relationship has been strengthened. I know I can count on him to bring issues directly to me, and he can certainly count on me to do the same."

Have you ever felt hurt because an individual did not talk with you directly about an issue, instead talking about it and you to everyone else behind your back and leaving you to learn about it through the grapevine? What happened to your level of trust?

WHAT IS COMMUNICATION TRUST?

Whether the situation involves an employee-to-employee or supervisor-to-employee relationship, painful misunderstandings, ill-placed outbursts, and undeserved hurts happen everyday on the job. They result in decreased risk taking and collaboration, breakdowns in information sharing, decreased performance, and diminished *communication trust*.

As we will discuss further in this chapter, communication trust is the willingness to share information, tell the truth, admit mistakes, maintain confidentiality, give and receive constructive feedback, and speak with good purpose. How we practice these behaviors demonstrates our willingness to disclose and the quality of that disclosure. Therefore, in our model we refer to Communication Trust as *"Trust of Disclosure"* (see Figure 1B).

Trust influences communication, and communication influences trust. The two are very closely related. When leaders readily and consistently share information and involve employees in the running of the busi-

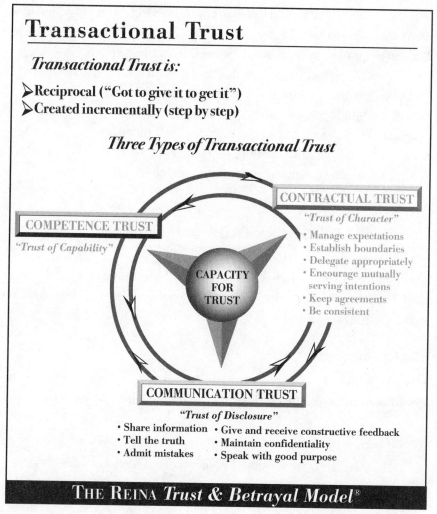

Figure 1B   Communication Trust

ness, it not only affects the trust between them but also affects productivity and profitability. People have to know what is happening if they are to work efficiently and effectively and be enthusiastic about what they are doing.

Likewise, employees need to communicate information up to leaders—information that leaders need to make decisions and solve problems. It is extremely embarrassing for leaders to be blindsided in a meeting by questions from the boss or a client regarding issues under their jurisdiction about which they should have known but were unaware. Leaders need their employees to keep them informed appropriately and in a timely manner, just as employees have the same need from their leaders.

People's perceptions affect the level of communication trust between individuals, within teams, and in the organization. It is human nature for people to make assumptions. In low-trust work environments, people tend to assume the negative regarding others' actions. In higher-trust work environments, people tend to give others the benefit of the doubt and assume the positive, until proven otherwise.

BEHAVIORS THAT CONTRIBUTE TO COMMUNICATION TRUST

There are six primary behaviors that contribute to building and maintaining communication trust in workplace relationships. We discuss them in the sections that follow.

Share Information

Have you ever experienced a breakdown in communication between headquarters and the field offices, management, and employees?

> *"Management should listen to concerns of employees in the field and act on them, rather than looking at the concerns as whining or complaints. I wish they would keep an open mind in dealing with these concerns, because not doing so builds resentment and breaks trust faster than anything. If management doesn't care about my concerns regarding the workplace, why should I trust them?"*

> *"I think the management weekly updates have helped keep us somewhat informed. However, I strongly feel we are told only what management thinks we need to know. I think decisions that we are told we will have input on may already have been made, and management is only going through the motions to make us feel good."*

Do we provide information willingly to others? Or do we simply tell them "only what they need to know"? Answering this critical question requires a high degree of honesty with ourselves. Some leaders assume that in the position they hold, they are obligated to tell employees only what they specifically need to do their job. This couldn't be further from the truth. When employees perceive that information is being withheld from them, they do not feel trusted by their managers. They need their leaders to be straightforward with them; this approach is in the best interests of getting the job done.

When employees don't have all the information or the correct information, they assume the worst and become anxious, especially in the midst of a change effort. This causes misunderstandings, needless concern, and distrust. When people don't have the facts, they tend to make them up, and rarely are they positive. Gossip and the grapevine go into high gear, deflecting time and energy away from day-to-day responsibilities.

Managing information is a challenge for leaders: they have to balance the desire and need of employees to understand what is happening in the organization with their own need to manage confidential and proprietary information that cannot be shared. Employees must manage such information as well. Leaders and employees preserve mutual trust when they are open, indicating and clarifying that they are sharing what information they are able to share.

The president of a large manufacturing operation asked us to assist him in assessing the climate of his organization following a significant change process. The changes the organization made were not producing the desired results. The president had a sense that there was some "disconnect" in the level of understanding among the employees regarding the change. He sensed that employees were not aware of the conditions that precipitated the need for change and the ways in which the change was designed to benefit the entire organization. Although the president felt the detachment, he was not clear regarding the specific factors contributing to the employee disengagement and was unsure of how to address it.

As we engaged with this organization and worked with people in all types of positions, we were able to confirm that a disconnect did indeed exist. When provided with a safe forum to talk about their perspectives, employees shared their experiences regarding how the recent changes had been managed:

> *"There was lack of communication and much miscommunication regarding changes that were taking place. People felt lied to. Human Resources had to pick up the pieces after being left out of the decisions. Even if management didn't have the answers, they simply needed to say 'We don't know.' It appeared as though leadership were operating in a chaos mode. To effectively steer this ship in the direction we need to head, the top management team needs to present a united front."*

> *"Every level of management has paid a great deal of lip service to the working troops. The information flow has dried up. Instead we must rely on the rumor mill or grapevine for information. We never really know how accurate it is. We feel as though we have been cut adrift and are floating aimlessly."*

The president's instincts were right: there was a disconnect between senior leadership and the employees at large. People mentioned that the lack of open information sharing contributed to employees' losing confidence and trust in leadership and the future direction of the company. As a result, employees were no longer able to trust what they heard and certainly were not able to contribute fully to the organization.

When information is not shared or there is a perception that information is not shared, employees feel betrayed. They feel as though they have not been trusted, and therefore their trust in leadership erodes. A government employee said, "I guess management doesn't trust that we can handle the information. So we are left in the dark."

The typical leader knows the importance of giving employees the information they need to do their jobs. Leaders are aware that they have a responsibility to help employees achieve the goals they are expected to achieve. If leaders know these things, one cannot help but wonder why leaders withhold information. There are numerous reasons. Some are conscious and deliberate; others are not. For example, some information may be sensitive or confidential and therefore inappropriate to share. In these circumstances, it is helpful for leaders to indicate to people that they are not at liberty to disclose all information. People are able to understand and respect the need for confidentiality and leadership's responsibility to maintain it. When a leader says, "I am not able to share all the pertinent information at this time," that degree of honesty actually enhances people's trust in their leader. Interestingly enough, even though they are not provided with "all the information," employees feel informed.

It is also true that there are individuals who consciously choose not to share information for personal reasons, the most common of which is fear of loss of control. They fear that not being the only ones "in the know" will reduce their value or power in the organization. This behavior is most common in periods of major change, when people are feeling particularly vulnerable and perhaps threatened. They respond out of a need to justify themselves and their role.

An individual's readiness to trust others may influence the degree to which he or she shares information. People who are trusting of others tend to be more forthcoming in sharing information. Individuals operating from hesitancy to trust others will be more inclined to withhold information.

Often leaders are not even aware that they are withholding information. This typically occurs when they are dealing with a vast array of issues and are working under tremendous pressure. Furthermore, they often assume that information-sharing channels are open and flowing when in reality they are not. Even though the withholding of information may not have been intended, people experience it as a betrayal, and trust is undermined.

Leaders are employees' best source for honest, accurate, and timely information. Sharing ideas and information with employees builds trust as well as enhances decision making, productivity, and the bottom line. Through sharing, leaders demonstrate trust in people to manage such information.

"I think management is taking the time and trying to listen to our concerns," one employee said to another. "The whole issue of communication between leadership and employees has vastly

improved. There is still some room for improvement. But I think the town hall meetings and companywide forums are important—they provide avenues for open communication between leadership and staff that includes employees from all entities of this organization. They allow for a larger view of what is happening in the organization. Often we focus only on our own department or unit and don't always take into consideration the impact our decisions and actions have on the whole."

Armed with a sense of knowing what's what, people are able to focus on performing their jobs with innovation and creativity, rather than on expending energy trying to fill in information gaps. This knowledge and clarity strengthens the foundation for trust in work relationships and the organization's capacity for trust expands. Withholding information to gain control, power, and perceived job security has the opposite effect and produces significant loss—it undermines trust in leaders' relationships with their employees. The organization's capacity for trust shrinks.

Tell the Truth

"At work, I cannot always honestly share my thoughts and feelings. I'm afraid of what will happen if I do. I have developed a tendency to say what I think they want me to say rather than how I truly feel. This isn't the way I want to be or how others generally see me, but this is how I feel safest in my current work environment. As long as I am professional and considerate in expressing my opinions, there shouldn't be any negative consequences, but unfortunately this is not always the case."

"I would like management to provide a process where people can voice their concerns, feelings, and needs safely. Recognize the need to openly talk about the issues and work them through. Allow subordinates to speak with superiors and with one another without retribution. People listening and talking with one another

without prejudging or overreacting—this is what creates trust in the workplace!"

Do we communicate openly and honestly? Do we create safe forums or work environments for people to express their concerns or voice their feelings without our prejudging them, making assumptions, or overreacting? Can employees speak the truth without fear of retribution? Particularly in times of change, people yearn for straightforward communication and need it from their leaders and one another. This means no lying, no exaggerating, no stretching or omitting or spinning of the truth. Lying and spinning destroy trust. If people don't tell the truth, trust can't grow. This is particularly important in today's global economy, where honesty is highly valued worldwide.

Experience shows that when the truth goes by the wayside, trust diminishes. People's natural openness is replaced by sarcasm and cynicism. Regardless of how savvy we may be in spinning the truth, others detect when they are receiving anything less than the full truth. Partial truth creates a major betrayal that may take a great deal of time to overcome.

Truth telling is the foundation for trust in an organization, and people deserve nothing short of the truth. Telling the truth sometimes takes courage, and employees look to their leaders to have those "courageous conversations." Especially in times of change, employees need their leaders to scrupulously and unflinchingly tell the truth—and nothing but the truth. As one health care finance manager put it, "Leadership means finding a way to be honest at all costs. That is the best way to lead. People want the truth! A good leader finds a way to deliver the hard messages." When people do not tell the truth, they actually betray themselves. Their sense of trust in themselves is compromised.

Because trust and honesty go together, a leader's behavior is crucial in building trust and fostering honest communication. Through their behavior, leaders can facilitate discussion of problems and concerns and then model responding in a nonjudgmental and engaging way. In so doing, they role-model this behavior for employees to practice with one another. Having the straight story and accurate information helps employees make better decisions, take the initiative to assume responsibility, be more productive, and make a strong contribution to the organization.

We have often heard employees, at all levels of the organization, express their concerns regarding the willingness of people—including themselves—to tell the truth. "We don't speak the truth at work," a marketing manager said. People tend to withhold the truth or "sugar-coat it to protect the current relationship or to avoid negative repercussions. The truth is too raw; people can't handle it. We are afraid of the truth. We don't trust what others will do with it."

Although in the short run avoiding the truth may protect the relationship, in the long run it does damage to the relationship and to the trust on which the relationship is built. Hence openness and honesty are essential for creating an environment of trust. These behaviors demonstrate respect and valuing of others. As a customer service rep expressed, "I find it easier to trust someone who is genuine about their feelings. I had a coworker in a former job who used to go 'overboard' with her compliments. It was so phony that you just knew she didn't mean anything she said. Not many people trusted her, and frankly, neither did I."

Avoiding the truth is a form of betrayal to ourselves and to the people with whom we are in a relationship. By not telling the truth, we compromise our sense of trustworthiness to others and to ourselves. The truth, although sometimes initially painful, can help people make a better adjustment to a situation, thus expanding the capacity for trust in a relationship.

We recently spent the day with a group of senior executives of one of the largest Fortune 100 companies. The purpose of the day was to explore what they, as top leadership, could do to build trusting relationships in their organization. A vice president looked at his colleagues and candidly said, "You know, it strikes me that we as a group sit in this room and spend more time talking about how we can put 'spin' on something rather than just telling the truth. And who are we trying to kid that our employees don't see it!"

These executives had become aware of the time and energy they spent in avoiding telling the truth. By adding spin, they were not being honest with their employees or themselves. As this group of executives was able to discover, spinning the truth doesn't work, no matter how bad the news is. It breaks down a leader's credibility. It decreases trust between the leader and people. As one of their employees sadly stated,

"We need honest answers from leadership. I have heard so much doublespeak and contradictory information lately, I don't know who to trust."

Admit Mistakes

"When I take responsibility and admit my mistakes, it gives my employees permission that it is safe to admit their mistakes. As a leader, the last thing I need is to be blindsided by covered up mistakes that my employees made and that I should have known about and could have corrected before they are shipped to our customers."

"We need to increase our speed to market," said the president of a personal products company. "This means we have got to find new, innovative ways of manufacturing our products. I need my people to think out of the box, to take some risks. Yes, they will make mistakes, but we need to treat those mistakes as an investment in our future position in the marketplace."

Do we readily admit mistakes? Do we take responsibility for our mistakes? How leaders deal with their mistakes and those made by others sets the tone for the rest of the organization and is a key factor in creating communication trust.

When any of us makes a mistake, it really is in our best interest to own up to it. It does not serve relationships to "stonewall" or cover up, which simply creates more significant problems. When energy is focused on covering up mistakes, precious time is wasted, and productivity, innovation, and creativity are lost. Such deception costs everyone, in many ways.

Avoiding mistakes at all costs is no way to run an organization, and almost guarantees a distrusting environment. There are no industries today where that can be tolerated. An environment where people are taking risks and stretching themselves to make progress is an environment where mistakes happen. If the individual and organization don't acknowledge those mistakes, they cannot learn from them. Remember the number of filaments that Edison tried in his efforts to invent the light bulb.

Those could be described as mistakes. He categorized those "mistakes," learned from them, and created an innovation. He could not have succeeded if he and his staff could not admit to mistakes. Leaders need to set the tone by admitting their own mistakes. They can choose to create a climate where mistakes are acknowledged or one in which mistakes are severely punished. Which choice fosters trust and supports business performance?

Leaders may be reluctant to disclose their mistakes or their concerns and feelings for fear of appearing weak. They may worry that this type of disclosure will compromise their employees' trust in them. In fact, for leaders at all levels, admitting one's mistakes goes a long way toward rebuilding trust with employees. Employees respect a leader who readily acknowledges his or her mistakes and makes amends for them. "In admitting when I make a mistake, it sets the tone and creates a safe environment. It shows employees that I am human and that I am vulnerable," said one senior manager in the computer industry. Admitting mistakes demonstrates a strong sense of trust in oneself. Remember, when others perceive that we trust ourselves, they are more inclined to place their trust in us too.

Trust is reciprocal. We get what we give. When we admit our mistakes, it is safe for others to admit theirs. Just as leaders must admit their mistakes, employees must own their errors as well. It does not build trust when people who repeatedly make mistakes hide behind excuses and abuse a leader's good nature and willingness to forgive.

Give and Receive Constructive Feedback

"Many people avoid giving feedback because they are afraid of confrontation or of hurting another's feelings. Giving feedback can involve lengthy conversations where issues are brought to the table. Many times, it's easier to avoid doing this. I'm not saying this is effective, but it happens in this workplace."

"I know it is going to be difficult for Joseph to hear how he came across in the meeting with the division team. But I have a responsibility to provide him that feedback so that he can grow from it. I don't want to rob him of that opportunity."

Do we give constructive feedback in a timely and effective manner, or do we avoid it for fear of confrontation? Do we give it with the intention of serving the other, or do we use it to serve ourselves?

"I appreciate leaders who are humble enough to receive feedback that isn't always positive; that creates trust among their people, and it helps me learn how to receive feedback. As an employee, I see receiving constructive feedback as an opportunity for me to learn or change what I do; it's not an attack on me as an individual."

Are we willing and open to receiving feedback—without getting defensive? Giving and receiving feedback is a critical factor in creating communication trust.

The president of a large manufacturing firm confided in us that his senior executive team meetings were too cordial. "Everyone is so courteous to one another—too courteous," he remarked. Upon further investigation, we quickly found out that there was a lot of unresolved conflict among the department heads. Because of their reluctance to confront issues openly and give each other constructive feedback, many of those issues were not addressed. The managers would talk to the president about their concerns but were unwilling to speak directly to the people involved. The managers hoped the president would intervene and do the talking for them. As the situation continued to go downhill, the level of trust among the senior executive team continued to deteriorate.

Does this sound familiar? Situations like this are not uncommon in organizations where people are unable or unwilling to give each other direct and constructive feedback. The result is that people don't know where they stand, and that undermines trust within the organization.

Positive feedback generates a sense of acceptance that is essential if we are then to take in corrective feedback. Given skillfully, with sensitivity and respect, feedback may open up channels of communication and further the development of trust. In addition, working with feedback, both giving and receiving, is an opportunity to become more aware of ourselves and others, which can expand our readiness to trust others and our sense of our own trustworthiness. When feedback is not a part of organizational life, we are robbed of this opportunity.

Providing constructive feedback sends a message that we are invested in the relationship that we trust that the individual will pay attention to what we have to say. (By "constructive feedback" we mean feedback that is intended to serve the other's growth.) But how we give it makes all the difference in the world. As one experienced employee stated, "I think it is important to give feedback in a nonthreatening, respectful manner. We need to acknowledge what was done, whether right or wrong, without making anyone wrong and then explore other ways of doing things. I also think that if you have feedback to give someone, it is important to give it to them directly instead of talking about them to everyone else." Speaking directly to the individual about his or her behavior and performance is critical to maintaining effective working relationships, especially if the other's behavior is having a negative effect on performance.

Individuals demonstrate a commitment to their relationships when they express their true thoughts and feelings about each other in a timely and appropriate manner. As one production worker on the shop floor of a northeastern manufacturing plant exclaimed to another, "If you ever get teed off at me, I want you to tell me. I'm a big boy. I can handle it." Or as an office worker exclaimed in a one-on-one communication session, "I don't know how to read you at times, and if I get upset with you, I shut up. That's not good. We need to talk things through with each other as they come up. We need to build on the trust we have had and keep building on it!" Giving each other effective feedback contributes to developing and maintaining trusting relationships that directly affect performance. To give feedback effectively, we need to be willing to receive it in return—nondefensively. When receiving feedback, we need to listen to the intent of what people are saying, rather than think of a comeback or response. We need to make an effort to show genuine interest in what we are hearing. Leaders support building this environment of trust around feedback by giving and receiving it themselves consistently.

But what gets in the way of giving and receiving feedback effectively? People who are hesitant to trust others and themselves tend to have difficulty giving and receiving constructive feedback. If they have unresolved issues with someone with whom they work, the amount and intensity of feedback they give may be out of proportion to a specific occurrence. Individuals with low trust in themselves may generalize about how this situation relates to past mistakes (whether they are similar or not). They may also attempt to project onto others their own feelings of inadequacy and fear, further clouding the issue at hand. The resulting distrust begets more distrust.

In receiving constructive feedback, people may find it difficult to trust themselves and others. They may not trust the messenger because of their low readiness to trust or because they are not convinced that the messenger is genuinely interested in their well-being. (For example, their manager tells everyone he has an open-door policy and that anything can be shared in confidence, but then takes punitive action against anyone who complains about anything.) Another problem might be that instead of hearing the issues presented, they cloud their perspective by consciously or unconsciously revisiting their past or bringing up prior mistakes they have made. They have difficulty separating the past from the present, possibly because they have unresolved issues.

These individuals' low readiness to trust gets projected externally and impedes their ability to develop effective relationships. Issues surrounding their performance don't get resolved but continue to mount. The issues of today get lumped together with the issues of yesterday. These individuals may have difficulty separating who they are from what they do and draw negative conclusions about themselves: "I will never be any good at this," or "I just can't trust myself in these situations."

Trust develops when people feel comfortable and safe enough to share their perceptions regarding one another's behavior without negative repercussions. They trust that they will not suffer the consequences of retaliation because they spoke the truth.

Working constructively with feedback helps develop our readiness and willingness to trust—in ourselves, our views, our perceptions, and our experiences. From this perspective, feedback is a gift—to those giving it and to those receiving it. Either way, when given with positive intentions and practiced skill, honest feedback helps us grow and develop, and nurtures communication trust.

Maintain Confidentiality

"I am appalled by employees discussing confidential information inappropriately. The eagerness, of some, to expose confidential information about a colleague or misuse personal information of coworkers is shocking."

"Patient information in our organization is treated with high standards of confidentially and dignity. In their reports, nurses report only pertinent patient information. Patient care always comes first, and it shows in the professionalism of the reports."

In any kind of relationship, confidentiality is essential to maintaining communication trust. We need to remember that when others have entrusted us with private or sensitive information, we have an obligation to honor that trust. There are times when maintaining confidentiality is a business responsibility, the breach of which may cost us our jobs. Other times, maintaining confidentiality is a relational responsibility, the breach of which may cost us our relationship.

Do we respect someone's request to maintain the confidentiality of sensitive information, or do we leak information to a close friend? Violating an agreement of confidentiality is an unabashed betrayal. It is a sure and fast way to destroy a person's trust *to the point where it may never be regained.* As one concerned employee shared, "If someone comes to me in confidence and shares something that has happened to them, I honor their confidence. If I don't, I know rumors will get started, things get out of hand, and damage will be done."

When trust is low, people fear that their confidential conversations will be used against them or that the information will be leaked across the organization. A midlevel manager explained, "I would like to go to my boss and confide in him about stressful situations that challenge me. But he appraises me, and I don't want to be perceived as weak." Another manager shared, "We, as a company, can't keep conversations in confidence. As a result, I'm afraid to share private information because it gets spread throughout the organization. That is how rumors get started and information gets distorted."

How do we deal with this kind of behavior? Such a breach of trust needs to be confronted with candor, respect, and sensitivity. Confronting others when there has been a breach of confidentiality is necessary if there is to be a trusting relationship in the future. The following illustrates how one colleague addressed a breach of confidentiality with another: "I bring myself to you with the highest integrity and confidentiality. I asked you on Monday to maintain confidence about X. After our conversation, I heard that you shared that information with others. I expect from you the same high degree of integrity and confidentiality that I bring to you. If I have a conversation with you in confidence, I expect you to keep it. Are we in agreement?"

Having this kind of conversation lets the other party know that you know what has happened. It establishes a clear boundary and sets explicit expectations (contractual trust) regarding future communication between the two of you. If we fail to address breaches of confidentiality, animosity and distrust result in our relationships with others. Left unaddressed, this kind of behavior can diminish any relationship. If this behavior proliferates in the workplace, it can destroy all trust and cripple the organization's performance.

Speak with Good Purpose

"GOSSIP!!! Yes, I am aware of gossip around here. Who isn't? You'd either have to be deaf, dumb, and blind or living in seclusion not to hear it. Although I don't condone it, I am sure I am a perpetrator as well as a victim of it. If I hear something about someone else, I usually ignore it. Sometimes if I am close to the situation being talked about, I will play the devil's advocate and defend the person being talked about. When I gossip about someone else, I tend to feel guilty, but only after everything is said and done, because honestly, no one thinks about it when they are actually doing it!"

*"We have an agreement, on this team, to talk directly to one
another when a problem arises rather than complain behind one
another's back. We have learned that when you hear others talking in a negative way, it is important to encourage them to stop
or talk to 'the person' directly. Before reacting to something that
you hear, it is important find out the whole story. What we often
hear through the grapevine is not accurate and can be quite damaging. It is we who must stop it."*

Do we gossip about fellow employees behind their backs? Or, if we
have a concern or issue with an individual, do we speak directly to the person? We speak with good purpose when we address issues or concerns
directly with the individual with whom we have them. We do so with the
best of intentions. Individuals who speak with good purpose speak constructively and affirmatively and stand up for each other. Conversely, when
we gossip, criticize, and shun others, we destroy trust between individuals, within a team, and throughout an organization. The consequences are
devastating to relationships, morale, and performance. In such work cli-
mates, the organization's ability to trust severely diminishes. "We talk
about each other behind each other's backs," admitted one supervisor in
the electronics industry. "When someone has an issue with another, we
don't speak directly to that person but blab it all over the lunchroom.
Backbiting is rampant around here!"

Do we share what is on our mind clearly and freely, or do we use
insinuating remarks or slighting digs to convey our thoughts indirectly?
When we are called to task for indirect remarks, do we take responsibility
or hide behind a white lie: "Oh, I was only joking. Don't be so sensitive!"
When we engage in dishonest communication by not saying what we mean
openly and directly, we misrepresent the reality of our feelings. In so doing,
we do harm to our relationships. This is a betrayal of ourselves and others.
This costs us our trustworthiness. Soon other people will not trust us and
will be guarded around us. They will withhold information about themselves for fear of being hurt or treated disrespectfully by us.

When we do not speak with good purpose, we betray our inner sense
of ourselves. When we hide behind inappropriate humor and sarcasm, we

betray our true voice, we betray what really needs to be said. The price we pay is the loss of a trusting relationship.

Leaders need to counter unfair criticism head-on, as do employees with one another. Leaders need to make it explicitly clear that engaging in gossiping and backbiting behavior is inappropriate, unprofessional, and unacceptable in their workplace. It breaks that precious entity that binds relationships—trust. As one savvy leader shared, "I have made my expectations clear, that people in this division address issues and concerns with one another directly rather than through a back door. To back up my expectations, I provided resources to help them develop the skills to do so mindfully. They now directly communicate problems and concerns to the appropriate individuals in an appropriate manner. Sure, there are slip-ups, and gossip does creep in. But it does not create the distraction and damage it once did. It is managed."

Speaking out against gossip builds a safe environment in which to trust.

COMMUNICATION TRUST BUILDS RELATIONSHIPS

We all have a need for effective relationships with those with whom we work and with whom we live. We have a need for connection with one another—to be heard, understood, supported, and given the benefit of the doubt when we trip up. Relationships are indeed a fundamental human need we share, and they are fundamental to meeting business needs. Business is conducted through relationships, and trust is the foundation to effective relationships.

A number of leaders we have interviewed work very hard to break down barriers and open communication with people. They have found that people welcome the opportunity to experience a leader's humanness, to have a window to who they are as a person. People want to see the different aspects of their leader. Experiencing their leader as human helps people feel safe and invites trust.

A leader's credibility unfolds through the development of trusting relationships. Trust develops through active engagement and participation with others. Enter into meaningful dialogue with your people. They want it! Find out what matters to them. Engage them in conversation about matters that are important to you and to them. Let them hear and see what is on your mind and what is in your heart.

Relationships develop through leaders' demonstrating a strong sense of trust in their people. The practice of communication trust helps leaders understand people better. Leaders can't take an organization single-handedly where it needs to go. They have to be able to count on effective relationships with people and to help employees learn to enhance their contribution to the organization. Inclusion and involvement need to become integral to leaders' daily operating style. Their words and actions reinforce trust and fairness. As one leader expressed, "Trust is the delicate fabric of human relationships. It is influenced far more by our behaviors than our words. It takes a long time to weave, but it can become frayed or torn very easily. Even a single action, perhaps misunderstood, can have significant effects."

A subtle yet common way leaders betray employees or employees betray one another or their leaders is by failing to practice the behaviors of communication trust. Understanding people means recognizing the importance and validity of their need for communication. Trust develops between leaders and their people and between employees when they understand that the other cares and is there to support them—to take risks and to fulfill his or her responsibilities. Communication trust contributes to the development of safe and productive work environments where an individual's capacity to trust in self and others increases, relationships flourish, and the organization's performance expands.

TRUST BUILDING IN ACTION

Reflecting on Your Experience

1. Where in your personal and work life do you experience high levels of communication trust?

2. Of the six behaviors that contribute to communication trust, choose one or two that you feel represent opportunities for you to build more trust in your relationships with others.
   - Share information
   - Tell the truth

- Admit mistakes
- Give and receive constructive feedback
- Maintain confidentiality
- Speak with good purpose

Application Exercises

A. The following questions are intended to facilitate dialogue as a team. Reflect on the following behaviors that create communication trust. Share those thoughts with your teammates. Observe how you practice each of these behaviors and its impact on communication trust.

1. *Share information.* How willingly do you share information with others? Do you receive the information you need? What happens to your communication trust when you don't? What can you do in the future to share information at a high level and encourage others to share with you?

2. *Tell the truth.* Do others tell you the truth? What happens to your level of trust when you question the truthfulness of others? What can you do to encourage more truth telling both by you and by others?

3. *Admit mistakes.* Are you willing to admit your mistakes? What happens when you do admit mistakes? What do you do when others admit their mistakes? What can you do to support the admission of mistakes within your organization?

4. *Give and receive constructive feedback.* How do giving and receiving constructive feedback contribute to communication trust in your organization? What can you do in the future to encourage constructive feedback?

5. *Maintain confidentiality.* How do you decide what to share and what to hold back? How do you balance this behavior with the need to share information?

6. *Speak with good purpose.* How do people speak of each other in your organization? Do they speak respectfully of others, or is there a lot of gossiping and backbiting? What can you do to promote speaking with good purpose in your organization?

B. *One-on-One Communication Meetings*. The following exercise is intended to facilitate communication trust within a group or team. This process is effective in dealing with interpersonal issues that impede communication and performance within a group. Construct a matrix of all the participants in the group so that every person has an opportunity to have a one-on-one meeting with everyone else. Set up one- to two-hour meetings. (Refer to the communication matrix in the following illustration as a sample.) Have participants speak candidly to one another regarding how they interact and work together. You may use the following sentences to add structure to the meeting. Have each person reflect on these in preparation for the meetings with each of their teammates.

- What I appreciate about you is . . .
- What works in our relationship is . . .
- What doesn't work in our relationship is . . .
- What I need from you is . . .
- Let's brainstorm together ways in which we can work together better.

This exercise works with groups as small as four individuals or as large as twelve. For larger groups, you might want to divide the participants into subgroups to expedite the process.

If there is low trust or antagonism within the group, it is advisable to lead these sessions with a skilled facilitator who does not have a relationship with any of the participants. It is important to conduct the sessions in a confined time frame to achieve optimum results. We strongly encourage that team members contract with one another before the sessions start to keep these conversations confidential. Establish working agreements ahead of time to ensure the psychological safety of the participants.

Trust Note

Trust influences communication, and communication influences trust. The two are very closely related. Leaders who readily and consistently share information and involve employees in the running of the business not only build trust within the organization but also boost productivity and profitability.

Communication Matrix

PURPOSE: To facilitate the logistics of everyone participating in this communication exercise

PARTICIPANTS:

1. Harry   5. Rachel
2. Maria   6. Jackson
3. Carlos   7. Joanne
4. Lee

PROCESS: The participants will speak to each other in the prescribed rounds during the following weeks:

	May 7–9	May 12–16		May 19–23		May 26–30	
Rounds	1	2	3	4	5	6	7
Participants	1↔7	1↔6	1↔5	1↔4	1↔3	1↔2	2↔7
	2↔6	2↔5	2↔4	2↔3	6↔5	6↔4	6↔3
	3↔5	3↔4	7↔6	7↔5	7↔4	7↔3	5↔4

EXAMPLE:

During the week of May 7–9, the following people talk with each other:

Harry and Joanne
Maria and Jackson
Carlos and Rachel

Trust Tip

When we gossip, criticize, and shun others, we destroy trust between individuals, within a team, and throughout an organization. The consequences are devastating to relationships, morale, and performance. Conversely, when we speak with good purpose, speak constructively and affirmatively and stand up for each other, we build trust, strengthen relationships, boost morale and improve performance.

4

THE TRUST OF CAPABILITY: COMPETENCE TRUST

"Why doesn't she just let me do my job!" Joyce said in utter frustration. "It seems like every day, the boss is looking over my shoulder, telling me how to do my job. Why did she hire me in the first place, if she isn't going to use my expertise? Doesn't she have anything better to do? I feel so discounted."

Have you ever felt micromanaged or underutilized because you were not able to use your talents to do your job in the way you know it needs to be done? Your education and years of experience are not valued, but are in fact devalued.

"I can't believe you promoted Hugh to the team leader position," Mark said in exasperation to his boss. "He doesn't know the job, accepts credit for work he didn't perform, and works half as hard as any other member of the team. I'm really shocked that you promoted someone like that!"

Have you ever felt frustrated because the competence (or lack thereof) of another was inappropriately rewarded, when they were unworthy of the credit or promotion they were given and particularly when other teammates were more capable and deserving?

"I'm not very confident Sam can do the job!" Suzette stated to her coworker on the team. "I don't think Sam has the knowledge or skills to pull his own weight in getting this project done on time and within budget. His lackluster performance thus far has me very concerned. We have a lot riding on this project's success."

Have you ever felt concerned regarding the capability of a coworker? Do you have trust in the people who pass work to you? Do you believe you will receive the work in a form with which you can be successful? Do you have trust in the people to whom you hand off work? Do you think they will build on your good work or screw it up and make you all look bad?

WHAT IS COMPETENCE TRUST?

Whether the situation involves an employee-to-employee or employee-to-supervisor relationship, these utter frustrations, extreme disappointments, and grave concerns happen every day on the job. They result in underutilization of skills and abilities, breakdowns of confidence in others' competence, decreased performance, and diminished *competence trust.*

As we will discuss further in this chapter, competence trust involves acknowledging people's skills and abilities, allowing people to make decisions, involving others and seeking their input, and helping people learn skills. How we practice these behaviors demonstrates our willingness to trust our capability and that of others. Therefore, in our model we characterize Competence Trust as *"Trust of Capability"* (see Figure 1C).

Most people feel good about their ability to do whatever job they are assigned. Unless they are given feedback to the contrary, they will continue to believe this. If they suddenly receive negative feedback after a long period of doing the job with little or no feedback or primarily positive feedback, they may initially ignore or discount the new feedback and

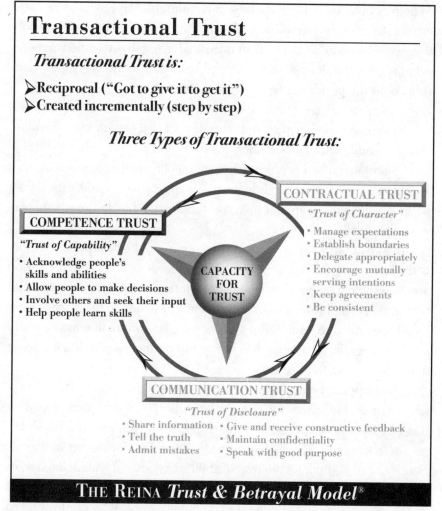

Transactional Trust

Transactional Trust is:

➤Reciprocal ("Got to give it to get it")
➤Created incrementally (step by step)

Three Types of Transactional Trust:

CONTRACTUAL TRUST

"Trust of Character"

• Manage expectations
• Establish boundaries
• Delegate appropriately
• Encourage mutually
  serving intentions
• Keep agreements
• Be consistent

COMPETENCE TRUST

"Trust of Capability"

• Acknowledge people's
  skills and abilities
• Allow people to make decisions
• Involve others and seek their input
• Help people learn skills

CAPACITY FOR TRUST

COMMUNICATION TRUST

"Trust of Disclosure"

• Share information   • Give and receive constructive feedback
• Tell the truth   • Maintain confidentiality
• Admit mistakes   • Speak with good purpose

THE REINA *Trust & Betrayal Model*®

Figure 1C   Competence Trust

continue performing their jobs as they always have. This is because people's sense of personal worth and identity is often directly linked to their competence in their jobs. The new information may not fit their picture of who they are and what they have to contribute.

Usually people are motivated to develop competence in what they do and how they do it. Most people want and need to know they make a difference and contribute to the overall good of the organization. It is important for leaders to be aware of this fundamental need in people and to help people apply their abilities in meaningful ways to meet business challenges. By giving employees the freedom and flexibility to do the jobs they were hired to do rather than micromanaging them, leaders not only acknowledge employees' skills and abilities but also increase their motivation and the performance of the organization.

Competence trust is an absolute requirement if an organization is going to get any work done, whether that work is a specific task or a more complex combination of activities. People count on each other to be able to do their jobs. When people can't count on one another to pull their own weight, and that lack of confidence is not appropriately addressed, then people's expectations are not met, communication breaks down, and performance declines.

Quite often when we think of competence in the workplace, we think of the formal mechanisms on which we have become dependent to develop our workforce: personnel policies aimed at tracking people's abilities and performance, and formal training programs designed to teach employees "what they need to know." But competence is more than education and training programs; it is more than hiring and promotion policies; it is more than information, tools, and technology, important as they are.

An important component of competence trust is the ability of individuals to deal effectively with the demands and expectations placed on them by leadership, peers, customers, and the organization. This ability relates to the skills, knowledge, attitude, behavior, confidence, and experience aimed at fulfilling the responsibilities associated with defined roles and holding oneself accountable. Often we hear leaders lamenting, "I can't trust my people in the field to do quality work. Why did I spend so much money training them? Didn't they learn anything?"

Competence trust is found where leaders and employees learn from one another, where they learn from their customers, suppliers, and competitors. This kind of trust develops where communication trust is strong, where information exchange is easy and open—up, down, across, inside, and outside the organization; and where contractual trust is prevalent, where leaders and employees are clear about what is expected of them and live up to those expectations.

You know competence trust when you experience it. You see it, feel it, and hear it. People respond swiftly to requests for information; they provide assistance with a complicated project without hesitation; they answer questions or concerns regarding an issue directly and candidly. Competence trust starts and finishes with knowledgeable people who are highly responsible, who hold themselves accountable, who are committed to continuous improvement, and who are aligned with the objectives and needs of their organization.

But what happens when there is a breakdown in communication and contractual trust, when communication is strained and information exchange is diminished? When people are not clear about what is expected of them and have difficulty living up to those expectations? Breakdowns of contractual and communication trust lead to breakdowns of competence trust. The boss may lack competence trust in those she supervises, fearing they haven't the capability to do the job at the level of quality expected. Likewise, her employees may have issues with her, perceiving her as not being a capable leader with knowledge and skills and from whom they can learn. Neither the supervisor nor the employees are meeting each other's expectations. There is a breakdown in performance in both directions. So what can we do?

BEHAVIORS THAT CONTRIBUTE TO COMPETENCE TRUST

Leaders and employees can practice four primary behaviors to build and maintain competence trust in their organizations. Let's look at each.

Acknowledge People's Skills and Abilities

"I have a lot of experience in this job, and one of the hardest things for me to do is to step back and let someone else do something. It is easier to just do the job myself than to guide someone through it correctly. Sometimes I have to just step back and let the other person struggle through as they learn to do the job their way."

Do we acknowledge coworkers' ability to do their jobs? Do we give them guidance and direction to get the job done right? Do we give them the room to grow? Do we allow people the freedom and flexibility to do the jobs their way?

"As a supervisor, I need to know where a person's skills lie to make me feel confident in delegating a task. So I talk with that person before I delegate to see if they have the experience needed or if this will require new skills for them. This helps me to know the type of support they will need. The look on a person's face when they have accomplished a new skill is priceless."

Respecting people's knowledge, skills, and abilities allows them to use their existing talents and to learn new skills to accomplish the goals they were hired to accomplish. Allowing people to do their jobs and to grow in those jobs is critical to keeping employees engaged. The leader's role is to keep people motivated by challenging them and giving them opportunities to increase their skills and knowledge.

When we acknowledge people's competence, we are actually providing a form of feedback. We are letting them know that we see what they have to offer and are therefore providing them with opportunities to use their talents. We thus build both competence trust and communication trust. Trust within the relationship grows, and the individual's trust in himself or herself is deepened.

Fredrick, a competent engineer, was promoted to a managerial position. For years he had enjoyed the hands-on fieldwork of his job. He liked having complete control of the projects assigned to him. Now, as manager, he has added administrative functions to his responsibilities. Fredrick doesn't have time for hands-on contact with the projects for which he is responsible, but he wishes he did. He is having a hard time delegating to his employees. He wants to delegate but has concerns about their abilities, and he is not taking the time to train them. When he does delegate projects, he is constantly looking over employees' shoulders, telling them what to do.

Fredrick has a higher readiness to trust himself than he has to trust others. Should this situation continue unchanged, Fredrick's hesitancy to trust his people will make it difficult for them to trust him. Remember, we have to give trust to get trust!

Do you trust in people's competence to do the task, to get the job done? Trusting people's knowledge, skills, and abilities is reflected in a willingness to allow them to use their talents to accomplish goals. Fredrick's challenge is to learn to trust his people to do their jobs and to grow in those jobs. It is important to be aware of your hesitancy to trust and need to control, if you have them, and of the impact of your attempts at controlling employees instead of trusting them. The more you trust them, the less need there is for control.

As you develop your people, they demonstrate your trust in their capabilities. You are actually investing in them and the relationship, and there are rewards. In your effort to invest in the development of your people's competence, you are in turn developing your own. As they grow and develop, so do you. As they assume additional responsibilities, you further explore professional interests and further develop your competence and trust as a mentor.

People with limited trust in themselves may not view themselves as competent. They may be unaware of their potential. When you see the potential in people, it allows you to trust in their potential competence. You provide them with a remarkable gift. For when you trust in them, you open the door for them to trust in themselves, for them to discover themselves further. With this foundation in place and with support and guidance, people flourish. Giving employees freedom and flexibility within clear parameters and trusting them to do their jobs pay dividends—to you, to them, and to the organization. It enables them to accomplish more than they may ever have expected. Their competence is enriched, and their capacity for trust expands.

When leaders trust in employees' competence instead of micromanaging, they give their employees the freedom and latitude to do their jobs. Under these circumstances, trust is more than reciprocated. Employees will usually exceed the leader's expectations. "A while back," a manager with a large consulting firm said, "I gave a junior team member the task of making a proposal presentation to a prospective client. Not being fully aware of his abilities, I took a risk; it took some trust. It was a long shot. However, the junior team member was highly motivated and did a lot of work in preparation for the event. He made a great presentation, and we got the contract. He actually exceeded my expectations and hopes. It took a leap of faith on my part." This leader gave trust and was not disappointed in return. He, the junior team member, and the organization benefited.

But what about the times when it doesn't work out, when you trust your employee with a major project and he or she drops the ball? How should you handle the situation? Obviously, you must review each situation individually and "with open eyes" to determine whom you can trust with what. You need to listen to yourself and follow your intuition. Sometimes we may trust in a person's competence more than he or she does. That is a situation ripe for your coaching.

Larry, vice president and comptroller for a dynamic restaurant group known for excellence, shares a hard lesson he learned: "Having competence trust is not blind trust—you've got to follow your intuition. I allowed Susan, who was outwardly very confident, to 'snow' me. Susan's confidence overshadowed a slipshod approach to her books. I trusted her, but I should have followed my instincts. She didn't perform up to my expectations." By the time Larry realized Susan was not performing up to par, it was almost too late. The books were due, and Larry's appointee had failed to deliver. Larry reflects, "The lesson for me is 'Do not be afraid to confront.' A lot of external distractions clouded my intuition. Because of my trust in this employee, I made an assumption, that Susan should know how to do this closing. Her assertiveness and confidence I mistook for competence. I needed to trust my intuition."

This story illustrates the hard lesson we all need to learn, some of us time and time again: when we don't listen to our inner voice, we betray ourselves.

Trusting in your own competence is directly related to the need to trust your intuition. Your beliefs about your abilities have a profound effect on those abilities. If you believe you have the competence and the confidence to meet certain goals for yourself, that belief will influence your success.

Your readiness to trust in your competence starts with your readiness and willingness to trust yourself. This also influences how trusting you are of others. Your readiness and willingness to trust influences your beliefs and perceptions about yourself and others. "If I see myself as trustworthy, I project that," a health care human resource manager observed. "My self-concept and worldview determine how trustingly I view others."

Risk taking, essential to business success, is directly related to trust in our own competence. Trust in our competence influences our thoughts regarding our ability to keep up with the changing demands of our jobs. We question, "Can I keep up? Can I learn the new system? Do I have what it takes?" In low-trust work environments, people are reluctant to take risks and admit mistakes for fear of looking incompetent. Working in this type of environment, an individual may over time begin to doubt or question his or her competence.

Margaret was her own worst critic. She was afraid of taking a risk for fear of making a mistake. When she did make a mistake, she would repeatedly beat up on herself. She didn't want to let the team down, yet her fear of letting the team down paralyzed her. She was so focused on the fear—in a way, she trusted her fear instead of trusting herself—that she continued to fail. Her supervisor asked if he could coach Margaret, and Margaret reluctantly acquiesced. "I urged her to stay in the present," her supervisor said, "to focus on the objectives, not on the obstacles, and to use the help of her teammates." As Margaret began to focus on the present and ask for help from her teammates, she started to make some progress. She started to trust herself and her teammates more—though not without occasional slip-ups. Ultimately, she was successful in accomplishing one major task and then another and another. She started to gain a sense of success and then pride in following through and accomplishing her goals. That was over a year ago. Margaret continues to grow, step-by-step, learning more about herself, trusting more in herself. Her confidence in her competence grows each day.

For the first time in her life, somebody took the time and patience to work with Margaret and to trust in her capability and potential. As a result of her supervisor's efforts and his trust in her, Margaret began to blossom. Sometimes another person's trust in us gives us the courage to trust in ourselves.

Allow People to Make Decisions

"I allow people to make decisions when they demonstrate good judgment, aren't uncomfortable asking for help when they need it, and are willing to give help as part of a team effort. If I have doubts or concerns, I tend to be very watchful and offer assistance. I am approachable, so they won't feel uncomfortable to ask a question. Likewise, I appreciate it when others consult with me when I have a question."

Do we allow people the freedom and flexibility to make decisions? Or, if we are not able to, do we at least include them in the major decisions, particularly those that affect their jobs and their lives? By allowing people to make decisions, we are giving them a chance to use their judgment to make choices that affect their work. When people are not included, they feel left out, discounted, devalued, and disempowered. Managers must trust themselves enough to let someone else make a decision. Part of this trust is managers' ability to handle an incorrect decision being made by another.

Sometimes you may not have prior experience on which to base a determination of an employee's competence, to assess whether you can trust that person's judgment. This is especially the case in a relatively new relationship, such as when working with new employees or perhaps when working on new projects with experienced employees. In these times, you must use your best judgment and trust it. When you make a judgment call, when you trust, it means that you empower employees to make decisions within the scope of their responsibilities, to the best of their ability, without encumbering them with your insecurities. Drawing on your judgment to trust their competence positions them to make a full contribution, to learn, grow, and further develop their competence. In this ever changing, competitive business landscape, leaders have got to develop and fully utilize their people's abilities. If leaders don't, they will lose their good people and demotivate and disempower the rest. An organization can't stay competitive with a disenfranchised and disempowered workforce.

Involve Others and Seek Their Input

Think of an occasion when someone asked for your advice or opinion. How did it feel? Pretty good? When you involve or seek the involvement of others, you demonstrate your trust in their competence.

Do you involve coworkers in planning, decision making, and problem solving related to the scope of their job responsibilities and your stated expectations of their performance? Do you allow your employees to discuss and even challenge your decisions with the intent of achieving what is best for the organization? When employees feel safe enough to challenge your decisions (in appropriate and respectful ways), this is an indication of the trust that exists in the relationship. Likewise, when people don't feel safe because of negative past experiences that diminished or broke their trust, they don't seek those people's input or involve them in decision making or problem solving. Their willingness to engage with others in dialogue to seek their views and to explore possible alternatives depends on the degree of confidence and safety they feel toward others.

We often hear employees voice resignation and frustration about not having input. From factory floors to high-rise offices, we hear employees say, "Either they don't trust us or they figure we don't have anything to contribute, so they don't ask us," or "Nobody ever asks me what I think!" When their ideas have not been solicited or, worse yet, when they have been solicited but not valued, people feel betrayed. The failure to recognize or value a person's actual or potential competence is a betrayal of both the individual and the organization: the individual is cut off from the opportunity to make a full contribution, and the organization is robbed of that individual's full talent. What a waste of human talent, a loss of human motivation and unachieved potential!

A leader must have enough self-trust and self-confidence in order to involve others and ask for their input. We have seen managers who would not turn to their employees for input or participation because they feared their subordinates might surpass them if they learned the "secrets" necessary to be a part of whatever process. The managers just did not have enough self-confidence that they would succeed using this approach.

In contrast, when we seek the input of others and involve them in problem solving and decision making, the benefits are multifold: we acknowledge their contribution, we gain from their expertise, and we empower the relationship. "Allow employees to take ownership and have pride in their work," advised a manufacturing vice president. "Challenge their thought processes. Give people the stimulus to do things." When you seek out the input of others, you demonstrate your trust in their competence. In return, you gain from their advice and enhance the trust between you and them. Trusting in people's ability deepens their sense of ownership and accomplishment in their work. Furthermore, you build a foundation of trust in the relationship. Their trust in themselves and your trust in them and yourself expand.

Help People Learn Skills

"We have many employees in our unit who have worked many years and are experts at what they do. Yet there is resistance when it comes to training new staff. It is imperative to the success of the unit that these new employees receive the necessary training. I know that I would not be at the level that I am today without the training I received from my coworkers."

"We have so much expertise and longevity in this unit. We can learn a great deal from one another if we are willing to share and listen to what we each have to offer."

Investing in people is a powerful way to demonstrate your trust in their capacity to develop their competence. As mentors, leaders need to find out about what motivates people and to work with them to develop their capacity and potential. Doing so enhances employees' development of trust in their own competence and hence their performance. Trust in leaders grows when employees are supported in gaining relevant knowledge and skills and in applying them on the job.

During our interviews with senior executives, they spoke of the changing work contract. They spoke of the struggle they face regarding what they can and cannot guarantee their employees. Long-term job security no longer exists. Assisting their employees to develop competence is one aspect many leaders said they could guarantee. One senior manager at the corporate headquarters of a large chemical manufacturing company tells his employees, "I can't guarantee you job security, but I can guarantee that I will try my hardest to make you all you can be." Another seasoned manager said, "There is no such thing as job security anymore. The only form of job security I can give them is for them to learn more skills than they have now."

Although leaders may not be able to guarantee jobs for life, they can make a commitment to develop their people. Leaders who do make that commitment make a wide array of developmental tools available: training programs, outside workshops or conferences, or visits to other organizations to observe their methods and practices. Many leaders enable employees to continue their formal education or to receive assistance from a professional coach. Leaders may ask individuals to head up a special project or provide a promotional opportunity as a further means of developing employees' skills and experience.

Leaders have an obligation to develop employees, and those employees in return have an obligation to pursue their own growth and development. "Leaders need to get their people to be more empowered," said one chemical plant manager. "To do so, individuals need to take responsibility for their own person. They need to be in touch with themselves and their needs. They need to make choices (with eyes wide open) to get their needs met versus blindly trusting in the organizations [in which they work] to get their needs met." When people see others highly involved in their own personal development, they tend to be more trusting of their competence.

Yet how do we engage employees who are not motivated in their jobs? Many people in organizations (particularly the aging baby boomers) are at the top or near the top of their careers. A good number of these "corporate soldiers" have already hit the R.O.A.D. (retired on active duty); they do what they have to in order to get by—no more, no less. How do we appeal to their interests in developing their skills and abilities? How do we bring them back and utilize their wealth of knowledge in the few years they have before retirement?

Giving these employees money bonuses, letters of appreciation, or employee-of-the-month recognition probably will have little or no effect. What is critical is finding out what is important to them as individuals. Can we sit down with them and find out what motivates them? Can we give these employees training incentives or retrain them to create job opportunities within and outside their department to help them better themselves?

When leaders trust in their people's competence, they influence and empower their employees to go beyond their current beliefs about their personal limitations. Employees' readiness to trust in themselves and others expands. The development of people's competence can be thrilling and exciting for all involved. It can also be quite challenging. Leaders and employees alike know that to develop the capacity of their organizations, there must be opportunities to stretch and grow, they often find themselves driven by day-to-day pressures and demands and therefore feel as though they "can't afford the time" to invest in development. Yet, leaders must make the time to develop their people's competence in order to grow the capacity of the organization—for the immediate and long term future.

A leader's ability to develop the competence of employees and thereby develop the capacity of the organization is critical to the organization's maintaining a competitive edge. Effective leaders create environments where people are not afraid to take risks and tackle new areas and new ways of doing things.

In developing competence trust in their organizations, effective leaders create the psychological as well as the physical safety for people to stretch themselves to accomplish business objectives. Within these safe boundaries, people are able to focus on what they were hired to do: produce products and services and satisfy customers.

"Create the space so that people can find out for themselves and learn. They may not get it right the first time, but they will get there," said a senior manager for an international chemical company. People need the freedom and the flexibility to learn from their mistakes. People's trust in their competence and in their leaders grows. Conversely, when the organizational environment does not support people's learning from their mistakes, competence trust in themselves and their leaders dwindles.

When there is fear in the workplace, people's readiness and willingness to trust their competence diminishes. They are unwilling or, as in the Dilbert cartoon, unable to exercise their given talents and realize their performance potential. Hindered or frozen by fear, their willingness to be creative and innovative shuts down. These people feel betrayed by the organization in which they work

In dealing with these challenges, it is easy to get discouraged. Leaders, however, cannot give up on people or themselves when disappointed in performance. If someone is not living up to performance expectations, it is a leader's job to continue to nurture the person's potential and to trust in the person's ability. Being an effective leader means being able to reach out to each individual, to develop people's strengths and work with their weaknesses. Competence trust is about trusting where people are and trusting where they have the potential to be.

DEALING WITH DISAPPOINTMENT

There are times when we are disappointed in a person's performance. "I asked you to do X; you gave it your best effort but came up short. I am disappointed." When that occurs, is their behavior a betrayal? When a person has honestly tried to accomplish a task but failed because of lack of skill or aptitude, we may feel let down, but their behavior is not a betrayal. It is not a betrayal in that they were not acting in a self-serving manner. They simply did their best. (If, however, the individual did have the ability but chose not to use that talent, it is a betrayal. Knowingly failing to meet expectations is an intentional breach of contractual trust.)

Leaders may be disappointed, even frustrated, by an employee's performance, but they must continue to provide support, which can take the form of helping the person see how he or she can enter into similar situations differently in the future or how the person may tap into others and surround himself or herself with the skills and support needed to be successful.

An old Chinese proverb is as true today as ever: "If you want one year of prosperity, grow grain. If you want ten years of prosperity, grow trees. If you want one hundred years of prosperity, grow people."

Contributing to the growth of others starts with our being aware of how we bring ourselves to our relationships with them. Do we behave as though we are second guessing what they are able to do? Do we hold back our trust? Through reflecting on these questions we may find that we need to shift and be open to trusting others more fully, which will allow us to see and reframe habits, thoughts, and perceptions that have caused us to hold back. We will then be able to choose to behave differently, in a way that serves us and our relationships.

Leaders' acknowledging employees' skills and abilities, allowing them to make decisions, involving them and seeking their input in planning and decision making, and helping them learn new skills—all these daily behaviors develop employees' capacity to contribute, leaders' capacity to develop others, and the organization's capacity to perform. The more we trust in our employees, the more trust they have in us. This level of trust gives birth to limitless possibilities.

TRUST BUILDING IN ACTION

Reflecting on Your Experience

1. Where in your personal and work life do you experience high levels of competence trust?

2. Of the four behaviors that contribute to competence trust, choose one or two that you feel represent opportunities for you to build more trust in your relationships with others.
   - Acknowledge people's skills and abilities
   - Allow people to make decisions
   - Involve others and seek their input
   - Help people learn skills

Application Exercises

A. The following questions are intended to facilitate dialogue as a team. Reflect on the following behaviors that create competence trust. Share those thoughts with your teammates. Observe how you practice each of these behaviors and its impact on competence trust.

1. Where in your personal and work life do you experience high levels of competence trust in yourself? In others?

2. Do you acknowledge your own knowledge, skills, and abilities? What happens when you feel less trust in your own or someone else's competence?

3. Are you reluctant to give others a chance to perform because you fear their failure? How do those decisions affect your workload? How might you help create situations where others have a much better chance of succeeding?

4. Do you allow others to make decisions, or do you assume that no one can make decisions as good as yours? How does this affect your trust in the competence of others?

5. How do you involve others in matters that affect them? In what ways do you seek their input? When you do, what is the effect on your trust in their competence? On their trust in their own competence?

6. In what ways do you develop your own skills? What actions do you take that help others develop their skills? What might you do differently in the future to enhance skill building even more?

B. *Each One Teach One.* This is a method of cross-training in which people proficient or experienced in certain skills contract with their coworkers to teach them skills they need. This approach is also useful when people go to outside training and come back and train their peers in what they learned. Teaching others what we learn challenges us to "know our stuff," helping us internalize and integrate our learning. It encourages sharing of information and expertise that builds competence trust and support in each other, while also developing the capacity of the team and maximizing the training dollar investment.

Instructions:

1. The next time you attend a training session, contract with a coworker who did not attend the session to teach him or her what you learned.

2. After completion of the training, review the material covered and prepare an outline of the key knowledge and skills learned.

3. Set up blocks of uninterrupted time to share what you learned with your coworker. Check for clarity and understanding as you proceed through the process.

4. Brainstorm ways each of you can support each other in applying the new knowledge on the job.

C. *Create Learning Contracts.* Employing learning contracts with people in training programs or in on-the-job training helps ensure application of skills and increases competence trust among team members. The following illustration is a sample matrix of questions people address prior to engaging in a specific learning process. It formally outlines skills and knowledge they want or need to learn to do their current job or take on additional responsibilities, resources they will use to acquire the skills and knowledge, projected dates to learn skills or have a basic understanding of the knowledge, and application of learning.

Learning Contract

Name: _____

WHAT I NEED OR WOULD LIKE TO LEARN	RESOURCES NEEDED	PROJECTED DATE	APPLICATION OF LEARNING

Signature: _____ Date: _____

Instructions:

1. Use the learning contract here as a tool for professional development.

2. After an employee returns from training, have him fill out the form and meet with him to discuss his learning plans.

3. Follow up with the employee to support him in his learning process.

Trust Note

People often measure their sense of personal worth and identity by their competence in their jobs. Most people want and need to know they make a difference and contribute to the overall good of the organization. Help people apply their abilities in meaningful ways to meet business challenges.

Trust Tip

Trusting others' competence is the acknowledgment of their skills and abilities; you are allowing them the freedom and flexibility to do the jobs they are hired to do, instead of micromanaging them. Doing so increases people's motivation and organizational performance.

PART III

WHERE
TRUST BEGINS

*Where does our readiness and willingness to trust
ourselves and others begin? How do we learn to trust?
What influences our decisions to trust ourselves and
others? These questions are answered in these next two
chapters, which discuss capacity for trust and what we
call the Capacity for Trust Attributes.*

5

OUR READINESS AND WILLINGNESS TO TRUST: CAPACITY FOR TRUST

Chandra began to doubt in her ability to keep up with the increased workload and changing demands placed on her. "Can I do this? I'm not sure if I can trust myself to learn these new systems and procedures in time to get the project done. I don't know anymore." Later, she reflected on her fears. She reviewed the strengths she knew she would bring to the job. She was able to see that what was most important to the position were the skills she possessed. "I will use this opportunity to build on them."

"Can I trust them? I don't know if it is safe to rely on my new teammates to come through for me and get the job done. I took a risk counting on my coworkers in my old job, and those guys didn't deliver as promised. I lost my credibility and reputation with my clients—I was burned badly! Now I'm a lot less willing to trust my teammates with such an important project."

Where does our readiness and willingness to trust begin? How do they affect our perceptions and our beliefs? How are they influenced by our experiences, positive and negative?

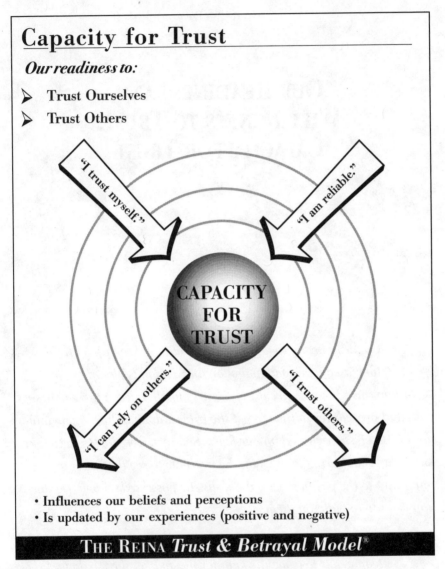

Capacity for Trust

Our readiness to:

➢ **Trust Ourselves**
➢ **Trust Others**

"I trust myself."

"I am reliable."

CAPACITY FOR TRUST

"I can rely on others."

"I trust others."

• **Influences our beliefs and perceptions**
• **Is updated by our experiences (positive and negative)**

THE REINA *Trust & Betrayal Model*®

Figure 2   Capacity for Trust

We have explored the meaning of transactional trust and the behaviors that build it. Here we explore where trust begins, our readiness and willingness to trust *ourselves* and *others* which we call our *capacity for trust* (see Figure 2).

Our capacity for trust is fundamental to understanding how we bring ourselves to relationships with ourselves and others. When we trust ourselves, we see ourselves as reliable, dependable, and well intentioned toward ourselves and others. When we trust others, we feel we can rely on their judgment and their intentions. We have confidence in them and their word.

Our capacity for trust is influenced by our life experiences, and it expands or contracts depending on the nature of our experiences, positive or negative, and the situations that we encounter.

Some of us enter trustingly into relationships until we have an experience that tells us it is no longer safe to trust. Others enter untrustingly into relationships until it is proven safe to trust. We refer to people's readiness to trust as their developmental predisposition.

How Our Capacity for Trust Develops

Our developmental predisposition to trust begins to form in the very early stages of our lives and is based on positive and negative experiences. The first two years of life are especially critical to this development. Through the loving care of primary caregivers, we develop our fundamental capacity to trust others. Some of us have early life experiences that represent support, comfort, safety, and nurturing. We found ourselves surrounded by those we could count on. We may therefore tend to be more ready and willing to trust others.[1] Others of us may have found ourselves in early life circumstances of inconsistent care, loss, lack of safety, little nurturing, and few people we could rely on. We may therefore tend to feel the need to wait and see before we trust others. We need concrete evidence that it is safe to trust.[2]

As we develop mentally and physically, we are able to be more self-reliant, and we learn to trust ourselves more. As we develop muscle coordination and become more mobile, we also become more aware of ourselves as individuals separate from our parents. As we master developmental tasks that are appropriately acknowledged by our caregivers, we begin to develop a sense of confidence in ourselves. Confidence from these experiences influences our willingness to take risks and to trust in our competence to resolve problems and overcome difficult situations.

As we continue to grow through adolescence and into adulthood, our capacity for trust matures from the concrete to the abstract, from simple to complex, largely based on our conditioning or lifetime experiences: "I trust it because I can see it" to "If I do something for you, will you do something for me?" to "You have my word that you can depend on me, no matter what!"

Our lifetime experiences influence our readiness and willingness to trust today. But our conditioning may also be influenced by the situations in which we find ourselves. It can be quite difficult to separate the impact of our experiences (our conditioning) from the dynamics of a current situation in which we find ourselves. The following story illustrates how our life experiences influence our capacity for trust.

Ed was a department manager who regularly betrayed people in both his commitments and in his communications. Finally he was removed from his supervisory position. Robert, the new manager, had to deal with his predecessor's mistrustful legacy. Because people in the department had a diminished capacity for trust due to the earlier boss's behavior, they were very skeptical and prejudiced regarding Robert and his current behavior. They didn't cut him any slack. They interpreted his every action with distrust and assumed he was acting in self-serving ways. When he made mistakes or even committed minor betrayals, they were unable to appreciate the big improvement in his behavior over that of their earlier manager, Ed.

Because of the employees' prior life experiences of a tyrannical boss who betrayed them constantly, they were conditioned to treat the new manager with caution and skepticism.

It is important that we are aware of our capacity for trust. It is at the core of how we bring ourselves to our relationships and how we practice trust-building behaviors. Our capacity for trust influences our perceptions and beliefs, our perceptions and beliefs influence our behavior, and our behavior is what builds or breaks trust with ourselves and others.

Trusting Ourselves

Trust in ourselves is indispensable to our sense of self and self-esteem. We might think of it as the glue that holds together our sense of who we are (our identity) and how we deal with others and our world. When we have a high level of trust in ourselves, we feel centered and confident. We view ourselves as dependable and reliable in fulfilling our expectations of ourselves and the expectations others have of us.

Trust in ourselves also influences our work relationships. People who have a healthy level of trust and confidence in themselves tend to be trusted more by others than those who have low trust in themselves.

We all have an inner voice that asks us questions about our capabilities; we might call this our "capacity for trust voice." This voice asks such questions as "Can I do this?" "Do I believe I have what it takes to achieve this objective?" "Am I capable of learning this new program?" "Am I right for this job?" "Am I able to live up to the new bosses' expectations of me?" "Can I keep up with the changes around here?"

Each of us has asked these questions of ourselves at one time or another during our working lives. You can be assured that these are questions employees are asking themselves, particularly during change or when the stakes are high. Although we may not answer these questions consciously, we answer them daily through our actions.

When we trust in ourselves, we are more inclined to answer yes to these questions. We may feel a bit anxious or tentative answering yes, but we know that we are able to draw on our relationships with others for the support we need. We find a starting point within ourselves that we can lean into and from which we can move forward. We ultimately find our way. When we answer no, we may find ourselves paralyzed by fear, wallowing in confusion and self-doubt and unable to find that starting point. We are also less inclined to ask others for support.

Our capacity for trust directly affects our attitude toward taking risks and trying new things. We know that an athlete is capable of accomplishing only what he or she believes is possible. For example, if a pole-vaulter does not believe that she is capable of clearing eighteen feet, the chances are pretty slim that she will achieve that objective. Likewise, at work, an employee may be given a task to complete on a short deadline. If she simply assumes, without honestly assessing the requirements of the task or attempting to meet the goal, that there's no way she is going to be able to complete it on time, she will prove herself right and fail to get the job done. However, if she works through her fears, realistically assesses the situation, trusts in herself, and strives to meet the goal, she may very well be successful.

A higher capacity to trust enables us to take risks, particularly during times of change and transition. We are able to deal with uncertainty and ambiguity, try new approaches, take calculated chances, and share pertinent information, to include our thoughts and feelings when appropriate.

Sandy was asked to take over the central operations center of a large telecommunications company. This job was a high-profile position and a promotion for Sandy. Although she had never seen herself in such a role, she did see how the assignment would serve as a stepping stone to reaching her professional aspirations. Sandy found herself considering the position with quiet excitement, coupled with strong anxiety and fear. She was not sure she could trust herself to do the job. She felt that she didn't have the necessary technical skills.

At one point, her fear almost took her over, and she came very close to turning down the position. She shared her concerns with her boss. Her boss helped Sandy see the skills she did have and how foundational they were to this role. The conversation with her boss helped her quiet her fears. Sandy was able to see the abilities she could count on and trust. She identified the people around her she could rely on to further develop her technical knowledge.

Sandy accepted the job, trusting in herself and those around her to develop and execute a sound strategy. She was successful in her new job and was given another promotion two years later.

TRUSTING OTHERS

When we trust in others, we view them as dependable and reliable in fulfilling our expectations. Our capacity for trust voice may ask, "Can I really trust my coworkers?" "Will they tell me the truth when it counts?" "Are they able to do what it takes when the chips are down?" "Can I trust them to do their part to get this project to the customer on time?"

Our capacity for trust in others is critical to our work relationships. It is the force that holds our relationships together. When we have a high capacity for trust in others, we are more willing and able to work in a fluid fashion. We share information and depend on others; we relax in our necessity to control people in making sure a job gets done. Leaders who have a high capacity for trust are willing to trust another person until they have clear evidence that he or she can't be trusted.

Our capacity to trust others influences how we work together and how work gets done. Healthy working relationships are based on trust, not legal contracts or money-back guarantees. We know that trust is a reciprocal process: trust begets trust. Generally speaking, the more we give, the more we get. Mutually trusting relationships grow the more we share information (communication trust), keep agreements (contractual trust), and respect people's abilities (competence trust).

When we have a more expanded capacity for trust, we are also more inclined to give people the benefit of the doubt when they have let us down. We suspend our judgment or criticism until we more fully understand the circumstances. For instance, when someone doesn't come through for us, our inner voice will be less inclined to angry thoughts—"I should have known I couldn't trust her"—and instead might say, "I wonder what might have happened to have caused this person not to deliver? Perhaps she was sick, had a family emergency, or had a computer failure." We remain open to the individual, continuing to trust until it is clear that it is no longer appropriate to do so. We approach the person with sincere interest regarding what happened rather than with readiness to blame and to make her wrong.

Although there are no guarantees in any relationship, personal or professional, it is easier to risk trusting others when we trust in ourselves. That trust in ourselves anchors us through both our highly trusting and satisfying relationships and those with disappointments and frustrations.

THE STARTING POINT FOR OUR RELATIONSHIPS

Whatever our individual capacity for trust, we must be aware of it, as it is the basis of our perceptions, beliefs, and behaviors. Heightened awareness of our capacity for trust helps us to pay attention to what we need in relationships and thus to be able to make a *conscious choice* to practice trust-building behaviors in response to situations rather than to react in ways that may not build trust. Trust building does not require us to change who we are or how we trust, but rather to make a conscious choice to practice the behaviors of transactional trust.

TRUST BUILDING IN ACTION

Reflecting on Your Experience

1. Think about your relationships with others in your personal life. How do you bring yourself to those relationships?
   a. Do you tend to assume that others can be trusted until proved otherwise, or do you wait for people to prove they are trustworthy?
   b. Whichever your tendency, how does it affect the quality of those personal relationships?

2. Think about your relationships with others in your professional life. How do you bring yourself to those relationships?
   a. Do you tend to assume that others can be trusted until proved otherwise, or do you wait for people to prove they are trustworthy?
   b. Whichever your tendency, how does it affect the quality of those professional relationships?

Application Exercises

The following two exercises are designed to help you as an individual become more aware of your capacity for trust and to help your team become aware of its collective strengths and areas of vulnerability.

A. *Individual Reflection.* Think about situations at work. Reflect on the following questions and record your insights and observations. You may use a matrix like the one illustrated here to organize your thoughts.

   1. Do you trust yourself? In what types of situations can you answer yes? In what situations is the answer no?
   2. Do you trust others? Again, in what situations can you say yes and in which ones no?

CAPACITY FOR TRUST MATRIX		
Professional Life	**Situations in Which I Can Answer Yes**	**Situations in Which I Answer No**
Do I Trust Myself?		
Do I Trust Others?		

B. *Team Discussion.* Post a blank Capacity for Trust Matrix on the wall. Have team members name different work situations and record their responses to each as they relate to the team or organization. The team then reviews and discusses their observations.

1. Ask the team, "What story does this tell about us?" What key insights emerge?
2. Discuss with your team key observations and insights contributed by each team member. Identify the team's collective strengths and areas of vulnerability.

Trust Note

It is important that we are aware of our capacity for trust; it is at the core of how we bring ourselves to our relationships and how we practice trust-building behaviors.

Trust Tip

Capacity for trust is our readiness and willingness to trust ourselves and others. Our capacity for trust influences our perceptions and beliefs, our perceptions and beliefs influence our behavior, and our behavior is what builds or breaks trust.

6

HOW WE TRUST: THE CAPACITY FOR TRUST ATTRIBUTES

"No one can do this job as well as I can. If I want it done right, I've got to do it myself!"

"Show me," she said looking for evidence that she could believe her coworker. "I need to see that you can deliver as promised before I'm going to take your word for it and possibly risk my reputation. I have been burned before!"

"Once you make a mistake on an assignment given to you by 'the boss,' he never forgets it. He immediately forms opinions and makes judgments about your capability without giving you the benefit of the doubt or taking into consideration the extenuating circumstances you might have been up against."

"Working with her is like a breath of fresh air. She does not make generalizations about people or place stereotypes on them, unlike others in our unit. She collaborates equally well with those who think and act like she does and with those who are very different. She actually appreciates the differences! She gives people a

chance to be seen for who they are and for what they have to offer. Trust in her team is flourishing."

How do we trust? Trust in our relationships with others begins with trust in our relationship with *ourselves*. Some of us have a well-developed trust in ourselves. We view ourselves as reliable, dependable, and consistent in our behavior. We trust that we will find our way through even the most difficult of situations. Others of us feel more vulnerable and less likely to trust in ourselves, particularly in situations that are new to us, that involve us with people with whom we have limited experience, or that remind us of painful experiences in which we were deeply hurt.

Our capacity for trust influences our willingness to take risks, accept the word or promise of another at face value, see the multifaceted aspects of a situation, or appreciate the differences in people. In short, our capacity for trust influences the way we practice transactional trust (contractual trust, communication trust, competence trust) behaviors, the behaviors that build trust. The nature of how we trust in ourselves and in others is best understood through a study of what we have come to call the Capacity for Trust Attributes, which we describe in the following section.

UNDERSTANDING CAPACITY FOR TRUST ATTRIBUTES

We all make decisions about whether or not to trust in a person or a situation. Yet we are often unaware of these decisions. The more unaware we are of how we trust and behave, the more vulnerable we are to letting others down unintentionally or even betraying them. By raising our awareness of ourselves and how we trust, we put ourselves in the strongest position to make *conscious choices* about how we behave, even in low-trust situations. By choosing to consistently practice trust-building behaviors, we are more able to be seen as trustworthy by others.

The capacity for trust attributes explored in this chapter help us become more aware of our predisposition to trust, the decisions we make

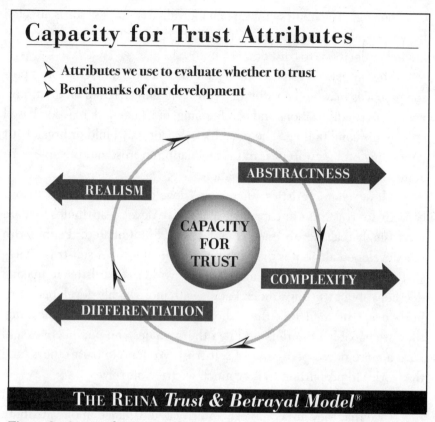

Figure 3 Capacity for Trust Attributes

in relationships, and how they influence the way we practice transactional trust behaviors. Four attributes influence our capacity to trust a person or a situation: realism, abstractness, complexity, and differentiation.[1] (Please refer to Figure 3). We will look at how each attribute affects our decisions to trust a person, group, or situation and how those decisions influence our behaviors.

These characteristics we call the Capacity for Trust Attributes develop from an individual's life experiences and are influenced by each unique situation. In other words, a person's degree of trust in another person or a situation depends on her developmental capacity (predisposition or conditioning). The more self-aware an individual is, the less she is affected by her predisposition or conditioning and the greater conscious choice she has in her decisions to trust others.

Most situations require some kind of behavior; the behaviors a person practices may be the result of a conscious choice based on his awareness of his predispositions and conditioning, or a knee-jerk reaction based only on his conditioning. The person's behavior may build or break trust depending on his awareness of his inclination to trust and the appropriateness of his behavior in the situation.

These characteristics mirror the developmental process in our capacity for trust. As our capacity expands, we develop attributes that are increasingly realistic, abstract, complex, and differentiated.[2] People with less developed attributes may exhibit a minimal level of self-trust. They also may use a self-centered model of the world as a yardstick in making decisions about trusting others. People with more highly developed attributes may tend to include the "other" as a significant source of meaning: they are capable of understanding others' values and perspectives and have a more developed sense of self-trust. We tend to trust others (and the world) in proportion to how much we trust ourselves.

We will examine each of these attributes separately, but you must recognize that they are complexly interrelated. Change in one attribute often affects change in one or more of the others. Ultimately, the capacity for trust is a function of the *combination of attributes* rather than merely the frequent use of *one* attribute. In other words, it is the interaction of realism, abstractness, complexity, and differentiation that increases capacity, not simply "being very realistic."

Each of the four attributes can be best understood as comprising a continuum from low to high, reflecting the contracted to expanded nature of our capacity to trust.

Realism

Realism indicates the extent to which a person places an unreasonable or reasonable amount of trust in herself or others. It influences how a person takes risks, collaborates, engages with others, and deals with her perfectionist tendencies.

A person with a tendency toward high realism may take calculated risks and develop trust in incremental steps. She is apt to assess the risks involved before placing confidence in others and is willing to check out her assumptions and reevaluate the judgments she forms about others and the situations with which she is dealing.

When we are in a relationship with an individual with a higher degree of realism, we experience her as giving us room to do our job, giving us new opportunities to be engaged in projects that stretch our skills and abilities, and asking us questions about our views rather than making assumptions about them.

A person with low realism may take unreasonable risks with a customer's project, believing it possible to overcome insurmountable challenges and that he can "pull it off at all costs." He may trust himself more than he trusts others to do important tasks. Or he may have an extremely low sense of self-trust and not take action for fear of punishment for failure to perform up to standards.

Either way, this person may fail to let others know of the risks involved in a situation; consequently, teammates may not have the full picture. Further, he may lack the skills or resources to complete the project successfully and may jeopardize the company's reputation and relationship with that customer (and others). Even if he does have the skills and resources necessary to do the job, by failing to communicate the risks and to keep others informed, he may break trust in his relationships with his customer or coworkers, in spite of results he delivered.

Such a person may take unreasonable risks or make unrealistic promises without knowing how to go about achieving the goals or keeping the promises. Conversely, a person high in realism tends to break the project down into manageable pieces; he trusts, realistically, that the goal can and will be achieved using available skills and resources. In order to ensure the success of the project, this person collaborates with others consistently.

Another aspect of realism pertains to perfectionism. A person with a tendency to trust highly in herself to the exclusion of others may be a perfectionist. Perfectionists often trust no one but themselves to do the job because they are "the only ones who can do it right," as one frustrated team member expressed. If they do delegate to others, they may remain heavily involved.

People in the workplace today are forever pressed to do more with less. Individuals attempting to have every task done perfectly are experienced by others as overly idealistic and "bottlenecking the process." On the other end of the continuum, a person with high realism does what is appropriate to get the job accomplished. Because these individuals trust in the abilities of others and believe in the positive intentions of others, they tend to collaborate more with others. In these relationships, we experience flow of information, exchange of feedback, and support to learn new skills.

There are times when it is appropriate and necessary for an individual to work in a highly self-reliant manner, when she must trust solely in herself. For example, there may be an extremely high-security project or one that requires a specific degree of expertise. However, by practicing communication trust behaviors that keep others informed and by managing expectations and boundaries, this person can maintain healthy levels of trust in her relationships.

As one individual shared with us following a high-security project for the CEO that he needed to deliver as a sole contributor, "I have found that letting others know that I will not be providing updates for security purposes actually helped me further build trust in my relationships. I learned how important it is to clarify expectations. In this case, I made it clear to my teammates that they would not be involved. They understood and respected me for managing expectations."

Abstractness

Abstractness indicates the degree to which a person relies on concrete facts, figures, and the five senses as opposed to philosophy, values, nuances, and intuition.

An individual whose capacity for trust tends toward low abstractness needs solid, tangible, or physical evidence before trusting the intentions and promises of others. Such individuals may have a "Prove it to me first!" attitude and a great need to feel that they are in control of themselves and the situation. For example, they may become overly controlling of others and heavily involved in the details of projects.

When we have a boss who tends toward low abstractness, we experience her as unable to trust us to do our job. She may not delegate, or when she does delegate, "she keeps looking over our shoulders, telling us how the job should be done," as one employee told us in exasperation. This person usually needs the steps of a process to be clearly defined and needs evidence of another's skills and abilities before she trusts the actions of others.

At the other end of the continuum, people who have a tendency toward high abstractness are generally willing to trust the word or promise of another at face value. When we have a boss with a high-abstractness capacity for trust, we experience him as willing to trust our work or take us at our word. We do not have to "prove it first"; we are given the benefit of the doubt. He is also able to deal with the uncertainty of situations and the ambiguity of process. We experience the freedom, flexibility, and empowerment to do our jobs. He is more comfortable letting go and trusting others to work independently.

Different job situations call for different degrees of abstractness. For instance, manufacturing production processes require a strong attention to detail and tangible elements. People who are drawn to this work commonly have a need for stability, consistency, and a sense of always knowing "where things stand." They generally rely on specific details rather than abstract impressions when building relationships with others. These preferences may represent a relatively low capacity for abstractness. People with low abstractness may see times of change and transition as threatening, particularly if they are not provided with information consistently and do not understand the impact of the change on them, their work, and their lives. They may be less ready to trust in the possibility of "what might be," an abstract concept.

Many senior managers operate at the high end of the abstractness continuum. They find it necessary to trust in the abstract to create the vision and set the direction of the organization they serve. They may believe that uncertainty and ambiguity are part of trusting relationships.

A reason for the common breakdown in communication and growing distrust between senior management and frontline employees today is a discrepancy in the awareness of how they each trust and therefore in what they need in their relationships. This is particularly true during change and transition: senior leaders may be asking employees to trust in the further direction of the company and in the idea that the changes will strengthen the organization. In this situation, senior leaders are asking their people to trust in the abstract idea of "tomorrow."

Those with a tendency for low abstractness may be inclined to focus on the perceived or known losses associated with change and transition: "What will happen to our 401(k)? What jobs will be cut?" Those with a tendency for high abstractness may be inclined to trust in the possibilities, trust that new opportunities will be presented: "What new positions will be created?"

Whether we tend toward low or high abstractness in our capacity for trust, what is important is our *awareness of how we are trusting*. When we are aware of our tendency for low abstractness, we know we need information and concrete facts. This self-awareness will allow us to choose to practice communication trust behaviors: we will ask questions, seek out others, tell the truth about our needs, and provide feedback that lets others know of our level of understanding and comfort.

When we have a tendency for high abstractness, we need to be aware of others' need to rely on their senses and concrete information. Their needs may not be the same as ours, so we must make an effort to pay attention to them. We build trust when we are sensitive to others' fears and vulnerabilities and practice transactional trust behaviors consistently. For instance, we tell the truth rather than a comfortable variation of it, we clarify expectations, and we communicate how skills and abilities will be harnessed and new ones developed.

For leaders to build trust with employees in low-trust situations, it is important to think about the employees'. perspective, use language they can understand, and give them tangible evidence that leaders keep their word and live by their principles. Likewise, the more leaders trust their frontline workers, the more employees will develop trust in leadership.

Complexity

Complexity indicates the extent to which a person bases his or her decisions to trust on black-and-white, right-or-wrong, good-or-bad criteria as opposed to the multifaceted aspects of a person or situation.

An individual on the low side of the complexity continuum may make simplistic decisions about herself or others. Although there are situations where the individual's constricted capacity may compromise trust, there are others where this tendency can actually build trust; following are several examples.

"The fire alarm went off. I smelled smoke. I knew I needed to get out of the burning office building and help Myrtle, our sixty-three-year-old receptionist, get out with me. We were on the top floor. The elevator was jammed. I didn't have time to think about it; I just reacted. I grabbed Myrtle by the arm and assisted her down seven flights of stairs. She is forever grateful. From then on, she's trusted me with her life."

"We were at a crossroads. Although it would have been easier to take a shortcut and use the cheaper material in the product, we took the high road. We could have cheated. After all, our client wouldn't have known. But we used the more expensive material in fabricating the item—because it was the right thing to do. We didn't even think about it; it wasn't a conscious action when we were faced with the choice. I believe that as a result, we maintained our trusting relationship with our client, and I sleep better at night."

"I was getting really anxious. The clock was ticking away; our deadline was rapidly approaching. Yet the team was going around and around, discussing all the possible alternatives. Somebody needed to make a decision fast. Take decisive action. Nobody was daring to jump in and stick their neck out—so I did! We needed to reduce the complexity of the situation to a simple right-or-wrong answer. Our time was up; we needed to get this decision to upper management—now! I went on my instincts; I didn't think about it, I just voted for solution A. You know what? It worked. From then on, my teammates trusted me and my decisions."

Even though there was not any deliberation in each of these low-complexity situations, the "knee-jerk reactions" contributed to building trust in all three circumstances. In contrast, we break trust when we make broad, sweeping judgments about others—for example, saying things like "Brett is a total liar" or "You can't trust that team." In these situations, one may have difficulty seeing both the relative strengths and weaknesses of an individual simultaneously. People with low development in this attribute may be unable to see the shades of gray in their relationships. They may assail a person's (or their own) overall competence for making one mistake in a specific area or beat themselves up and exclaim in exasperation, failing to see that they and their coworkers were on a steep learning curve.

If we are unaware of our negative assessments of a situation or person, including ourselves, our assessments rarely change. Through our lack of awareness, we may make up our minds about others and ourselves, rather than giving them or us a second chance.

People low in complexity tend to be their own worst critics, belittling themselves when things don't go as they had expected. If they've had a disappointing experience, they may not trust that they have what it takes to work through complex problems, holding themselves back. Others may view these individuals as strong willed, inflexible, rigid, and unwilling to compromise once their minds are made up.

By contrast, individuals high in complexity tend to see the multiple sides of a person and the relative performance of each individual. They tend to be able to manage contradictory information about people. These individuals can appreciate that someone is reliable under certain circumstances but not others. They are likely to take into account the varied aspects of people's personalities and any extenuating circumstances that may influence their behavior. For example, Alex, a manager who has a complex capacity for trust, knows that he can trust Bart, a very competent technician, to do an excellent job once he gets to work, but can't trust him to be on time. He knows that Michayla is good at solving computer problems but is not as strong interacting with customers.

In sum, individuals high in the complexity attribute tend to be able to trust selectively depending on people's strengths and weaknesses and to approach relationships with a mix of skepticism and positive expectations. They are more inclined to give the benefit of doubt, to ask questions, and to test assumptions.

Differentiation

Differentiation indicates the degree to which a person is able to distinguish between qualities of self versus qualities of others. There are two aspects to the differentiation attribute. The first is conveyed by the question, Do I assume that whatever is true for me is true for them?"; the second, "How well do I differentiate individuals from various groups they might be a part of? Do I assume that whatever I perceive to be true for a group is also true for each of its members?"

Regarding the first aspect of this attribute, a person low in differentiation assumes that whatever is true for himself is true for others and may indiscriminately project his views on others. On the job, this tendency can hinder trust in a working relationship, as these individuals generally trust only people highly similar to themselves. If the person assigned to a project with them is dissimilar to them or exhibits a behavior that they disapprove of, these individuals may not personally feel very trusting toward that person and act accordingly. They may not be receptive to collaborating. Their distrusting actions may impede their working relationship and in turn compromise the company project. This is especially true with long-term projects, because when individuals low in differentiation negatively evaluate a person, they keep their mind made up regardless of whether or not the other person changes over time.

Regarding the second aspect of this continuum, a person low in the differentiation attribute who assumes that what is true for the group is true for each of its members may be guilty of a form of stereotyping and prejudice. These individuals make broad-based, blanket statements or generalizations about individuals or groups without any basis for their validity or specific facts to back them up: "Management can't be trusted," "The union has no clout," "People in Department X are difficult to relate to," "You can't count on anyone in that department," "Those people are always trying to get something for nothing." Or they may take one small bit of truth about one individual and attribute it to everyone in the group. They also may not be able to modify prior assumptions about others.

Here is an example of a low-differentiation capacity for trust at work:

Hank is a shop steward. Eugene, a new employee, reminds Hank of someone who betrayed him the past. Consequently, Hank is reluctant to open up to Eugene and acts in distrusting ways toward him. Eugene reciprocates with similar behavior. As a result, the working relationship between the two is poor. What Hank doesn't realize is that his own projection onto Eugene, and Eugene's actions in response, created the very thing that Hank feared—distrust. Hank never differentiated between Eugene and the memory of Hank's past betrayer and therefore acted similarly to Eugene.

On the other side of the differentiation continuum, persons who have a highly differentiated capacity for trust tend to avoid stereotyping and are able to distinguish individuals from the groups to which they belong and can understand and appreciate individual differences. They tend to be capable of reevaluating people over time. They are also able to make distinctions between groups (ethnic, religious, social, educational status, and so on), and do not make sweeping generalizations about groups.

OUR CAPACITY TO TRUST CHANGES OVER TIME

As our capacity for trust grows and we heal from relationship disappointments, we tend to rely on trust criteria that are more realistic, more abstract, more complex, and more differentiated than earlier in our development.[3]

That isn't to say that we don't ever exhibit behavior at the low ends of the realism, abstractness, complexity, and differentiation continua. There may be situations where our capacity for trust diminishes. However, with self-awareness we can choose to practice transitional trust behaviors consistently. For example, we ask questions, seek to understand, clarify our expectations, tell the truth, and define boundaries, rather than make judgments based on assumptions and criticism.

Our capacity to trust is not static but dynamic. It expands and contracts as it is updated by our positive and negative experiences. Each of us develops a unique trusting pattern or blueprint, reflective of our experiences, which is unlike anyone else's. The positive and negative experiences we encounter, particularly during our developmental years, mold our capacity to trust and therefore our pattern of trust behavior—our unique configuration of the four capacity for trust attributes.

Developing our capacity for trust through self-awareness is a slow developmental process. It requires that we take the time to learn to listen to ourselves so that we can acknowledge our feelings, take responsibility for them, and trust ourselves. The Seven Steps for Healing, which we explore in Chapter Eight, are a framework for healing from life's betrayals and nurturing our capacity for trust.

TRUST BUILDING IN ACTION

Reflecting on Your Experience

In order to better understand how each of the four attributes influence the development of our capacity for trust, think about the following questions:

Realism

1. Why are some people willing to take risks?

2. How willing are you to take risks?

Abstractness

1. Why are some people willing to accept the work or promise of another?

2. How willing are you to accept the work or promise of another?

Complexity

1. Why are some people willing to make a judgment of another based on one interaction?

2. How willing are you to make a judgment of another based on one interaction?

Differentiation
1. Why are some people more comfortable with other people whose thinking is different from their own?
2. How comfortable are you with people whose thinking is different from your own?

Application Exercises

Think about and discuss with your team the following questions:

1. Reflect on your experience in relationships. What are examples of behaviors that illustrate how high and low development of the capacity for trust attributes influence trust positively and negatively?

2. Think about the people on the job with whom you work the closest. How can you use the capacity for trust attributes to help you better understand your working relationships with them?

CAPACITY FOR TRUST ATTRIBUTES™		
Attributes	**How the Attribute Positively Influences Trust**	**How the Attribute Negatively Influences Trust**
Realism		
Abstractness		
Complexity		
Differentiation		

Trust Note

The capacity for trust attributes develop from an individual's life experiences and are influenced by each unique situation. In other words, a person's degree of trust in another person or a situation depends on his or her developmental capacity (predisposition or conditioning).

Trust Tip

The more self-aware an individual is, the less he is affected by his predisposition or conditioning and the greater *conscious choice* he has in his decisions to trust others.

WHEN TRUST BREAKS DOWN:

HOW TO REBUILD AND SUSTAIN IT

How does trust break down? What are the behaviors

that contribute to such a breach? After it is broken,

how does one rebuild trust: in oneself, between

two people, or within a team or organization?

How is trust sustained and even increased over time?

The chapters in Part IV answer these questions.

7

HOW TRUST IS BROKEN: BETRAYAL

"I'm really upset with Sue! She didn't deliver her part of the project as she promised. She let down not only me but also her other coworkers. There is no longer trust on this team."

"I don't understand why John went to Craig to talk about the concern he has with me. Why didn't he come to me directly and give me a chance to address it with him? It hurt to hear about this from Craig. Now I wonder who else has John talked to about me. Can I really trust him?"

"I devoted two-and-a-half days to developing our new strategy with my team. We all agreed to our direction and to the action steps for which each member was responsible. Half the team is actively following through on their deliverables; the other half is questioning the decisions we made, raising points that have already been thoroughly discussed. I am getting worn down by

this dynamic of unnecessarily second-guessing and questioning. I don't feel like I can trust their word."

"We trusted Bill, and he betrayed us!" Lori said angrily, referring to her boss. "He lied to us. I've got a hollow feeling in the pit of my stomach, the sense of disappointment and anger that comes from being hurt. I don't like working in an environment where I'm lied to and where there's betrayal. I spend too much energy watching my back! I don't know what or who I can believe anymore."

"I have left three voice mail messages and have sent two emails requesting the information necessary for this meeting. She promised to get it to me last week. Here I go again, chasing her down."

When trust breaks down, it is frustrating and painful. We may even feel betrayed. We shut down and are unwilling to put ourselves at risk. Further, it is difficult to work with people whom we don't trust, to work in an environment of distrust and betrayal.

But betrayal means different things to different people. What do we mean by betrayal? We define betrayal as a breach of trust or the perception of such a breach. It can be intentional or unintentional. Intentional betrayal is a self-serving action committed with the purpose of hurting, damaging, or harming another person. Unintentional betrayal is the by-product of a self-serving action that results in people's being hurt, damaged, or harmed.

Betrayal is a dark word that means negative things to many people. Yet the word *betrayal* is no darker or more severe than the impact of betrayal. Some people run away from the word or avoid using it in their everyday language. Others seek to understand it, recognizing that betrayal is a natural part of relationships.

If you find yourself having difficulty relating to the word *betrayal*, you may consider other language, such as *distrust, breakdown,* or *disappointment*. What is most important is that we become aware of the shapes and forms betrayal takes, that we understand the impact it has on relationships and performance and, ultimately, what we can do in response to

Betrayal

> ➢ **A breach of trust or the perception of a breach**
> - **From major to minor**
> - **Intentional or unintentional**

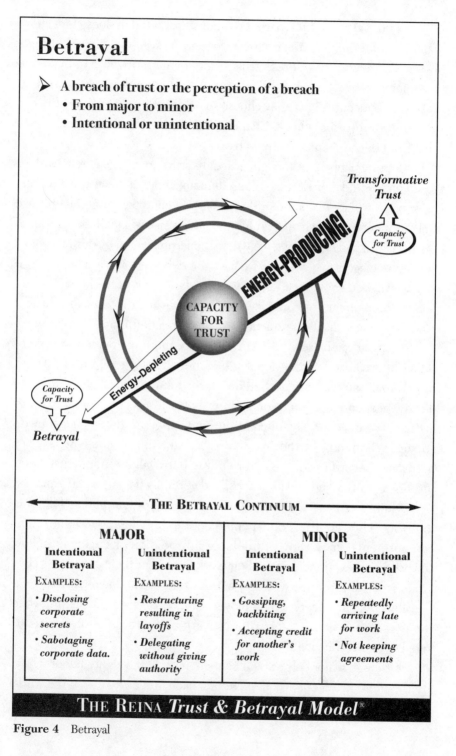

THE BETRAYAL CONTINUUM

MAJOR		MINOR	
Intentional Betrayal	**Unintentional Betrayal**	**Intentional Betrayal**	**Unintentional Betrayal**
EXAMPLES:	EXAMPLES:	EXAMPLES:	EXAMPLES:
• *Disclosing corporate secrets* • *Sabotaging corporate data.*	• *Restructuring resulting in layoffs* • *Delegating without giving authority*	• *Gossiping, backbiting* • *Accepting credit for another's work*	• *Repeatedly arriving late for work* • *Not keeping agreements*

THE REINA *Trust & Betrayal Model*®

Figure 4 Betrayal

it. Yes, betrayal is a natural part of relationships, but that doesn't mean we can't do something to prevent or reduce it. As we become increasingly aware of behaviors that break trust, we become more able to make the conscious choice to behave differently. And when we are aware that betrayal has occurred, we may choose to deal with it rather than bury our hurt or turn the other cheek. Chapter Eight explores steps we can take to heal from betrayal and to rebuild trust.

Betrayal happens. Although most of us strive to engage in relationships based on a foundation of trust, we are human, and that means trust will get broken; we will let one another down. We will fail to keep agreements; we will misunderstand each other's communication; we will leave people out of key decisions and be left out; we will feel micromanaged by our managers, and our managers may feel that we have not delivered. We will be betrayed and we will betray. Betrayal comes with trust; it is part of the human condition. It complements our interactions like the yin and the yang, the ebb and flow, the expansion and contraction of human relationships.

Betrayal can be seen as occurring on a continuum from major intentional betrayal to unintentional minor betrayal (see Figure 4). Major intentional betrayals are carried out to hurt and harm. We feel them in our deepest core. Unintentional minor betrayals are incidental to other actions. We may not pay much attention to them initially—but they do add up! When they do, they may have the same impact and cost as major betrayals. Regardless of the nature of the betrayal, it erodes trust, compromises or even ends relationships, and certainly damages performance.

Major betrayals are often the by-products of fear and self-serving interests. They are caused by people deliberately failing to honor their commitments, knowingly withholding information or deceiving fellow coworkers, or even sabotaging their work to further their own ends. They are hurtful, ill-intended words or actions that break down trusting relationships. As one concerned employee said, "It is especially painful when we are stabbed in the back without warning by those closest to us. It knocks you off your feet."

Although major betrayals do happen, most betrayals are minor. These are the more prevalent acts that happen each and every day in the workplace. People gossiping about one another behind their backs, arriving late for meetings consistently, hoarding pertinent information, not responding to requests made by others, blaming and finger pointing, and abdicating responsibility are examples of minor forms of betrayal. They alienate employees from their managers, their peers, and their subordinates.

These subtle betrayals seem innocent and unimportant. They are often swept under the carpet and ignored; people may say, "Oh, let's not waste time on that little stuff. Let's get on with it; we have too much to do." While we may try to deny their existence, they do not go away on their own. They can and do grow to more severe hurts and contribute significantly to the negative feelings that employees have toward their bosses, each other, and their companies.

These seemingly minor acts break down relationships *if not addressed*. Their cumulative weight is that of major betrayal. This occurs when minor betrayals stay alive in behavior and in people's minds, resulting in a pattern of trust-breaking behavior. Over the course of time, they become bigger than the actual event or a single act.

How we might position an experience along the betrayal continuum depends on our perception of the betrayer's intent and the impact on us—in other words, the degree to which we perceive that the individual intended to cause hurt, damage, or pain to us and the degree of hurt, damage, and pain actually caused or inflicted. For instance, accepting credit for someone else's work may be a minor intentional betrayal in one circumstance, but if the person who falsely accepts credit gains greatly at the other's expense (for example, if he or she gets promoted as a reward for something that in reality a coworker deserved credit for), it becomes a major intentional betrayal.

The opportunity for betrayal in any relationship at work or in our personal lives depends on the degree of trust we have in that individual, situation, or organization. An important aspect of trust has to do with our wondering if our expectations will be met. If an individual has few or no expectations and trust is low, the chances of being betrayed are not great. Consequently, that person is not particularly susceptible to disappointment, hurt, or betrayal. However, if he or she has higher expectations and greater involvement and loyalty in the relationship, the person is more vulnerable to betrayal. The more we have invested in a relationship, the

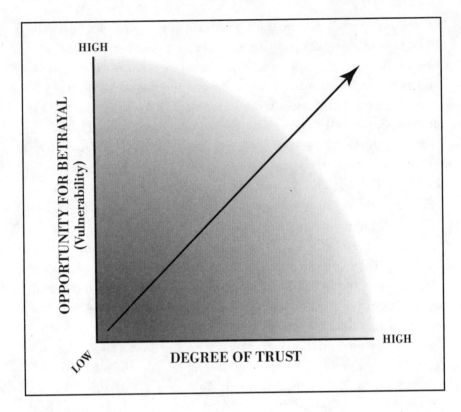

more deeply hurt we may feel by a breach of trust. The illustration here reflects the correlation between the degree of trust and the opportunity for betrayal.

The High Cost of Betrayal in the Workplace

Organizations depend on trust and effective relationships among their people to function and to thrive. We must trust that company executives will keep people's interests in mind when they make decisions to promote the health of the company. We need to know that we can rely on the skills and talents of others, that we can ask tough questions and get honest answers, that we can go directly to an individual with a problem or concern, and that we can give and in return receive feedback that strengthens the relationship and performance.

When we trust in this way, we can focus on doing our jobs, developing our relationships, and contributing to ourselves, those we work with, and our organization. We are able to be in a "flow state." Sure, we have our ups and downs, but the foundation of trust serves as the basis for consistency. We know we can count on one another.

Betrayal destroys the essential fabric of the relationships that keep our organizations operating and our people engaged. Major betrayals demolish the healthy trust that has existed; minor betrayals eat away at it bit by bit. Trust is energy producing; betrayal is energy depleting. Trust feeds performance; betrayal eats away at it.

Major betrayals are traumatic experiences that diminish people's energy, cloud their thinking, sap their motivation, and derail their productivity. Minor betrayals also contribute incrementally to distractions; people are left wondering, "What is going on here?" Rather than focusing on doing their normal jobs, betrayed individuals attend to protecting themselves and possibly taking revenge on whoever betrayed them. Trust begets trust, and betrayal begets betrayal. When we hurt, we hate and want to get back. We want to get even! And sometimes we do.

In a climate of betrayal, productivity plummets and negatively affects the bottom line. The news headlines are filled with corporate scandals and ethical breaches that cost companies, customers, employees, and stockholders billions of dollars. The hallways, break rooms, and dining halls are filled with the whispers of betrayal and people wondering, "How much longer can I cope? When will something be done? I thought I belonged here; now I'm not sure. Maybe I don't have what it takes after all."

Yes, betrayal hurts. It hurts because we have suffered a loss, a significant disappointment. We may have lost an opportunity, our hope of what might have been, or a relationship. To guide employees out of betrayal toward trusting again, it is important first to understand the nature of betrayal. In an effort to rebuild trust, it is necessary for leaders to understand what betrayal is, the relationship of betrayal to trust, and the effect major and minor betrayals have on an employees' capacity for trusting themselves, others, and relationships.

THE EFFECT OF BETRAYAL ON
OUR CAPACITY FOR TRUST

Whether a betrayal is major or minor, the experience affects our capacity to trust ourselves and others. People's emotions vary in intensity, depending on their perceptions of the severity of the betrayal. As one employee sadly shared, "Betrayal makes me feel angry, sad, and lost. It destroys my faith in the betrayer, but also makes me question my own judgment for trusting in someone or something unworthy or undeserving of my trust." Betrayal destroys confidence and morale and replaces it with self-doubt.

Leaders are in denial if they don't believe that people have feelings about business transactions. We must not forget that business transactions are conducted through relationships, and feelings are an element of relationships.

Betrayal goes to the core of human vulnerability; it cuts through us to our deepest emotional layers. For example, one vice president of an international telecommunications company reflected on being betrayed by his boss: "I had to get out. I got myself transferred as soon as possible. I couldn't work for someone I didn't trust." Betrayal is deeply felt—so much so that people use physical words to describe their emotional states. As a leader in a pharmaceutical company said, "I really got beat up in that board meeting this morning."

Major Betrayal: Trusting Others

As we've already seen, major intentional betrayals are deliberately planned to manipulate others for self-gain. The perpetrators know that their actions will hurt others, and they justify them with self-serving arguments. Our level of trust in these individuals decreases dramatically, and our capacity to trust others can plummet.

Sharon, a designer for a major advertising agency in New York, was severely shaken when a trusted friend and coworker stole her ideas for an ad campaign she had been working on. Sharon was further incensed when her colleague received a large year-end bonus as a reward for her deceitful actions. From that point on, Sharon cut all per-

sonal ties with this individual and became extremely cautious about
sharing her ideas with anyone.

Our level of trust and vulnerability determines the depth of betrayal we feel. In Sharon's case, she trusted her colleague very much—perhaps unwisely and unrealistically. As a result, she was quite vulnerable and was caught off guard.

Though unintentional betrayal is a by-product of a self-serving action, it can have hurtful consequences. Losing a job or being demoted may be the by-product of downsizing, restructuring, or a merger, but people end up hurt nonetheless. Once an organization starts downsizing, the consequences are never-ending. Like betrayal, the negative consequences and the negative energy are larger than the act itself. The betrayal is implosive; it sucks productive energy from employees—especially those worrying about whether they are going to have a job next month. Typically, it is not the downsizing or restructuring itself that causes betrayal; rather, it is *how* the change is managed—the failure to acknowledge the impact of change on individuals and the lack of support people experienced to deal with it. As one manager expressed, "We were downsized twice in one year. When people left, we lost relationships. Yet we have been expected to behave as if that were not the case, to simply focus on getting the job done. The loss of those relationships hurt, and it hurt even more that leadership did not recognize that."

Betrayal is systemic; it affects the whole system and everyone in it. For example, organizational changes affect the morale of the whole company, whether individuals in the company are affected directly or indirectly. People develop deep relationships with coworkers and come to care about them, perhaps love them. It hurts to lose those relationships.

Betrayal shuts down the whole system, removes trust, and destroys relationships. In some situations this occurs over time; in others it can happen in an instant. As one frustrated employee said, "I can do five hundred things to build trust in a relationship; then I do one act, and all the trust is gone in a split second."

Every day on the job, leaders betray employees, and employees betray their leaders and one another, unintentionally. If you as a leader give an employee the responsibility but not the authority, trust, and support needed to do a project, you have destroyed the full potential of that employee's contribution to the company. You have sent a message to that employee that says you don't trust his or her skills. Likewise, employees betray leaders and their coworkers when they don't fulfill their work-related agreements. How often do we hear employees lament, "I was counting on you, and you didn't come through."

A major betrayal, intentional or not, is shocking and devastating. It grabs us when we least expect it. What we thought was dependable is not dependable; what we thought was permanent is not permanent. Our world is turned upside down, and we are tossed into emotional chaos. We wonder, "Where can I place my trust now?" "Whom can I trust?"

Major Betrayal: Trusting Ourselves

A major betrayal can decrease our capacity to trust ourselves. Because it slams us over the head and pierces us at our core, we feel vulnerable and wounded. It is a profound experience. It shakes our confidence, causes us to doubt ourselves, and causes us to question our trustworthiness. It deeply wounds a relationship. Betrayal is usually taken personally, and it is rarely forgotten.

Major betrayal touches the very center of our vulnerability. As one shaken coworker said, "You make yourself vulnerable to the other person, and he uses your own sword to betray you." Being rejected against our will can severely damage our self-esteem, leaving us feeling powerless. Losing a job or being passed up for a promotion can bring up feelings of worthlessness and may be devastating to our capacity to trust. As one distraught employee explained, "My experience of betrayal is that I am standing on a rug, and the rug is suddenly pulled out from under me. I am tumbling helplessly out of control."

Through self-exploration and self-awareness, we are able to shift out of the negative feelings of betrayal and view them as stepping stones to personal and spiritual growth. Most of the time, however, rather than working constructively with our pain, we typically give ourselves over to anger and resentment[1]. When we act as victims after being betrayed, we lose the opportunity to learn and grow from the experience. If we take the traditional response to betrayal and operate out of fear or the desire to control or manipulate, we end up sabotaging ourselves as well as others.

A personal crisis can teach us a lot about ourselves. Whether betrayal occurs in our private lives or our work lives, it can be an opportunity for inner growth, if we are willing to work through the feelings and endure the pain. In the next chapter, we will explore steps we can take to help heal themselves; in Chapter Eleven, we will explore the steps leaders can take to help others heal from betrayal.

Minor Betrayal: Trusting Others

One minor betrayal will probably not decrease our capacity to trust others. However, as minor betrayals accumulate, they will eventually affect our capacity to trust one another and will create distrust among us. Trust breaks down over time when we sense that another's intentions and motives are not sincere and that the person in fact has ulterior motives.

Distrust breeds distrust and ultimately betrayal. When a leader comes from a place of fear and caution, worrying about whether she can trust an employee, her behavior can backfire and cause the very distrust and betrayal she seeks to avoid.

Most betrayals are not intentionally malicious and are not designed to hurt others. They occur when we are overworked, stressed-out, and trying to do more with less. Yet these minor betrayals can create significant hurts, which lead to major betrayals. And major betrayals result when people realize the extent to which they have been quietly misled. The discovery of deception, dishonesty, or indirectness may prompt an abrupt exit from an effective working relationship between individuals. When people are allowed to get away with breaching trust in minor ways, it becomes easier to betray in major ways. The cumulative effect of these minor betrayals eats away at trust and damages working relationships between individuals and in the organization.

How We Betray Ourselves and Others

When we have betrayed another, the first person we have betrayed is ourselves. We betray ourselves by overriding our own needs and failing to speak our truth. We may not have asked questions for the clarification we needed. We may not have requested the additional support necessary to meet the deadline, so we are working sixteen-hour days. We may have agreed with a decision just to go along with the group, when we knew it would put us up against a wall. We may have agreed to moving the dates for this business trip knowing it would cut into precious family or weekend time. Or we may agree to a job assignment we know we will not enjoy because the boss asked us to, and we want to be seen as a team player. After all, it's only for one year. That one year turns into a very long year!

When we agree to terms and conditions that we know are not mutually serving to *us*, we override our own needs. We may push beyond our physical limits by working excessive hours, eat poorly because fast food was all that was available at 11:00 P.M. on our way home from work, and drop exercise because we can't take the time out for it. We become skillful at overriding our own personal needs to get the job done. We become pressed and anxious, and we simply try to do too much.

Often at the core of behaviors that cause us to override our needs and to betray ourselves is fear: fear of not being good enough ("I have to do more"); fear of not being seen as competent ("I won't ask for help because then they'll be right"); fear of not being seen as cooperative ("I won't disagree with others' views"); fear of not being considered for promotion ("I'll take on the extra assignments to show them what I can do, even if it means I don't take a vacation this summer!").

When we override our personal needs and become pushed, anxious, and overextended, we lose our center—our sense of being grounded. That sacred relationship with ourselves is compromised. As one senior vice president said, "I have been pushing so hard I can't feel myself anymore." When we are not aware of ourselves, we are not able to be aware of others. It is in this space of disconnection from ourselves that we let others down in our haste, pace, and pushing; we lose our footing.

THE INFLUENCE OF OUR PERCEPTIONS AND BELIEFS

Our capacity for trust influences our perceptions and beliefs, which in turn influence our readiness and willingness to trust ourselves and others. When our capacity for trust is constricted, we are not as ready to trust ourselves or others. This is when we are most vulnerable to betraying ourselves and others. The following questions illuminate how we may bring ourselves to relationships with others when we are not ready and willing to trust.

Do We Expect to Be Rejected?

If we expect to be rejected or criticized, we may constantly test people's loyalty and commitment to us. Rather than being open to what we might experience and assuming the best, we assume and look for the worst. "You'll have to prove to me that you're trustworthy first." We find ourselves constantly on the defensive; we are ready to run from or "beat up on" those individuals who may present a danger to our delicate sense of safety and identity. People who have a low capacity for trust in themselves may project their inability to trust onto others. People who need solid or tangible evidence in order to trust their coworkers exhibit a concrete capacity to trust. They will not trust until it has been proven that it is indeed safe to trust. In this situation, trust may be a long time coming. It bears repeating: trust is reciprocal; if we are not willing to give it, we may not get it.

Do We Contribute to Conflict?

Our expectations of conflict generate the very conflict we fear. Our attitude influences our interactions with others. Do we enter a potential disagreement on the defensive, assuming that the other person is not aligned with us? As one factory worker said to a coworker, "If you are looking for a fight, by golly I'm going to help you find one!"

Thought is creative. When we perceive that others are going to bring us harm before we have even examined our assumptions about their intentions, we may tend to bring ourselves to them with judgment and criticism. When we have low capacity for trust in others, we may exhibit protective behaviors that cause other individuals to react in a similar fashion. We may not give trust the opportunity to form.

Are We Mostly Preoccupied with Our Own Problems?

If we are constantly preoccupied with our own problems, we may be totally unaware of our self-absorption and the consequential impact of our behavior on others. For example, if we are fostering an attitude that the world is treating us poorly, we rarely feel responsible for the pain we cause others. We are too consumed by our own issues to be aware of or sensitive to those of others. People with a low capacity to trust in themselves may feel victimized by their circumstances and the unresolved patterns of betrayal they have experienced in their lives. They may come across as needy and emotionally draining to their coworkers. Their preoccupation with themselves causes them to be unaware of their actions. These people break promises, miss deadlines, and are insensitive to the problems they cause others. When the problems are brought to their attention, they may fail to take responsibility, tending to justify and rationalize their behavior.

Do We Create Difficulty Unnecessarily?

If people are preoccupied with a frantic search for certainty and pre-dictability, they may be unable to understand the complexity of dynamic relationships at work. For example, in conversations with coworkers, these individuals may have little tolerance for differences with others. They may come across as self-righteous, speaking in absolutes and thinking in sim-plistic, black-or-white, good-or-bad terms. If they disagree with or don't understand the points they are hearing, they may react with a verbal attack. For these people, life is a battle to be won, and the goal is being right and winning at all costs.

People with this approach tend to have a low-complexity capacity to trust and may have a limited ability to deal with the uncertainty of new situations. For example, when facilitating a team meeting, they may come across as domineering: "My way is the right way." They may have difficulty leading a dialogue session that lacks a formal structure.

Do We Discount People?

If we feel hurt, embarrassed, or frightened in our association with some-one, we may conjure up an elaborate mental smoke screen to protect our-selves from feeling the memories of past painful experiences. By devaluing the other individual(s), we are able to distance ourselves from them. History has shown that in war, countries discount other nations or ethnic groups by labeling them the enemy and portraying them in non-human, demeaning terms. It is easier to drop a bomb on our enemies if we convince ourselves that they are subhuman and evil.

In the workplace, people fostering this perspective tend to have a low or undifferentiated capacity for trust. They are unable to distinguish individuals from the groups in which they are members and may prejudge others without fully understanding them. Because these people have a low capacity to trust others, they don't cooperate with others. As a result, they don't readily share information and resources to accomplish the job, working relationships suffer, and the organization is cheated of the affected employees' potential performance.

Betrayal Can Be a Teacher If We Let It

As we have seen, betrayal happens every day; it is a natural part of human relationships. Although betrayal does not feel good and certainly complicates life, it can provide us with invaluable lessons. Betrayal can be a gift and teacher if we let it. Choosing to embrace betrayal and to work through the pain will strengthen us and deepen our understanding of ourselves and relationships. Knowing how to deal with betrayal is essential to maintaining healthy levels of trust in relationships. Healing from betrayal and rebuilding trust are the topics of the next chapter.

Trust Building in Action

Reflecting on Your Experience

Reflect on a time in your life when you felt let down, hurt, disappointed, and betrayed, intentionally or unintentionally, and consider these questions:

1. What happened? How did you feel—emotionally, psychologically, spiritually—when it happened to you? What did you do about the situation? How did you respond to the experience of betrayal? What short-term and long-term impact did the experience have on you?

2. Describe a major and a minor personal or work-related betrayal that you have experienced. In what ways did your experience of them differ? What were the feelings you had in response to each of these experiences?

Application Exercise: The Betrayal Continuum

The following two exercises are designed to help you as an individual become more aware of the kinds of betrayal you see and experience and to help your team or organization become aware of its issues and areas of vulnerability in order to begin to deal with them.

A. *Individual Reflection.* List the kinds of betrayal that you see and experience in your organization, team, or individual relationships. Don't overthink the appropriate category in which to place the kind of betrayal; list it in the first place that comes to your mind. You may have a behavior listed in more than one place.

B. *Team or Organizational Betrayal Continuum.* Draw the betrayal continuum template on a large flipchart or scroll paper on the wall. Have team members record their experiences under each type of betrayal as they relate to the team or organization. Then review and discuss their observations.

1. Ask the team, "What story does this tell us about us?" What key insights emerge?

2. Discuss with your team key observations and insights. Identify the team's critical issues and areas of vulnerability.

Trust Note

We betray others when we are absorbed with ourselves. In our absorption, we lose sight of others. As a result, when we betray another, we first betray ourselves.

Trust Tip

In order to fully understand trust, you must understand betrayal. Betrayal is a natural part of human relationships. Critical to the health of human relationships is how we effectively deal with betrayal when it happens!

← BETRAYAL CONTINUUM →

MAJOR		MINOR	
Intentional Betrayal	**Unintentional Betrayal**	**Intentional Betrayal**	**Unintentional Betrayal**
EXPERIENCES:	EXPERIENCES:	EXPERIENCES:	EXPERIENCES:

CHAPTER

8

HOW TRUST IS REBUILT:
THE SEVEN STEPS FOR HEALING

*Chest aching, stomach churning, Roberta splashed water on her
face as she fought back tears of shock, horror, and deep hurt. She
could not believe what she had just heard. She honestly thought she and
Carlos were totally aligned. What a way to find out they were not!*

*The company president had given Roberta the responsibility of
overseeing the design and development of a major building complex.
Roberta asked Carlos to work with her on developing the proposal out-
lining the approach to the project. She had tremendous respect for Carlos's skill and talent, and they had worked well together in the past.*

*Roberta felt that she and Carlos had developed a solid proposal
and looked forward to reviewing it with the president. At the start of the
review meeting, she could not believe her ears when the president mentioned that Carlos had stopped into his office that morning—behind
Roberta's back—and had announced that he had major concerns about
the proposal and about Roberta's ability to oversee the project. Roberta
was flabbergasted.*

Betrayal catches most of us off guard. As in Roberta's case, major betrayals often seem to come out of the blue and knock us off our feet. To cope and get through the initial shock of our experience, we may be inclined to repress our pain or become swept up in confusion and hurt. Many of us become skillful at distracting ourselves by keeping busy with work and materialistic concerns in an attempt to shield ourselves from feeling our pain. Others will seek outside entertainment or turn to drugs, alcohol, or food.

WE HAVE CHOICE

When we have been betrayed, we often feel helpless and hopeless. We feel as though we have no control over what was "done to us." We indeed do not have control over the behaviors of others; however, we do have control over how we *choose to respond*. We may choose to remain angry, bitter, or resentful or to assume the posture of a victim, locking into what "they did to us." We may even choose to betray in return in an effort to get back at the betrayer. We may choose to embrace the pain of betrayal. We may seek to understand it and to work through it to heal, to deepen our understanding of our relationships with ourselves and with others.

When we deny ourselves the opportunity to heal from our pain, we betray ourselves. We rob ourselves of the opportunities that healing provides: the insights, the lessons, our restored capacity for trust, and potential future opportunities. When we choose to embrace our pain and work through it, we are rewarded with a renewed sense of trust in ourselves and a deeper appreciation of relationships with others. We regain our wholeness. Although none of us is likely ever to seek to experience betrayal, we can be grateful for it because of the gifts the healing provides. As Ginger said during one of our trust-building programs, "I am grateful for my experiences of betrayal because of how they contributed to the person I am today. They led me to the relationships I hold most precious and to the place I am in my life." Betrayal can be a gift and a teacher, if we allow it to be.

In organizations, we see people at all levels feeling betrayed. We see leaders feeling betrayed by inconsistencies in the systems of which they are a part. We see employees feeling betrayed as a result of the way decisions have been made or changes orchestrated. As noted elsewhere, betrayal is often not a result of what happened but rather of *how* it happened. Leaders may honestly believe that the decision to downsize, merge, cancel a product line, restructure a department, or bypass someone for promotion was absolutely in the best interest of the long-term health of the organization. However, when they ignore the impact of those decisions and particularly the impact of the manner in which those decisions were carried out, people feel betrayed. Betrayal occurs when *decisions that affect people's lives are carried out without awareness and sensitivity to their impact.*

In such cases, a double betrayal occurs: the leader's self-betrayal in failing to honor the integrity and spirit of leadership, and a betrayal of the people and organization the leader leads and serves. Both result in loss.

Few of us know how to deal with the emotional pain of betrayal, because our culture doesn't encourage reflection and genuine expression of our feelings. Experiencing a major betrayal is like experiencing a death. We have feelings of loss—of plans, jobs, dreams, relationships, trust in others or ourselves. Our hearts ache, our capacity to trust may be bruised, and our innocence is tarnished.

Trust is not necessarily the same as naiveté, but before a betrayal, we may be oblivious to the risks involved in trusting. Some psychologists say that trust cannot be fully realized without betrayal. It is only after individuals have experienced betrayal and completely know the risks that trust can be fully established. We have found this to be true in our trust-related work with thousands of people. Honoring the trust in relationships is like taking care of the health of the body. Having dealt with two bouts of cancer ourselves, we can attest that a person can't really appreciate his health until he has been seriously ill. That same line of reasoning suggests that we can't really know and appreciate trust until we have experienced the loss of it.

This does not mean that we should run back and restore our trust in relationships with our betrayers. On the contrary, before we approach anyone else, we need first to allow ourselves to take in our experience, honor it, and work with it. We need to allow ourselves to go through a process of healing. Because a major betrayal is like a death and when we experience a loss, we need to go through a grieving process. When we do so, we open the door to healing and to new possibilities with relationships. We are then available to assist others with their healing.

Whether we are the betrayed or the betrayer, the experience of betrayal provides an opportunity to discover more about ourselves. This is something many of us want, need, and seek. We want to understand and arrive at meaning that enriches us. But we often ask ourselves how: How do we deal with the depth of pain we are feeling? How do we resolve past hurts so that we see hope in rebuilding relationships? How do we understand what happened?

As noted, experiencing a betrayal has much in common with experiencing a death. There is a sense of loss. Healing after a betrayal, as after a death, requires some form of grieving. In her examination of death and dying, Elisabeth Kübler-Ross defined the steps of the grieving process: shock, anger, denial, rationalization, depression, and acceptance.[1] Our Seven Steps for Healing (see Figure 5) build on Kübler-Ross's observations and provide manageable steps to help us acknowledge and move through our hurt, with support to reframe our experience, take responsibility, let go, and move on. It is through the seven steps that we learn the lessons betrayal has to teach us about ourselves, relationships, and life.

Each of the seven steps represents a phase of the healing process, and although they are numbered sequentially, we do not work through them in a linear fashion. Different people go through the steps in different ways. You may be in multiple steps at the same time, or you may have completed one step and moved on to the next, only to reexperience aspects of the earlier step. Feelings come in waves; there are highs and lows, ebbs and flows—and movement toward *healing*.

THE SEVEN STEPS FOR HEALING

The Seven Steps for Healing are intended to serve as a framework to help us work through the painful feelings of betrayal toward renewal. They address healing on the individual, team, and organization levels because healing needs to occur at all levels. For teams and organizations to heal from betrayal, individuals need to heal first. In this section, we explore how each step assists us in healing. The Trust Building in Action section at the end of this chapter explores how leaders can use the seven steps to assist teams. In Chapter Eleven, we explore how the steps can be used to help organizations heal from betrayal.

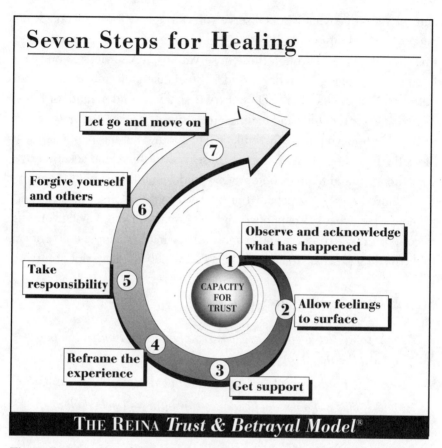

Seven Steps for Healing

Let go and move on

7

Forgive yourself and others

6

Observe and acknowledge what has happened

1

Take responsibility 5

CAPACITY FOR TRUST

2 Allow feelings to surface

4

Reframe the experience

3

Get support

THE REINA *Trust & Betrayal Model*®

Figure 5 Seven Steps for Healing

Step 1: Observe and Acknowledge What Has Happened

"I couldn't ignore what had happened. In spite of the fact that I wanted to run away from it all and continue working harder and harder, I couldn't ignore the deep pain I was feeling in the pit of my stomach. It was as if someone punched me in the gut and ripped out my insides. I was hurting. I was angry, and I hated my coworker's stealing the credit for work I had done and then lying about it to make me wrong."

Moving from betrayal to trust starts with self-discovery. The first step in moving out of betrayal is awareness. Notice what you are experiencing and acknowledge what is so. Observe your thoughts: "I was taken advantage of," "He double-crossed me," "I gave my best to this company, and this is what I get?" Through these observations, acknowledge your true feelings: "I'm angry," "I'm depressed," "I feel taken advantage of," "I feel betrayed," "I feel like hell!" Do not try to analyze, understand, or intellectualize your thoughts and feelings; just "simply notice" them. Ignoring or denying how you honestly think or feel about what has happened will block the healing process. You must consciously observe and acknowledge your thoughts and feelings before you can do something about them.

There are two aspects of the betrayal that you must observe and acknowledge: what has happened and the impact on you. Giving yourself the opportunity to observe and acknowledge what has happened is critical to the healing process. You cannot heal that which you have not observed.

Step 2: Allow Feelings to Surface

"I was livid! Yet deep down I was really hurting. I hated the person for what they had done to me, and I hated myself for being so naive that I didn't see it coming. I couldn't sleep, couldn't eat, my stomach was in knots, my head was throbbing—I ached all over. All I wanted to do was wallow in self-pity. 'Why me?' I said. I didn't deserve this!"

Give yourself permission to feel. After all, when you have been betrayed, you hurt. Once you are consciously aware of your feelings, allow yourself to feel your pain—all of it. You have experienced a loss; acknowledge and grieve for that loss. You need to honor and respect your emotions. They are central to the healing process. They are real and have a right to be expressed. The most effective way out of the pain is *through* the pain. Use your body as an instrument of healing by allowing yourself to feel your emotions. If you feel anger, get angry. If you are afraid, feel afraid. It's okay to feel lousy.

Recognize that nobody else can do it. This is a job nobody can do for you. In our professional lives, there are many tasks we can delegate to people, but grieving is not one of them. This is your work. You may attempt to avoid grief, but the only effective way to experience true healing is to work through it. For those of us willing to embrace the grieving process, there is light at the end of the tunnel, and renewal awaits us. Healing does provide deeper value and meaning to the pain you are experiencing, though that may be hard to believe while you are in it.

Give yourself quiet time alone. Each of us needs to create time and space in our lives to get in touch with and explore our feelings. For some people, reflective time spent writing in a journal may be therapeutic; others may prefer physical exercise. What is important is not *what* you do but *how* you do it. Choose an activity that helps you get in touch with your feelings rather than escape and avoid them.

Say no to guilt. The betrayal may occur only once, but we may relive it in our minds a thousand times. If you are like many people who are hard on themselves, you may become obsessed with guilt and worry. You replay over and over again the injustices that you suffered. By doing so, you hurt yourself even more. Although it is important to feel your feelings in order to grieve, feeling guilt and worry are of no positive value and are not helpful emotions for healing. They drain your energy, cloud your thinking, and clutter your emotions.

Step 3: Get Support

> *"I need help! I can't go on trying to do my job as if nothing happened, feeling like this. I need to talk with someone—someone I trust—which isn't too many people these days. I can't confide in my coworker Tammy; she would blab it all over the department. I can't go to my supervisor, Tom; he may use it against me in my performance review. Who can I rely on that I can have confidence in? I'll seek help outside the organization, maybe a coach or counselor."*

Healing from betrayal is difficult to do alone. We all need support to help us fully observe and acknowledge what happened, to allow our feelings to surface, and to understand them. Yet it may be difficult for us to reach out. When we have been deeply hurt, we are feeling vulnerable, and our instinct may be to draw back. We may find ourselves less trusting of others and ourselves and may therefore feel disinclined to share our experience.

Although this reluctance is completely understandable, you must find a way to reach out. This is a time to be good to yourself, and getting support is one way of doing that. It may be helpful to consider the options available to you and select the one with which you are the most comfortable. You may turn to a colleague, friend, or family member. Alternatively, you may turn to a counselor, support group, member of the clergy, or professional coach. Often someone you perceive to be a neutral third party may allow you to feel safest to express yourself and reach out for support.

Share your feelings with this "trusted adviser." In dealing with major betrayals, have him or her assist you in reconnecting with painful feelings from your past that are related to your present circumstance. Use this support to help you confront feelings of helplessness, hopelessness, and powerlessness so that you may reestablish your self-esteem and return to a fuller sense of self. Have the person help you see the choices and options available to you.

In dealing with an accumulation of minor betrayals, you may have to work through them while they continue because you have limited control over them. A good coach or counselor can help you redefine your expectations and options given your current situation. For example, you may have a supervisor who behaves inconsistently or a coworker you cannot rely on. Support in this context includes helping you clarify what is reasonable to expect, identifying best- and worst-case scenarios, and recognizing what options you have. Although you cannot change others' betraying behaviors, you have options to consider regarding how to respond.

Step 4: Reframe the Experience

"Why did this happen to me? What surrounding circumstances led to this betrayal? What messages do I need to hear at this time in my life? What lessons do I need to learn?"

Reframing the experience of betrayal is an important aspect of the healing process. It is here that we use our hurt and pain as stepping stones to healing. We begin by putting the experience into a larger context. We reframe it by considering the bigger picture, the surrounding circumstances—those that were in our control and those that were outside our control. We do so by asking guiding questions that help us see the betrayal differently.

Healing is a journey of inquiry. Your reflecting on reframing questions will enable you to make meaning out of what you experienced. The following are some of the questions that people we have supported through healing typically ask: Why did this happen? What extenuating circumstances might be at play? What is the purpose of this event in my life at this point? What options do I have for doing things differently? What lessons do I need to learn? What can I take from this experience in moving forward?

Reflecting on these questions will help you sort out your thoughts and emotions and arrive at greater insight. Take yourself to a place of stillness. Listen to your inner voice; it will answer these questions. Look for the greater purpose. Reframing your perspective on a betrayal can help you see that there is a greater purpose to this experience. Through reframing, you are able to transform your experience of betrayal from a trauma to a rite of passage. You will be able to use the hurt and pain as stepping stones to your spiritual growth and as an opportunity to develop your capacity for trust in yourself even further.

That which does not kill us makes us stronger! We gain inner strength and resilience. We see the benefit to our personal development. Whether the betrayal was intentional or unintentional, we learn to listen to and trust in our higher self. We see life's process as one that helps us renew, heal, and transform our experiences. We deepen our capacity to trust ourselves. We deepen our understanding and respect for relationships.

Step 5: Take Responsibility

"What was my role in this experience?" Marjorie asked herself. What did I do or not do that contributed to this betrayal? What could I have done differently? What do I need to say or do now to put this issue to rest? How do I protect myself in the future from this happening again?"

When people are in pain, they tend to project their feelings onto others. Take responsibility for your role in the process. After feeling betrayed, many people are obsessed with blaming the culprit, pointing fingers or getting revenge. There is no benefit to this perspective. Rather than dwell on who is at fault, you must take responsibility for your reactions and your part in the process. It is far more supportive of your healing to accept responsibility for working things through than it is to place blame and cast judgment. Healing and growth require you to be accountable for your behavior and the choices you made that may have contributed to the betrayal—yes, even though "they" may have been misguided or wrong. You must always consider what your part might have been. That exploration supports your finding "your truth."

In any relationship between two people, both contribute to the unfolding dynamics. When we accept responsibility for our reactions and resulting choices, we are in a better position to examine what led up to the precipitating event and how we may have contributed to it. We may ask ourselves: What role did I play in the process? What did I do or not do that contributed to the betrayal? Am I owning or disowning my part? Am I making excuses or diverting blame away from myself? Do I have a need to make the other person wrong? What could I have done differently? What actions can I now take to take charge of the situation?

We all have choices in any situation, even when we are hurting.

Step 6: Forgive Yourself and Others

"I need to forgive myself—for being so naive. I was working hard and doing all I could to keep up, and I was blindsided. Now I know better. I may forgive George, because carrying the anger is wearing me down. But I will never forget the lessons I have learned—nor should I. They are too darn valuable to forget."

Forgiveness is a gift we give ourselves. Not everyone sees forgiveness this way. Some may see it as letting the other person off the hook. Our view is that forgiveness is a gift we give ourselves to free ourselves from the burden of bitterness and resentment. In this light, forgiveness

℞

HENNEPIN COUNTY MEDICAL CENTER
701 PARK AVENUE
MINNEAPOLIS, MN 55415
612-873-3000
180-00018 (11/04)

☐ Spanish
☐ Somali

DATE   MO.   DAY   YR.   TEAM CTR./CLINIC

N MRN: 1363387 F 11/2/1950 (57y)
U WERNZ, PHYLLIS A.
M 1/30/08 1330 EIDMAN, KEITH E
B Enc: 874923 Bne Min HCMC
E HAR: 2700918146 CSN: 300926
R D: _____ Ti_____
A _____ Init: _____
M
E

Ergocalciferol 50,000 Units
#12

Do NOT Refill ☒   Signature _Keith Eidman_

Refill _____ Times   Print Name _____

Staff Physician (Print) _____

DEA #* _____   Provider No: _____ (6 Digits)

*(required for controlled substances filled outside HCMC)

018349

is more for us than for the other person. When we forgive, we are the ones who benefit first. Forgiveness gives us an opportunity to heal our wounds more rapidly. If in order to forgive we are waiting for an apology from the person who betrayed us, we become the victim once again, this time holding ourselves hostage in waiting for an act of contrition or admission of guilt.[2] An apology may certainly be warranted and may support our healing. However, we can move through the seven steps in the absence of it *if we choose to.*

Forgiveness is healing. Holding on to negative feelings of anger, resentment, and bitterness can deplete our spirit and interfere with our capacity to trust. However, with forgiveness, we not only help heal ourselves but also create an opportunity for healing to happen between us and the person who hurt us.

Forgive others. In the process of forgiving, we experience hurt, hate, and healing.[3] In our hating, we cannot forget how much we hurt. With a major betrayal, we may want our betrayer to hurt as much as we do. With a minor betrayal, we simply may not have the energy to wish the betrayer well. Though none of us wants to admit it, when we hate, it is extremely difficult to heal. To shift from hate to healing, our personal insight is critical. We need to shift our focus from our betrayer to our wounded selves. We need to detach from the person who hurt us and let go.

Forgiveness may be likened to a kind of "spiritual cleansing," a cleaning of the clutter of the wrongs our betrayer did to us and a separating of the person from the deed. Through the lens of compassion, we may choose to look at our betrayer differently. We may see her as a person who is struggling and in her own pain. We may offer the benefit of the doubt; we may consider, Is it possible that she lost her sense of herself? Is it possible she betrayed herself in the process of betraying me?

When we can do this, we are able to see our betrayers as people with needs, feelings, and vulnerabilities rather than as evildoers from the dark side. And when it comes right down to it, we are mirrors of each other. At the bottom of it all, we are like them and they are like us. They just may have been stressed, up against a wall, and doing the best they could, and lost their footing, just as we have—many times.

Full healing occurs when we invite the person back into our lives. This is challenging because it depends as much on the other person as on us. Both parties have to be willing to come together. If the other person is not, we must heal within ourselves.

To achieve reconciliation between the two parties, we expect our betrayers to listen to and hear our claims, acknowledge and honestly apologize for what they did, understand the depth of the pain they caused us and feel the hurt we felt, and make new promises that they intend to keep. They must give back more than what was taken.

Forgiveness is *not*, however, condoning the betrayal behavior. Forgiving does not mean we are saying that the act of betrayal was okay. We are saying only that we understand.

Forgiveness is a gift we give ourselves. When we don't forgive, we betray ourselves and others. This dynamic restricts the flow of life energy in us, in the people with whom we are in relationship, and in the organization we serve. Forgiveness is about healing. When we don't allow ourselves to heal, we betray ourselves.

How do we know forgiveness has begun? When we can think about individuals who betrayed us and wish them well! In situations where people are unwilling and unable to come together with us, we can still forgive them and free ourselves—in our minds and in our hearts.

Forgive ourselves. Most of the betrayals that occur at work are unintentional. Hurting others does not mean we are bad people. Most of the time we hurt others through oversights, rushing, and cramming to do more with less time, energy, and money. The more self-aware we are, though, the more we feel the pain we caused others.

Forgiving ourselves is as important as forgiving others. In forgiving ourselves, we need to be candid, clear, courageous, and responsible. We need to be candid by honestly facing the facts, admitting our wrongdoing and our faults, and acknowledging the pain we caused. We need to be mentally clear and put our inner critic on mute. We need to clear our heads to make way for an open, forgiving heart. We need to forgive ourselves for the wrongdoing we did. We need to be courageous and face ourselves and others we have wronged and let go of any shame. Finally, we need to be specific about what precisely we are forgiving ourselves for. Perhaps we were selfish by focusing solely on what was in our best interest or did not keep a promise or did not speak the truth. We can not forgive what we have not identified needs forgiving.

Step 7: Let Go and Move On

"It is time to let go and move on. I've learned some lessons—difficult as they were. I have spent enough time, energy, and emotion on this experience for a lifetime. I would not want to go through this again, but I am grateful for the experience and the lessons it provided me. It has strengthened me, and I'm glad it's over!"

The process of forgiving, letting go, and moving on deepens our relationship with ourselves. How do we know we are ready to move on? When we are able to reflect on the experience of betrayal and have a sense of inner peace. Yes, there may still be a dull pang of pain, yet the tears no longer flow.

In looking back over the experience of betrayal, we reflect on what we learned about ourselves and others that we will use in the future. We identify what we will do differently next time. We gain clarity about our approach to future relationships. No, we don't forget. But we remember in support of our relationships.

Choose to act differently. Like learning a new skill, learning to relate to yourself or others in a different way, with heightened awareness, takes practice, time, patience, and self-care. Start with small steps. Experiment with what works and what doesn't. Focus on what is in your power to control. Trust in yourself and in the process of healing.

Focus on being. We spend much of our professional lives focusing on where we would like to go in our careers and what we need to do to get there. We spend little or no time reflecting on who we are and what kind of person we are in our relationships. Many of us neglect this area. If we want to develop as leaders of people and if we want to have trusting relationships, we need to know ourselves. We do not heal by trying to be something other than who we are, but by being fully aware of who we are and honoring that knowledge.

Lighten up. Be careful not to take yourself too seriously. You should of course be conscientious about your work, your job, and your behavior, but taking yourself too seriously puts distance between you and others. Cut yourself and others some slack!

The Seven Steps Help Us Heal

When it comes to going through the pains of betrayal and rebuilding trust in ourselves and our coworkers, there is no spontaneous healing. In fact, it takes a lot of hard work and courage. However, working through these seven steps will help us heal, let go, and move on.

The process of forgiving, letting go, and moving on realigns us with our sense of self. By being more fully aware of who we are, we expand our capacity for trust in ourselves and in others and the depth of our relationships. *We are the gift to ourselves.*

Each of us will heal in our own way. We will need to spend more time on some steps than on others, especially when working through our feelings. Because intense feelings come in waves, we may progress through several steps, only to go back and deal with additional feelings that may surface. Working through one experience may kick up the pain from previous experiences. We may also be working on multiple steps at once. The sequence through the steps is not important. What is important is that we, in our own way, go through the process with honesty and integrity. By facing betrayal in a conscious way, we can move toward greater understanding of the value of the experience and develop a greater capacity for trust in ourselves and in others. Only in this way can we find value and meaning in the pain and form enriched relationships in the future. We are then able to embrace the gifts healing offers.

Trust Building in Action

Reflecting on Your Experience

1. Consider the Seven Steps for Healing. Were you able to complete all seven steps when you were betrayed? If yes, what were your feelings as you completed each step? How did it feel when you were able to move on?

2. If you were not able to complete all seven steps, where did you stop? What contributed to your halting at that point? Were you frustrated at not completing the steps? What ideas did you gain from this chapter that will help you complete the steps?

3. In the future, how are you going to use the seven steps? How do you see their use as a pathway to healing painful experiences?

Application Exercise

The following questions are intended to facilitate dialogue and begin the healing process as a team. The nature of this process requires that the seven steps be facilitated by skilled facilitator(s). It is essential that they ensure the psychological and physical safety of the group to enable the healing process to begin. Implement confidentiality agreements or ground rules with the group before beginning the process.

1. *Observe and acknowledge what has happened.* How can we start the healing process? Reflect on the circumstances that caused you or your teammates to feel betrayed. You may use the betrayal continuum at the end of Chapter Seven to list and categorize betrayals within your group or team. Share those findings with your teammates.

2. *Allow your feelings to surface.* What feelings are present regarding each of these betrayals? Notice how you feel when you are betrayed. List the emotions you feel. Do you feel angry? Vindictive? Hurt? Sad? In pain? Acknowledge your feelings. When you share your experience with others, remember to use "I" statements rather than blaming others: "I feel angry" rather than "You made me feel angry." This is easier said than done. When we are in pain, we want to strike back and get revenge on the person who caused that pain.

   Notice how your teammates feel about being betrayed. Listen to understand what they are saying. It is helpful not to get defensive or make excuses for what happened. Simply acknowledge what they are saying. For the healing process to begin, people need to know that they are heard.

3. *Get support.* What kind of support, if any, do we need? After allowing feelings to surface, notice if you feel rejected or abandoned. The betrayal experience may trigger a fear of loss, separation, or abandonment based in our past as well as in the present (loss of security, status, or a paycheck). What support do you need to help you deal with these feelings? Individually, you may want or need to talk to

someone you trust about your feelings. You may seek professional assistance (human resource professional, employee assistance program counselor, psychotherapist, and so on). As a team, it is important to have skilled facilitator(s) assist group members in dealing with their feelings.

4. *Reframe the experience.* How can we reframe the experience? Look at the big picture. What were the surrounding or extenuating circumstances that led to the betrayal? Which circumstances were beyond your control? Which were within your control?

5. *Take responsibility.* What do we need to do to take responsibility? What part did you play in the process? What did you do or not do that contributed to the betrayal? Is it possible that you did not express yourself clearly or set firm boundaries with the other person? Do you have a need to make the other person wrong so you can be right? How did you betray yourself or the other person in the relationship? What actions can we take to take charge of the situation?

6. *Forgive yourself and others.* How can we forgive ourselves and others? Are we ready to forgive? What needs to happen for forgiveness to take place? Realize that each of us has positive and negative sides, strengths and weaknesses. Notice the worst negative trait of your betrayer, and ask yourself if you have ever lost your sense of self and behaved in that way. We betray ourselves when we try to negate the fact that we have a shadow side and attempt to disown the part of ourselves that we find distasteful. Acknowledging your weaknesses helps you forgive and have compassion for yourself and others.

7. *Let go and move on.* What do we need to do to let go of these feelings and perceptions? What needs to be said or done to put this experience behind us? Have each team member reflect on these questions and share his or her needs with the group. Define and record action steps and implementation strategies to bring closure to this process.

Trust Note

Forgiveness is a gift we give ourselves. Forgiveness is about healing. When we don't allow ourselves to heal, we betray ourselves and others. We restrict the flow of life energy within us and within the organization.

We can help ourselves forgive others by asking these questions:

- What needs to happen for forgiveness to take place?
- What do I need the most?
- What do I think the other most needs?

Trust Tip

Life's most painful experiences often provide life's most powerful lessons!

9

HOW TRUST IS SUSTAINED: TRANSFORMATIVE TRUST

How do individuals and organizations sustain and increase trust over time, even during change, disappointments, and uncertainty? What does it take to develop a good working relationship into a great one? What does it take to transform our relationships and the organizations in which we work?

CREATING SUSTAINABLE TRUST

When we consciously and consistently practice the behaviors that contribute to the three types of transactional trust, and when we practice the Seven Steps for Healing after trust has been broken in our relationships, we create the conditions that cultivate *transformative trust*. That is, the amount of trust reaches a critical point and increases exponentially. It becomes self-generating and synergistic. Trust is integrated into the way people interact and do business every day. People's interactions with one another produce more trust than there was originally invested in their relationships. An organization's ethical actions in dealing with difficult situations earn more trust (and good will) than the leaders could imagine (or than money could buy)!

Trust is the foundation of an organization's culture; without it we struggle to maintain effective relationships, align on a common vision, and achieve goals and objectives. When trust is low and distrust becomes the norm, relationships are de-energized, morale suffers, and strategies and interventions to improve performance and bottom-line results are diminished. In contrast, when trust is high, relationships are energized, and organizations function at optimum performance. The presence of transformative trust does not mean that betrayal does not occur. There will always be disappointment, letdowns, and betrayals. They come with the territory of relationships. However, the presence of transformative trust means that the organizational culture and its people are committed to practicing transactional trust. They minimize betrayals and practice the Seven Steps for Healing when betrayals do occur. They make a conscious choice to work through betrayals, treating them as an opportunity to strengthen interpersonal relationships and organizational effectiveness and efficiency.

Trust is both the adhesive that holds organizational relationships together and the oil that lubricates its performance. Although of course trust building and healing are important during stable times, they are critical during times of change, as illustrated in this story.

Faced with a strategic business decision handed down from corporate headquarters, the Smith Company, a division of a Fortune 100 company, had to lay off 100 people from its 420-person operation in a one-company town in rural America. It was a decision in which local leadership was not involved. This was the first of this type of change ever in the ten-year history of the division.

Although the local managers were not involved in the initial decision to reduce the division's workforce, they were fully responsible for implementing the change. They were committed to doing so in a way that honored their people, all that the departing employees had offered the organization, and the relationships that had been formed. They carefully orchestrated each phase of the downsizing process.

These leaders were sensitive to their employees' needs and acknowledged the impact of this change on their lives, both for those who were leaving as well as for those remaining. "We know this is affecting your lives dramatically," the division manager said, holding back tears, but allowing himself to express his emotions. To ensure that people remained fully informed, top management set up open lines of communication and held special meetings and forums every step of the way to make sure everyone heard the same message at the same time, in person, and had a safe place to talk.

Management worked diligently to assist the employees, whether they were directly and indirectly affected. The managers set up career counseling and outplacement centers, visited with management in other organizations to explore job opportunities for those leaving, and invited companies into the plant to meet with job candidates. Venues were established to support those remaining behind. Skilled facilitators helped address transitional needs and set up closure meetings for employees to say good-bye to those who were leaving.

Within five months, management made sure that all the displaced employees who wanted to continue to work were placed in new jobs, inside or outside the corporation. They held open discussions with those remaining in which the impact of the changes on them were explored. They clarified new sets of expectations and boundaries. Working with the employees, management formed agreements regarding new processes and relationships, and established channels of communication and information sharing, and provided training to teach new skills.

Throughout this traumatic time in Smith Company's history, the behaviors of the leaders of the organization cultivated transformative trust. Their conviction to honor their role as leaders, their courage to tell the "hard" truth at all times, their compassion in remaining sensitive to the impact of the change on people's lives, and their awareness of the organizational community made a difference. Leaders were able to cultivate trust in an adverse situation because they demonstrated awareness and caring about the people in their organization and how they were affected by this experience.

As we have discussed, trust starts as a transaction: "You have to give it to get it." Yet when relationships are honored and the behaviors of transactional trust are consciously practiced consistently, the level of trust reaches a critical point. It experiences a multiplier effect whereby we receive more than we originally gave. Every time trust is offered, greater trust is returned. Trust between people takes on a dynamic energy and force of its own. We feel good about our relationships and are excited about our work and our colleagues on the job. We feel believed in and therefore believe in what we are doing. We feel acknowledged and respected. As a result, we show up for work alert and excited, knowing that what we do makes a difference.

Victor walked over to Patrice and knew the news was not going to be well received. She had already emphasized that she needed the lab report by this afternoon. The problem was that the equipment had failed (again), and Victor knew it was going to take many hours before he could complete the required tests.

Patrice listened as Victor outlined the issues and waited until he finished before she spoke. "Victor, thanks for alerting me. Let's focus on what can be done to get this work completed on time. Did you know that the biochemistry department at another hospital in our Area Health Service region just purchased a new machine? Let's call them to see whether they can help out."

Victor felt huge relief and was also pleased he had discussed this with Patrice before the deadline arrived—which was his usual practice. Patrice smiled. Victor had certainly started to practice the behaviors that had been promoted at the last team meeting, namely to remember to "renegotiate directly with the requestor" when one cannot honor a commitment.

In work environments where transformative trust unfolds, we learn to communicate effectively with one another, even if we are relaying bad news. We take responsibility to keep our agreements or renegotiate if we cannot. We learn to manage our assumptions and fears and our need to protect our positions and expertise. We become more willing to trust in relationships between individuals, within teams, and across the organization.

Just as betrayal decreases our capacity for trust by striking at the very core of our being in a painful way, transformative trust increases our capacity for trust by speaking to that same core of our humanness in a nurturing way. Betrayal and distrust come from a place of deprivation or scarcity, whereas transformative trust comes from a place of abundance.

Transformative trust in organizations is the hope and vision of the future as today's leaders raise the level of awareness among themselves and their people regarding behaviors that develop trust, those that destroy it, and the choices they make to rebuild it. In doing so, people honor, respect, nurture, and trust workplace relationships.

This is not easy work. Together, we are partners in the process of learning and discovering more about the complex dynamic that is transformative trust. In this chapter, we explore what this means to leaders and employees alike every day on the job. We further explore how we can bring ourselves to our work and to one another to make a difference.

The Four Core Characteristics of Transformative Trust

How does transformative trust happen at the level of interpersonal relationships? How does it happen at the organizational level?

When we express conviction, exemplify courage, extend compassion, and embody a sense of community in our relationships with our leaders and coworkers, we experience profound results: our relationships and organizations transform! Although the development of transformative trust is simple to discuss, it takes work to create it. As we've noted, consciously practicing the behaviors of transactional trust and the Seven Steps for Healing gives rise to transformative trust. Likewise, the characteristics of transformative trust support the practice of the transactional trust and healing behaviors. They work hand in hand.

We use the metaphor of a spiral to understand the interplay of transactional trust, the Seven Steps for Healing, and transformative trust. (Please refer to the Seven Steps for Healing figure in Chapter 8.) The spiral represents the upward and downward movement of relationship.

When there is a conscious practicing of transactional trust and the Seven Steps for Healing, the spiral moves upward, representing the generating of trust. Relationships are energized, and people are productive. When there is a failure to practice transactional trust behaviors, a breakdown of trust and a failure to work through betrayals result, and the spiral moves downward. Relationships are de-energized and results compromised.

Sustainable trust building takes an intention and commitment to be aware of ourselves and others: intention in the way we integrate trust-building strategies and practices into how our organization does business; commitment in how we consciously and consistently practice the behaviors of transactional trust that affect the business drivers of our organization.

As a colleague pointed out, "Building trust is more than just showing up. It is showing up as a total, whole self." Our role as leaders gives us an opportunity to create transformative trust in our organizations. This level of trust cannot be mandated; it must be invited. It is not created instantly; it takes time to develop and mature. We have found that four core characteristics are present when the level of trust in relationships and organizations is raised to transformative trust; we call them the four C's: they are *conviction, courage, compassion,* and *community.*

In the high-pressure world of most organizations, creating transformative trust requires leaders and employees alike to demonstrate and support the core characteristics of transformative trust.

It takes the four C's to move individuals, teams, and organizations out of betrayal and toward a trusting workplace environment. It takes conviction to acknowledge the truth about dynamics people have experienced. It takes courage to honor relationships when the going gets tough and we are truly challenged. It takes compassion to forgive ourselves and others for mistakes and transgressions. It takes a sense of community to reframe painful situations and take responsibility to help us understand what we have experienced, draw on it in constructive ways, let go, and move on.

It takes the four C's of transformative trust to practice the behaviors of transactional trust (contractual, communication, and competence trust) day in and day out. When we trust in ourselves, listen to our hearts, and act out of the goodness of our souls, we are being true to ourselves. When we speak and act with conviction, courage, compassion, and community, we help others heal, and we help ourselves heal. What results is powerful!

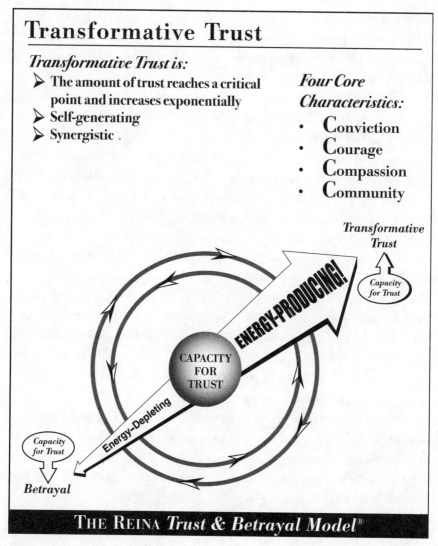

Figure 6   Transformative Trust

Transactional trust—working with the four C's—increases people's capacity for trust, nurtures healing, and transforms the quality of relationships.

Conviction

The strength of our convictions starts with self-awareness. When we are not working from our convictions, we are betraying ourselves. Our convictions stem from our awareness of our higher purpose and of what is most meaningful to us. Through our convictions, we come to know the things we will "go to the wall" for. That is where our conviction resides. When we are true to ourselves and have passion and conviction in what we believe, people concur in what we are saying and trust us. They trust that we are guided by our convictions and are committed to making those convictions a reality. Being clear in our convictions builds trust with others and strengthens our capacity for trust in ourselves.

Awareness of and trust in oneself are the greatest assets a leader can have, especially in times of change. Yet when we stray from our convictions, our personal truths, we betray ourselves and others. When we don't listen to our own voice, trust our instincts, and live by our convictions, we break our spirits and diminish our capacity for trust.

The people we work with and lead are affected by how we live our convictions. It takes conviction to give relationships a chance, to keep agreements and follow through on them or to renegotiate when we are honestly unable to meet them. It takes conviction to be consistent in our behavior and to be in harmony with our personal values as well as the organization's. It takes conviction to speak up and confront behavior that we know undermines trust in our relationships. And it takes conviction to say "I'm sorry" when we have hurt another.

When we are authentic in our words and actions, we live by our convictions. Unfortunately, in many work environments, authenticity is punished. So what happens? We go underground with the truth, become inauthentic in our words and actions—we betray ourselves. Trust in ourselves and in others diminishes.

Living by our convictions every day is hard work. It takes discipline, focus, energy, and effort. Yet it is through daily discipline that we achieve confidence and competence and expand our capacity for trust.

When we are clear about our convictions, we are in a position to help others arrive at the same level of clarity within themselves and become empowered. The result is an expanded capacity for trust in self and others.

Courage

Courage comes from the French word *coeur*, which means "heart." Sometimes it takes courage to trust our hearts and to do what we know is right.[1] We must be willing to take action in tough situations in spite of the potential consequences.

It takes courage to let go of the need for control and delegate greater responsibilities to our employees—responsibilities that we enjoy and take pride and pleasure in doing and for which we remain accountable. But to help employees learn and grow, we know we must demonstrate our trust in their competence. In so doing, we help them find the courage to trust in themselves.

It takes courage to be true to our values: to speak up and point out a betrayal resulting from the organization's not practicing its values, to point out lapses of integrity and to take the lead in correcting them, or to see how we may have betrayed others and to take responsibility even though we did not intend to let them down. It takes courage to step into the process of healing, to feel our feelings, to consider our part, and to find the compassion to forgive.

It takes courage to tell the truth in the face of adversity and not put a spin on it: to tell employees that things are tough, that the company just lost a major portion of its business to an offshore operation and may have to lay people off, some of whom have been working at the plant most of their adult lives, or that the company has just been sold to a larger firm and will undergo major restructuring. It takes courage to speak from the heart, to share that this is a painful time for us as individuals and as members of the organization, that we deeply care about our people and don't want to let them down, yet we just don't know what will happen.

Leaders have a rich opportunity to provide a deeper understanding of relationships at work, to recognize betrayal and participate in the renewal of trust with their people. It takes courage to recognize betrayal and to take the first step to heal broken trust and mend relationships.

Betrayal can be a gift and a teacher if we allow ourselves to receive it and embrace the learning it offers. It takes courage to work through the pain and to gain the benefit of betrayal.

Compassion

Do employees know we care about them? As leaders attempting to navigate change in our organizations, do we have the compassion to acknowledge the uncertainty, confusion, vulnerability, and pain that we feel and that our employees must feel? Do we remain sensitive to how our actions affect others? Do we give the benefit of the doubt when seeing disturbing behavior? This level of relating produces the very type of climate organizations are attempting to create: one that is flexible, adaptable, and trusting.

If a sense of compassion pervades the organization, the level of trust between people is so strong that they no longer rely on the traditional ways of conducting business. For instance, they are not as inclined to rely on a formal contract. "In fact, operating strictly by the contract impedes performance," the division manager of a telecommunications company noted. Compassion gives us awareness and understanding of others. This awareness enhances our capacity for trust and that of the organization. Relationships are strengthened.

When compassion exists, we feel safe to talk honestly. There is a freer exchange of feedback with the intent of helping one another develop. It takes compassion to receive feedback in a constructive way—to appreciate the intentions of the other party, to listen actively, to put our defenses aside in an effort to take in and understand what is being offered.

It takes compassion particularly when we have been hurt and are being asked to forgive the one who hurt us. When we are able to look beyond our own pain and stop blaming others for their shortcomings, we release energy in a way that opens the door to forgiveness.[2] We become lighter. Trust begins to grow; our relationships are energized.

The authors used to think that forgiveness was about giving the other person a break. We have learned it is more about freeing ourselves from the burden of distrust, freeing the energy within ourselves from blame and from holding on to the notion that someone else is responsible for the bad things that happen to us.

The act of forgiveness which is an act of compassion is an act of creation in itself. It is the process of letting go that frees up our energy for more productive purposes. Forgiveness permits the rebuilding of trust to begin. In this sense, trust is an act of creation. By making the first move to rebuild a relationship, by extending trust, we create trust. By being willing to forgive others who have broken trust with us, we begin to rebuild relationships. We are not talking about naively forgiving or granting blind trust here. We may forgive the person, but we won't forget the behavior that broke the trust.

At the transformative level of trust, we have compassion for our coworkers when we are able to walk in their shoes. We recognize that we and they are human. We consider that at any moment in time, people are probably doing the absolute best they can do, even if we sense that we might have done it better. And, under different circumstances, they might have done better themselves. Compassion understands that given the opportunity, people want to contribute and make a difference.

Community

Where there is transformative trust, people see that they are part of a larger whole. They see the underlying meaning in what they do and their contribution to the larger system. At the transformative level of trust, relationships align people and provide a sense of community.

When we feel connected through a foundation of trust, we automatically cooperate with one another. We take responsibility and honor our agreements in the spirit of relationship. We feel secure counting on one another to get the job done. Through our connection with one another, we shift our focus of operation from *I* to *we*. Trust grows; relationships are energized.

At the transformative level of trust, the workplace community promotes openness and honesty. We feel safe to discuss deeper issues of interest and matters of importance to us. We willingly admit mistakes and mention errors to be corrected because we know that not doing so would be a betrayal of our community. We feel free to ask for help without fear of looking incompetent in the eyes of others. In our connection to our workplace community, we recognize and act on the opportunity to give and take, learn and teach, help and be helped.

At the transformative level of trust, we invest in our community. We know that the only way to achieve the organization's objectives is through the collective knowledge and experience of the community—people working together in relationship.

RENEWAL OF TRUST

We seek to create work environments where we can use our skills and abilities in fulfilling our potential while also pursuing the organization's business objectives. These are conditions where we can thrive. The behaviors

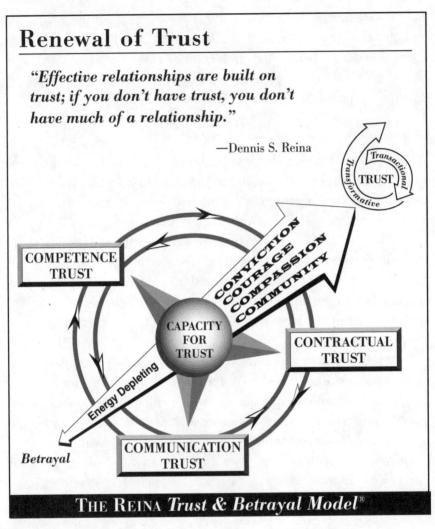

Figure 7   Renewal of Trust

of Transactional Trust, the Seven Steps for Healing, and Transformative Trust are integrated. People experience a *renewal of trust* that enables them to unleash their vast creative and productive energies for the good of the organization. When people experience such a renewal, they are in a stronger position to bounce back from traumas and can more readily deal with constant change and challenging times—together. The foundation of trust becomes *the* constant (see Figure 7).

People Want Trust in Their Relationships

We do not know what the future holds for our organization; we can only anticipate the challenges we face and do our best to prepare for them. We do know, however, that regardless of what the future holds, it will take people to make it happen. And people, regardless of where they work or what they do, want very much the same thing: trust in their relationships.

Are we willing to be catalysts for transforming the quality of relationships between leaders and employees, among teams, and across departments in our organizations? Are we willing to establish work environments where people are excited about what they are doing and the people with whom they are working? Are we willing to create organizational communities where people have an opportunity to express who they are and to be fully present at work? Are we up for the challenge? These are the possibilities for leaders, employees, and organizations embracing the four C's of transformative trust.

We have the opportunity to develop trust at work, but it isn't easy. However, the Reina Trust & Betrayal Model serves as a framework with which to begin. By trusting in ourselves and choosing to trust in others, we embrace the journey.

Trust Building in Action

Reflecting on Your Experience

Think about the four core characteristics of transformative trust and the people with whom you work. How would practicing those behaviors transform your relationships and your organization?

Individually reflect on the following questions and record your answers to discuss later with your teammates.

1. At work, where do you see *conviction* expressed?

2. What behaviors on the job exemplify *courage*?

3. How do you and your coworkers extend *compassion* to one another on the job?

4. At work, where do you see a sense of *community* being embodied?

Application Exercise

Draw the template of transformative trust characteristics on flipchart paper on the wall (see diagram). Have team members post their insights and observations regarding the preceding questions under each core characteristic as they relate to the team or organization. Then do a "gallery walk" of the characteristics of transformative trust.

1. Ask your team, "What story does this tell us about us?" What key insights emerge?

2. Discuss with your team key observations and insights. Identify the team's critical issues and areas of vulnerability.

TRANSFORMATIVE TRUST CHARACTERISTICS			
Conviction	Courage	Compassion	Community

Trust Note

Practicing the transactional trust behaviors gives rise to transformative trust. Likewise, the characteristics of transformative trust support practicing the transactional trust behaviors. They work hand in hand.

Trust Tip

In transformed organizations, trust is integrated into the way people interact and do business. People's interactions with one another yield more trust than was originally invested in their relationships. An organization's ethical actions in dealing with difficult situations earns more trust (and good will) than its leaders could imagine!

TRUST BUILDING IN THE FIELD

How do we apply trust-building behaviors and principles to relationships between individuals, within teams, and across organizations? What lessons do we learn in rebuilding trust? What works and what does not? Part V illustrates wisdom gained over the last decade from applying the principles of the Reina Trust & Betrayal Model in organizations around the globe. The stories are real; just the names have been changed to protect client confidentiality.

10

REBUILDING TRUST
WITHIN TEAMS

Trust or the lack of it affects how people work together. How do leaders rebuild trust within teams, even during times of change? How do we revitalize our relationships within teams when trust has been lost? What does it take to restore broken trust and heal betrayals with our coworkers? How do we restore trust within groups where people are unwilling or afraid to speak up, acknowledge the issues, difficult as they may be, and work toward viable solutions?

Your heart is pounding. Your stomach is in knots. The tension in the room is so thick, you need a chainsaw to cut it. The team must reach resolution on a key initiative. The boss is presenting his views on the topic, and everyone in the room is nodding in agreement. Yet twenty-five minutes ago at the water cooler, these same people were complaining that it was a "stupid idea," that it would never work. The boss finishes his presentation and asks the group, "So what do you think?" Team members anxiously shift in their seats, look around the room, avoid eye contact with each other. Everyone is quiet. Meanwhile, the voice inside your head is screaming, "Will somebody please say some-thing!" You begin speaking only to clamp shut again, succumbing to the other voice inside your head, which says, "Don't do it. It's not safe. What if the boss doesn't like what you say and blows up again?" A similar mes-sage is being played in the heads of every individual around the table. "I'm not going to speak. You do it! I'm not taking any chances."[1]

Have you experienced a team meeting like this? It is a far too com-mon scenario. When there is insufficient trust within a team, where peo-ple do not feel safe to speak their mind for fear of retaliation, members do not share openly. Instead, they have private conversations around the water cooler with the few people they trust, or keep their views totally to themselves. Or ideas and concerns get buried deep under cynicism and resentment. As a result, team members don't feel good about the team, they don't trust one another, and the team's effectiveness suffers.

THE IMPORTANCE OF TRUST TO TEAM EFFECTIVENESS

People come to teams with a range of expectations and emotions, from excitement and hope to doubt that the group will have the resources and support needed to get the job done to people who've had bad experiences who come in with cynicism. These expectations and emotions often con-cern how safe we expect the team to be, and reflect our previous experi-ences, positive and negative. We wonder if we can trust team members' intentions, if we can trust the organization to support the effort with which the team is charted.

Perhaps you have had a positive team experience: members treated one another with dignity and respect, and people shared information and views with one another openly, acknowledging what each had to offer. Your team may have had a strong foundation of trust that carried it through the challenging times. Team members felt good about each other and what they had accomplished.

Perhaps your team experience was one in which people were not treated with dignity and respect. Perhaps people did not follow through on their commitments, failed to complete team assignments, or jockeyed for position to make themselves look good. Perhaps members just stopped showing up for meetings, withdrawing their participation without a word. You may have experienced having your ideas put down before you were able to express them fully. You may have felt the pain of no trust and the loss of any hope that it could be built.

Trust in relationships is something for which we all yearn. It is a fundamental human need. Because teams are constituted on relationships, it comes as no surprise that team effectiveness largely stands on a foundation of trust. Trust is the glue that binds team members together. It helps foster a sense of belonging and influences members' willingness to communicate openly, commit to the team's goals, take risks, and support one another.

Many leaders realize that teams can be effective in helping organizations meet their objectives and adapt to change, and teams are thus widely used in organizations today. They are not always successful, however. Often a lack of trust prevents teams from developing to their fullest and most effective extent.

Being a member of a team represents a risk for some people. Some may have had no prior experience of being a member of a team or of being on a team like the one they have been asked to join. Worse, they may have had a negative team experience. In this chapter, we will explore how the three types of transactional trust can be used to strengthen existing trust and rebuild trust after betrayal. We'll look at a sampling of the behaviors related to each form of transactional trust to illustrate how they are applied and practiced in teams.

CONTRACTUAL TRUST WITHIN TEAMS

Contractual trust is where the business of relationships starts; this is particularly true within teams.

Manage Expectations and Establish Boundaries

"I try to be clear regarding my expectations of my teammates. But when I learn about what is expected of me by being criticized for what I've done wrong, especially when my teammates did not

clearly state their expectations, my trust with those members
breaks. In fact, I feel betrayed."

"What do my coworkers expect of me? Can I meet those expectations? Can I do my part as a team member? Will I be accepted?" At the
onset and throughout the time of a team's work together, members have
a strong need to know what is expected of them and what they may expect
in return. Members often have many questions on their minds regarding
what is acceptable behavior: Who is expected to do what? How are the
tasks divided, roles established? How are decisions made? Will I have
access to information? Are agendas known, or are they hidden? How will
meetings be facilitated? Is it okay to miss a meeting occasionally to handle other obligations? How late is late to a meeting? Can I renegotiate
project deadlines? What is taboo here? Is it okay to say, "I don't know"?
How will the team work together?

Contractual trust is the starting point for trust building in teams; if
the team hasn't established contractual trust, it cannot move forward.
Team members don't clarify and agree on roles and responsibilities,
leading one person to think that he or she is doing the expected job,
whereas others see it differently. People are not forthcoming about their
needs, leading to hidden agendas and "workarounds." Agreements are
"blown off," accompanied by excuses. Team behavior in general is
inconsistent.

The team's purpose defines the reason for the team's existence;
expectations define the objectives and scope of work for members. Team
boundaries define roles and responsibilities. Therefore, understanding
expectations and boundaries is crucial to the foundation of trust within
that team.

When trust is high, team members feel they are "in the know." They
have discussed their expectations and achieve agreement and alignment
around them. With this understanding, people then have an opportunity
not only to achieve their goals but also to perform at a high level.

When expectations are not clear, team members may feel confused,
anxious, and vulnerable. When people learn what is expected of them
through hearing what they did wrong, their trust breaks down. When the
purpose of the team has not been clearly established, team members have

difficulty being aligned toward the same objectives and may in fact operate at cross-purposes with each other.

It is important to create alignment so that team members can rally behind the objectives and goals. The following practices work well:

- Quarterly planning sessions give members a clear idea of the direction in which they need to head.
- Monthly progress reviews allow people to take stock of their accomplishments and the challenges to be overcome.
- Daily ten-minute stand-up meetings allow people to manage their day-to-day work, announce intentions, identify needs, and make requests of each other.

These can be conducted in person or, in the case of virtual or geographically dispersed teams, online using community-building tools.

Keep Agreements

"When I honor my agreements, it speaks to my dependability in carrying out my commitments. When I keep my agreements, I feel good, and my teammates know I can be counted on, that I am trustworthy."

Keeping agreements means that team members are willing to be accountable for their actions. When members honor their agreements, large or small, it strengthens trust within the team.

Working agreements make explicit how team members would like to work together. Team members set out a contract regarding how they will behave. Many groups have ground rules or team charters that govern team member behavior both at meetings and in other settings. These working agreements help create an environment of predictability and trust within the team. As is true of any agreement, their power comes alive when the words are taken off the pages and put into practice—when they are lived on a daily basis.

Team members create contractual trust when they keep their agreements or renegotiate broken agreements, walk their talk, show up for meetings and complete their assignments on time and keep their commitments and promises.

Encourage Mutually Serving Intentions

"In the past, team members were focused on what was in their best self-interest. Over the last year, we have done a lot to identify and work through our individual and collective needs and interests. I honestly have to say that people now show more thought and consideration to what is in the best interests of the team. Trust is much stronger than a year ago!"

When team members encourage mutually serving intentions rather than operate with hidden agendas, they jointly support each other in being successful. They take the time to discuss and address their needs. There are no hidden agendas. As a result, trust is nurtured.

Unfortunately, hidden agendas are often a part of a team's life. Individuals do not fully disclose their interests and needs and then work to meet them covertly, or team members may withhold information, thinking that this self-serving action will help them maintain power and look like experts as they position themselves for promotion.

Hidden agendas break down trust and lead to betrayal, but they arise only when there is insufficient trust in the first place. In an environment of trust, people can talk openly about their expectations, intentions, hopes, and fears. They may even enlist group members to help them. Group members feel free to say no without fear that some other member will try to circumvent their decisions.

The top management team of a small hospital system was having difficulty operating effectively as a team. The president was aware that there was a low level of trust within the team, but he did not know why.

In our work with this team, we learned that the president's relationship with the CFO carried a hidden agenda that compromised the level of trust within the team and in him. The CFO was highly competent, but she was a tyrant in the way she treated her coworkers. She would verbally attack her colleagues on issues during team meetings, rather than speak to them constructively in private. She was condescending and often abrasive. The other team members were unwilling to confront her for fear of retaliation. They were dismayed that the president allowed this behavior to continue.

Upon further investigation, we discovered the president's hidden agenda. He used the CFO to do his "dirty work" for him. The president did not want to come across as the bad guy in delivering the tough messages to his team. So he had the CFO confront members with his issues. Over time, the team all but shut down, information flow decreased, and trust "dropped through the floor." The president lost all trust and credibility in the eyes of his key people. Eventually he was asked to resign. The CFO left a short time after.

The president's self-serving actions destroyed contractual trust within the team. We helped this team heal and move on. They drew on the Seven Steps for Healing as a framework to guide honest, constructive discussions. Team members acknowledged what happened and expressed their feelings, reframed their experiences, and took responsibility for their parts. Transactional trust helped them link trust-building behaviors to their business strategy. During the following two years, the team used the Reina Trust & Betrayal Model to monitor and evaluate its progress and to guide members' behavior. What they experienced was transformative.

COMMUNICATION TRUST WITHIN TEAMS

Team members need to communicate openly with one another. They need to ask questions, honestly say what is on their minds, challenge assumptions, raise issues, or simply say they don't understand and ask for help. Only in a trusting environment will people feel free to relate in this way.

Share Information

"Samantha likes to withhold information from her teammates, thinking she holds greater power and control over them. What she doesn't realize is that when she doesn't share appropriate

information, she breaks trust. When there is an absence of infor-
mation, her teammates have a tendency to make it up—and it's
almost never positive!"

When a team member withholds information, that behavior is perceived as self-serving, and the person's trustworthiness and commitment
to the team is called into question. Performance and the trust among team
members suffer. When team members share information, it is powerful.
It contributes to the individual and shared learning. The following example highlights the power of sharing information; this is a supervisor's
observation of the way members from two teams shared insights from an
intensive training program.

"One of the teams openly shared the information they were learn-
ing in class. In fact, the members scheduled periodic feedback ses-
sions with their teammates who were not attending the classes, to
share what they learned. They became coaches for each other
back on the job. As a result, the free exchange enhanced the cohe-
siveness, trust, and performance of the entire team."

"The other team tried to enhance performance through com-
petition. They viewed information as power, so instead of sharing
information, they withheld it. Doors closed (literally), and people
shut down. These behaviors led to a secretive and "cutthroat"
working environment. The level of trust and performance within
this team declined."

"The team that shared information did more than develop
communication trust. Team members kept their agreements and
built contractual trust in coaching each other; further, this coach-
ing enhanced the skills of each team member and developed their
competence trust in one another. Having built all three types of
transactional trust, this team outperformed the one that withheld
information."

Open communication was desperately needed to turn the other team around. We engaged the group in the Seven Steps for Healing. Once members observed and acknowledged the patterns that had broken trust, we helped them reframe the experience and develop an action plan to take responsibility. As a result, team members began to open up and share pertinent job information and give constructive feedback on each other's performance. We facilitated one-on-one communication sessions over the next month (see the application exercise at the end of Chapter 3). Each team member had a chance to talk about his or her working relationship with every other group member. Members revealed what they appreciated about each other and what they felt was not working. They brainstormed how to work differently and agreed on ground rules for everyone's behavior. They ended their sessions by each summarizing expectations for the others. Over the next year, the group progressed from being a low-trust to a high-trust team, and its performance excelled.

Tell the Truth

"Telling the truth takes courage!" The supervisor said to Michael. "This means telling the 'real' truth rather than a convenient variation of or spinning of the truth. When that happens, we all notice. It certainly breaks our trust."

Telling the truth, the whole truth, is often frightening. We may question how it will be received and understood. We wonder how people will react. When we lean into our fears and take a risk by telling the truth, we honor our own voice, demonstrate respect for others, and strengthen our trust.

Although there may be a risk in being honest, there is a greater risk in being dishonest. If we speak the unvarnished truth, we may risk looking bad in the eyes of our employees or our teammates. However, if we fail to tell the truth, we risk losing our credibility. We betray ourselves and the spirit of teamwork.

Effective leaders model the behavior they expect from others. If we want truth telling, we must first tell the truth. If we want our people to open up, we must do so ourselves. We don't need to be "bleeding hearts," but we can appropriately disclose our thoughts and concerns about changes in the business environment. When we do so, it shows that we are human and do not have any hidden agendas.

The vignette at the start of this chapter illustrates what happens when team members are not forthright and not able to tell the truth. Collusion, a form of betrayal, takes place. The assumption underlying collusion is that team members cannot deal with openness or handle the truth. As a result, the truth goes underground, and trust in relationships plummet.

The first step to dealing constructively with collusion is to acknowledge what is happening within the group, name "the elephant in the living room," so to speak. Once individual team members have been made aware of the dynamic, they have a responsibility to themselves and others to raise the issues. They may say to their teammates, "I think there are some issues that we have not explored openly. I would like to suggest we discuss them." For a team that has a habit of colluding, it is essential to bring issues to the surface in order to break this pattern of denial. Trust has a chance to develop only when we are willing to uncover the truth and speak about it unflinchingly.

When team members do not tell the truth, they betray the very principle of teamwork. This betrayal affects all three types of transactional trust. It is extremely difficult to manage expectations and follow through on agreements. When you can't count on what others say, you are reluctant to commit anything to them. Furthermore, when people are not honest, others do not trust their judgment or involve them in planning or decision making. In the end, everyone loses, and team performance suffers.

Admit Mistakes

"As a leader, it takes a lot of courage for me to admit a mistake, but I have found that it allows my team to see that I am only human. And it sets the tone for them to find the courage to admit their mistakes. Mistakes are bound to happen when things are rapidly changing and we are taking risks and learning as we go."

In high-trust teams, team members take responsibility for their mistakes. These teams have regular checkpoints to monitor their progress. Leaders set the tone for the team by providing safe opportunities for people to admit mistakes. They work with their employees to correct their mistakes and to learn from them. Leaders openly surface and deal with issues in constructive ways. Within such a safe environment, employees are more willing to take risks, be creative and innovative; and they are acknowledged and rewarded accordingly.

Maintain Confidentiality

"When a team member entrusts me with confidential information, I have an obligation to honor that trust—with her and within myself. If I don't, it not only destroys the trust between us, but has negative ramifications throughout our entire team."

When team members share information in confidence, they assume it will not be shared with others. We have an obligation to uphold that agreement. Doing so builds trust; failing to do so breaks trust and results in a great deal of pain and disappointment for all involved. There is no middle ground. A person's ability to maintain confidentiality affects the degree to which others will tell him or her the truth and share information.

Rhonda was a member of a self-managed team of a production plant. She was a dedicated worker, but liked to talk—a lot! The team members made some ground rules regarding how they wanted to operate. One of the agreements concerned confidentiality: "What gets talked about in team meetings is team business and stays in the room." Rhonda attended a skills training the plant was sponsoring. During one of the breaks, she inadvertently shared some of the internal dynamics regarding a few of the team members. Word got back to the team through the grapevine that she was disclosing internal team business to the rest of the company. By the time the information got back, it was distorted. Team members were livid! Unfortunately, Rhonda was out sick for two days after the training. Meanwhile, the story and the tension within the team escalated. When Rhonda returned to work, she found out what had happened. Instead of calling the team together to discuss the facts, she was terrified and did nothing. None of her team-mates brought the issue to her either. The team's trust in Rhonda dimin-ished. She was perceived as having breached the team's confidentiality. Her team members did not confront her directly and were passive-aggressive in their interactions with her. They shunned her, refusing to share with her information she needed to do her job. She was cut off socially from the group. This went on for months. The interpersonal dynamics turned sour. Morale fell, and soon the group's performance suffered as well.

This illustrates the pain that results from a breach of confidence. Rhonda let the team and herself down. As can be expected, the team was angry and hurt. However, the other members' treatment of Rhonda was as inappropriate as her breach of confidence. Rather than confront Rhonda constructively, the team chose to shun her, shut her out, and betray her. Just as trust begets trust, distrust begets distrust.

However, in the midst of betrayal there is opportunity, if we are will-ing to see it. "These acts of betrayal can be catalysts for change; they can actually increase trust," a plant manager pointed out. "It takes courage and the responsibility of all parties to take ownership for their roles in these circumstances."

Speak with Good Purpose

"When I first started working here, gossip was rampant!" Georgia shared with the new team member. "It used to be so bad, I didn't want to get up and come into work in the morning. People used to talk behind one another's back, criticizing them for the very mistakes they themselves were making!

"Since Mr. Reynolds took over as supervisor two years ago, he put an end to the backstabbing. He established regular meetings where we would all identify and hash through the issues. We developed working agreements to guide our process. At the top of the list was 'Speak directly to the person you have an issue or concern with!' Now that is one of our team's key guiding principles."

To speak with good purpose means that we must have a positive attitude, understand what the team is seeking to accomplish, and think highly of our fellow team members. Without these, we won't be able to contribute much to the success of the team. If we don't speak with good purpose, we will undermine and distract our team from its work.

When team members speak with good purpose, they speak directly to one another regarding their concerns or issues, rather than to everyone else. They talk constructively and affirmatively and stand up for each other. Genuine support and praise for one another goes a long way toward creating a trusting environment that produces results. By supporting one another and receiving support in return, team members build an interdependence based on mutual trust.[2] Further, team members recognize each other's efforts and acknowledge the contributions they make to one another and the organization. They work harder, individually and collectively, to achieve the team's objectives and to serve their organization.

Teamwork is complex, and relationships are challenging. There are times when team members annoy, anger, or perhaps disappoint one another. If we contribute to these feelings in others, we hope they will bring them directly to our attention so that we can take an active role in resolving them. Sadly, that is not always the case.

Some people choose to voice their frustrations by gossiping and backbiting. These are surefire ways to destroy trust in a team. Through our experience with hundreds of teams and research using our trust-measuring instruments, we have found gossip to be the number one factor that destroys communication trust in work teams. People use these indirect tactics for a variety of reasons. One individual may be uncomfortable confronting another or may feel a need to put another down in order to raise his or her own standing. Yes, it is necessary to give voice to our frustrations. However, we have an obligation to the relationship with our team members to speak directly to the individuals involved. As one food service manager lamented, "I think people don't want to talk to me about the issue because they feel I don't want to hear it." If team members have things to say about an issue, they owe it to themselves and the team to bring it to the surface so that it can be discussed openly. When team members become aware of gossip and backbiting, they have a responsibility to stop it. When they don't, they betray themselves and their colleagues.

Competence Trust Within Teams

Competence trust is an absolute requirement for work to get done effectively in teams. Broadly speaking, it is the ability to do what needs to be done. Narrowly speaking, it means being able to rely on someone to complete a specific task.

Acknowledge People's Skills and Abilities

"As a leader, when I trust the skills and abilities of my team, it allows them to trust in their potential competence. It actually provides them with a remarkable gift. When I trust in them, it opens the door for them to trust in themselves. I have learned that in order to trust in the competence of others, I have to trust in my own competence."

People generally enter teams wanting to make a contribution, but they may be concerned about their ability to do so. They may wonder, "Will I be able to learn the new skills required of me so that I don't let down my team or my boss?" These are very real concerns and can cause much anxiety. Worse, fear and self-distrust feed on each other, and left unchecked, they can create a self-fulfilling prophecy. The very thing we fear, we create or bring upon ourselves. When we focus on our fear, we lose sight of our skills and abilities and lose sight of our trust in ourselves. We betray ourselves.

Team members can help one another deal with these anxieties. With marketplace demands and technological advancements ever on the increase, it is not unusual for a team's work to require a skill set or knowledge base that the team does not currently possess. However, a leader or team members may recognize the capability of one of their own to acquire it. When others see you as competent and they trust in your basic ability, their trust can help you trust in your own ability to learn new skills.

When people feel that their competence is trusted and their work is appreciated, they get excited about what they are doing and the people with whom they are doing it. They feel able to take risks and explore new arenas. The opportunity to contribute and make a difference is energizing to people.

Bill was scared to death. His stomach was in knots, his palms were sweating, and his breathing was shallow and fast. He had never given a public presentation, and in thirty minutes he would be speaking to sixty-five managers on behalf of his team. He did not want to let the other members down. The team had been working on this project for six months, and this presentation was key to getting approval on the project funding.

The team leader, Sarah, offered reassurance. "You are respected by the managers of this organization, and I know you will do a wonderful job. Relax and enjoy yourself." Well, Bill did not relax until he was halfway through his presentation, and he did not enjoy himself until it was over, but he did a wonderful job, and the presentation was well received. The team won the approval!

Bill's team members saw an ability he had to connect with people and earn their respect, a gift he was not aware of himself. The trust his team members had in him enabled him to step into his discomfort zone, giving him an opportunity to develop new abilities and discover new ways of seeing himself.

Unfortunately, team members don't always recognize each others' skills and abilities. There are times when they don't see one another as the whole people that they are. Their narrow perceptions limit the potential of their teammates as individuals and the team as a whole. When team members feel discounted or experience other members' being discounted, they need to communicate their concerns. When people discount one another, their comments say more about them than about the person they are attacking and are often the result of these individuals' own insecurity, fear, lack of information, or need to control.

In such situations, it is important to facilitate an open dialogue to clear the air. If members consistently feel discounted, they need to feel safe enough to express their frustrations and vent their concerns without being further discounted. The bully needs to be confronted head-on; consequences for his behavior need to be spelled out unequivocally, and discipline needs to be enforced. When team members are encouraged, they will start speaking up, taking a stand. As they experience some success, their confidence and competence in handling these situations will grow, thereby freeing up their energy for more productive purposes.

Involve Others and Seek Their Input

"When I ask my teammates for their advice, they feel acknowledged because I trust their opinions. It demonstrates my trust of their competence."

In high-trust teams, members involve one another and seek their input in the team's day-to-day work. They share information, exchange ideas, and brainstorm solutions. By actively involving one another in their processes, they support one another's goals and contribute to the total performance of the team. This support builds confidence and competence trust within each individual and the team as a whole.

In low-trust teams, members do not readily involve others or seek their input on decisions. People operate in "silos," with little to no collaboration. Competence trust is constricted.

One indication of a low-trust team is the "not invented here" (NIH) syndrome. When this syndrome is present, team members ignore or discount others' ideas or suggestions simply because they didn't think of them first. Team members do not benefit from collective learning when they do not value each other's input. Team and overall organizational performance suffer when people don't leverage each other's competence. Furthermore, when leaders don't value the contributions of their team members, they discount their employees and discredit themselves.

The manager asked the team to develop procedures for inspecting parts on the production line. Rallying to his request, the team worked hard for almost five weeks to develop the procedures. The team felt proud of what it had accomplished. At the end of the five weeks, the supervisor ignored the team's work and instituted his own procedures without any explanation to his team. Team members felt discouraged and defeated: "Why should we work to give him what he asks for? He'll simply ignore it anyway!"

The supervisor initially sought the input of his team, yet his actions did not respect the members' work or the value of their contribution. He demonstrated poor judgment and a lack of competence trust in them. Giving people an opportunity to contribute, whetting their appetites and firing their enthusiasm and then dashing their spirits, dishonored the relationship. It wasted people's time and energy and destroyed their trust in him as their leader.

We can learn powerful lessons from painful experiences like this one of what not to do. In contrast, there are many leaders who are trying to do the right thing. They encourage their employees to share information, exchange ideas, and brainstorm solutions. These leaders actively involve their employees in decision making processes, so they are able to support one another's goals and contribute to the total performance of the team. This support builds confidence and competence trust within each team member and the team as a whole.

Help People Learn Skills

"When I help my employees learn new skills, I am investing in their competence and the capacity of my team. Likewise, I encourage the employees to teach one another and share knowledge—this creates a positive feedback learning loop within my team. Everyone benefits, and the team's competence increases."

If, in contrast, team members don't feel acknowledged for the skills, knowledge, and experience they bring, they stop giving their utmost to that organization. They may go through the motions, but internally they shut down and resign themselves to giving as little as possible. After a prolonged time, when members don't feel valued for the capabilities they bring to the team, they begin to question their own competence. Their willingness to learn and take risks falters. Their capacity for trust in themselves decreases.

To retain talented employees who are engaged and satisfied, effective leaders know that they need to acknowledge their employees' contributions and challenge these individuals' to develop their capabilities. To build the capacity of their people, leaders need to push employees into their "discomfort zones," where most powerful learning takes place. Further, leaders need to support their employees in their discomfort. In doing so, they help employees acquire yet more knowledge and learn to trust more in themselves. In turn, the leader demonstrates that he or she is safe to trust.

TRUST: THE MOST CRITICAL TEAM INGREDIENT

Trust is the foundation to team effectiveness. Without it, a team will not do more than go through the motions of teamwork. Transactional trust anchors a team in its purpose and creates shared responsibility and accountability. Contractual trust sets the tone and direction for team functioning; it establishes the playing field and the rules for engagement. Communication trust establishes information flow and how people will talk with one another. Competence trust allows teams to leverage and further develop skills, abilities, and knowledge.

Can teams have one type of trust and not another? Yes, but not for long. We have learned through our trust-measuring instruments that it is possible for a team to have a high level of one type of trust and a low level of another at some points in its functioning. However, if low levels of trust are not rebuilt, the unresolved betrayal will erode the pockets of high trust.

High-trust teams strive to be aware of their behaviors. They link trust-building behaviors to their strategy. Trust building is an integrated part of their work. High-trust teams monitor themselves and practice the seven steps to address disappointments when they occur. And they reap the rewards of their awareness and behavioral choices: joy, satisfaction, growth, results, and *effective* relationships.

TRUST BUILDING IN ACTION

Reflecting on Your Experience

Individually reflect on the following questions and be prepared to discuss your insights and observations with your teammates.

1. Think of a team in which the trust among team members was high. How did that high level of trust affect the effectiveness of the team? In what ways did the high level of trust cause members to be more productive?

2. Think of a team where trust was low, perhaps as a result of having experienced betrayal. What was the impact of this low trust on the team's effectiveness? How did the low trust reduce the team's productivity?

3. Did members of the low-trust team have explicit agreements? Were they upheld? Were there areas where the team needed agreements but was unable to negotiate or commit to them?

4. How was the high-trust team able to share information? How did that sharing of information contribute to the team's effectiveness? What happened to team members when they made a mistake, whether they admitted it or not?

5. Did the low-trust team identify and systematically use the competence of its members? If not, what was the effect on team cooperation? Was any attention given to improving the capabilities of team members?

Application Exercise

Assess the Team's Transactional Trust. Use the transactional trust template on the next page to assess the level of trust within your team and to get each team member's perspective on how well the team is practicing the behaviors that contribute to each type of trust. Suggested steps are as follows:

1. Draw a circle in the center of a piece of flipchart paper and label it "Our Team's Transactional Trust." Then draw three branches extending from the center point of the circle, and label each with one of the

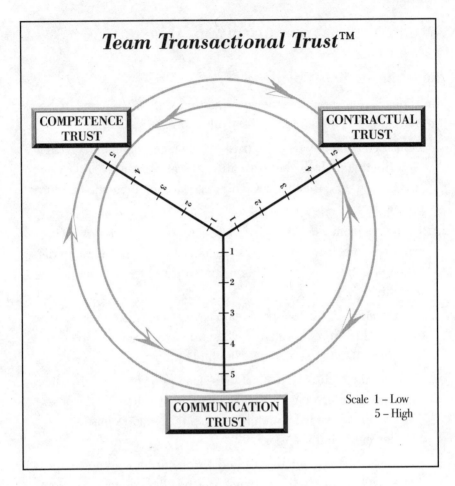

Team Transactional Trust™

COMPETENCE TRUST

CONTRACTUAL TRUST

COMMUNICATION TRUST

Scale 1 – Low
       5 – High

three types of transactional trust: "Contractual Trust," "Communication Trust," and "Competence Trust," as in the figure here.

2. Give each team member three colored dots and have all team members place their dots on each vector of the transactional trust template according to the degree to which they perceive the team practicing the specific behaviors that contribute to contractual, communication, and competence trust. Team members rate the level of trust on a scale from 1 to 5 (1 is low, 5 high).

3. Have the team step back and take a look after everyone has had a chance to rate the team's level of trust. Ask the team, "What story does it tell us? Where are we strong? Where are there opportunities

for improvement?" Have the team discuss the behaviors that are the weakest under each type of trust and discuss ways to strengthen these behaviors.

Please note: This is a quick snapshot of team members' perceptions of the level of trust in your team. It does not by any means replace such valid and reliable instruments as the Reina Team Trust Scale, an online research-based assessment survey that measures the quantitative and qualitative levels of trust within teams.

Trust Note

Team members have a strong need to be able to communicate openly with one another. They need to be able to ask questions, honestly say what is on their minds, challenge assumptions, raise issues, or simply say they don't understand something and ask for help. Only in a trusting environment will people feel free to relate to one another in this way.

Trust Tip

Trust is the glue that bonds team members together; it is the grease that lubricates the team's performance!

11

REBUILDING TRUST
WITHIN ORGANIZATIONS

*"I can't believe he did this! I am so angry! I just found out that
our president, Mr. Smith, cut our benefits package and is now
reneging on our 2.5 percent merit increase that he promised
months ago. I work hard for this company and was counting on
that pay. And I read in today's news that he is getting a year-end
bonus package worth millions—on top of his salary! I think he is
personally greedy and disconnected with the majority of employees within this organization."*

Budgets are decreasing, employees' benefit packages are being cut,
and some unscrupulous leaders are getting wealthy while many employees are paying the price. Fortunately, most leaders are conscientious, trying to do the right thing in the face of all odds. How do these leaders
rebuild trust within their organizations, given the changing business landscape? What can they do?

It was a Tuesday in November, cold, damp, and overcast, as many are in the Northwest. At the plant, anxiety was high and morale was low. In the lunchroom, people speculated about what was to come next. "Have you heard when the next cut will be? Who do you think will go this time?" A worker from across the table chimed in, "I have given seventeen years of faithful service to this company. From now on, I don't trust anybody—it's every man for himself!" Out on the production line, employees were moving the product, but performance was nothing like a year earlier, before the restructuring began. The plant manager peered out of his upper mezzanine office window overlooking the production floor. "Overall labor costs are lower, but production is declining, and morale has hit rock bottom!" he muttered to himself. "What am I going to do?"

Stories like this are commonplace. Change is happening in all organizations. Leaders face the challenge of managing change in a way that is the least damaging to trust.

Traditionally, leaders have approached change with an assumption that what is good for the organization is good for the people. Yet many change efforts based on that assumption have failed to produce desired results. Not wanting to repeat mistakes, leaders are becoming aware that sound business decisions must be executed with sensitivity to human needs. Tough decisions still have to be made, yet it is possible and necessary to implement them in a way that doesn't destroy trust. Aware leaders are more inclined to manage change with respect and sensitivity for all involved. When leaders fail to do so, they betray the people they serve and their leadership role.

THE IMPACT OF CHANGE ON PEOPLE

Organizations depend on relationships to get work done. Relationships depend on trust to succeed. Sometimes the mechanics of managing change overshadow relationships and compromise people's dignity, respect, and trust. The following examples illustrate this.

Camille was conducting an outplacement seminar designed to offer support to people who had just lost their jobs. Ten minutes before the session was to begin, Camille stepped into the hallway for some water when a manager approached her. "Camille," he asked, "can you hold up the session for fifteen minutes? I have two employees who need to be in your workshop today but haven't been informed yet."

The manager in this vignette was insensitive to the needs of his employees. He was going to rush into informing them that they were losing their jobs and then send them immediately into a workshop about résumé writing.

Over a number of months, as the La Petite Company downsized one of their divisions, they sold unneeded hardware and furniture. Following an employee's last day, the furniture was removed from his or her office. Jacque, a purchasing agent within this division, knew he was going to go through some type of job transition but did not know when it would happen or what it would be like. He was hoping for a transfer to another branch of the company. The next Monday, Jacque came into work and discovered that his desk and chair were gone. When he inquired about the missing furniture, he learned that he was out of a job.

Organizational change doesn't have to happen this way. As we've mentioned elsewhere, the betrayal people often experience is a result not of change itself but of *how* it is managed. Employees want to be a part of the process, not apart from the process. They want to hear the truth and have an opportunity to ask questions and become informed. All employees, leaving and staying, need to have trust in their environment. How leaders manage change affects whether trust will be built or broken and desired outcomes achieved.

WHEN PEOPLE SEE CHANGE AS LOSS

People may experience change as a loss—the loss of relationships with those laid off or the dissolution of the "family" company environment that once existed. People may resent that they are doing more work for the same pay with fewer benefits and that opportunities to earn more are limited.

With every change comes gain, loss, and grief. In organizations, often one person's gain is another person's loss. The people initiating the changes are usually the ones to gain. If I am the one gaining, it is harder for me to see how the other person loses. In our culture, we are taught that it is not good to cause other people to lose, so we mentally minimize their loss. This phenomenon makes it harder for us to see the pain many employees experience with change.

Often the organization in which people work is not the same place they "signed on for" initially. People may experience changes as losses. They need to talk about and grieve those losses. They need to acknowledge that what they once had is no longer. *The longer the employee's tenure, the greater the feelings of loss and the greater the need to grieve.* In a world where everything is changing rapidly, many people who previously looked to their workplace as a source of stability now regard it as out of control. It frightens them.

DEALING WITH THE EMOTIONAL SIDE OF CHANGE

Dealing with the emotional side of change is difficult but necessary. Many leaders are uncomfortable watching their people experience the pain of change and are uncomfortable experiencing their own pain. They often consider this to be touchy-feely stuff, not the stuff of "real business." During times of change, leaders tend to retreat to the "hard side" of business for many reasons: it is where they are most comfortable, where their role is more tangibly defined, where they are skilled, and where they are the safest. In the retreat to the safe side, they fail to honor themselves, their relationships, and the real needs of the people they serve. They fail to honor the essence of leadership. Their search for safety results in a betrayal of themselves, their role, and those they serve.

Aware leaders recognize the high cost of betrayal to individuals, to relationships, and to performance. It robs individuals of their ability to believe in themselves. Their ability to contribute wholeheartedly to the organization is diminished. When people feel betrayed, they pull back.

Morale declines, as does productivity. People's capacity to trust themselves is diminished with their readiness to trust their leaders.

Effective leaders acknowledge their employees' feelings of fear and loss and work to restore their confidence. Otherwise, the betrayal continues, and people's capacity to trust in their leaders and their organization further plummets. Survivors go into a state of resignation: they take fewer risks, blame others, go through the motions, and are not as productive as they once were. If employees have been burned before, they are less willing to give their all and come through when needed. If leaders do not deal with feelings of betrayal, they will unwittingly destroy two of the very qualities they need to be competitive: their employees' trust and their performance.

HELPING PEOPLE HEAL FROM BETRAYAL

We have explored how people experience betrayal. Quite often, it occurs during change. The Reina Trust & Betrayal Model provides a framework to honor relationships while managing change. Here we explore how the Seven Steps for Healing (see Figure 5 in Chapter 8) can help you work through betrayal and manage change.

Healing begins when we observe and acknowledge that betrayal (intentional and unintentional) has occurred and that we understand its impact on others. As a leader, you can take certain actions during the healing process that can have a positive impact on people. The Reina Trust & Betrayal Model will help you and others remain aware of the behaviors essential to healing that are too easily dropped, especially during times of rapid change. Our model also provides a common language and perspective that engages people in healing. Although leaders have significant responsibility to rebuild trust, they do not have sole responsibility. Rebuilding trust is everybody's job!

Step 1: Observe and Acknowledge What Has Happened

"Mr. Smith needs to effectively address the 'pay package' issue at the organizational level. If benefits or merit pay are going to be negatively affected, he needs to manage the message through an effective and timely information program. Tell all that you can as

soon as you can! I think he underestimates the level of awareness
and impact this has on employees."

Aware leaders acknowledge the negative impact of change. They realize that employees are whole human beings with feelings. They know that people who do not feel supported to deal with their feelings and concerns are less able to heal from their experience of betrayal. They are not able to fully show up for work.

Start with awareness. Similar to healing at the individual level, the first step to healing at the organizational level requires awareness. One of the greatest mistakes leaders make in challenging times is to assume that once a major change has taken place, trust will return on its own. This view is both unrealistic and irresponsible.

Assess the health of your organization. Observe and assess the climate within the organization. Notice what your people are experiencing and acknowledge it. Pay attention to what is building and breaking trust. Many organizations that we serve use the Reina Organizational Trust Scale, which measures the level of trust in the organization as perceived by management and employees. Find out what is important to people. Listen to what they are saying at the water cooler, in the break rooms, and on the shop floor. When witnessing anger, don't just notice the anger. Listen to it. Quite often anger represents deeper feelings of hurt and disappointment. Remember, people in pain need to be listened to. They need someone they can trust to turn to for support and understanding. They need help to understand their own experience.

Acknowledge feelings. Effective leaders consciously acknowledge their employees' feelings of frustration, disappointment, and betrayal. It is only after acknowledging the feelings of betrayal that leaders are able to respond to them. Leaders must work very hard not to get defensive or try to justify or rationalize what happened. They must remember that people are entitled to their feelings. It is the role of a leader to listen, observe, and acknowledge. This is the first step to healing the wounds.

Step 2: Allow Feelings to Surface

"I don't always feel heard—that I can address my concerns
directly with certain managers and be taken seriously. It is
important to me that I am able to do so. There are occasions

*when my supervisor has to address issues with a particular man-
ager on my behalf, because I wasn't deemed 'important' enough
by him to talk to. This attitude discourages me and other employees from addressing serious concerns in the future."*

Give people permission. Give employees permission to express their
concerns, issues, and feelings in a constructive manner. Create safe
forums, staffed by skilled facilitators, that support the expression of fear,
anger, and frustration. Giving your employees a constructive way to discuss their feelings and experiences helps them let go of the negativity they
are holding, freeing up that energy for rebuilding relationships and
returning their focus to performance.

Help people verbalize. Help employees give voice to their pain—
pain they are afraid or unable to share with anyone. When you give your
attention to understanding your employees, you let them know that you
respect their pain.

This is the difficult work for leaders, but it is important and necessary
work in facilitating healing and navigating change. Your employees don't care
how much you know until they know how much you care—about them and
their well-being. People in pain need to have their feelings heard. They need
to know that you are able to relate to what they are saying and feeling. When
you do not acknowledge your employees' emotions, they feel unheard,
resentful, and distrusting toward you. Another layer of betrayal occurs.

Step 3: Give Employees Support

*"Our leader took the time to hear our story. She really listened
and asked us questions. It really helped to tell her how we felt.
She heard how frightened we were about what was happening
around us. It feels good to know that she understands our needs.
When she shared her views, I was able to see things in a much
different way. I am beginning to have hope for the future."*

Recognize your employees' transitional needs. People have needs
that must be met before they can adapt to change. They have informa-
tional needs regarding the new direction the organization is taking and

the strategies it proposes to get there. They have relationship needs associated with belonging and their role in the new organization. And they need their skills and abilities to be valued. When leaders expect people to embrace change without these fundamental needs' being addressed, people feel betrayed.

Back your employees. Your leadership position allows you to be your employees' advocate. Represent your people's interests, defend them from unwarranted criticism, and lobby for resources critical to their jobs.[1] By backing your people, you are building contractual trust and meeting the implicit expectations people have of leaders. Furthermore, you demonstrate that you can be trusted to fulfill future commitments, that your people can count on you to do what you say you will do.

Step 4: Reframe the Experience

"Our president, Mr. Allen, took the time to visit every field office in our region to explain the business reasons for GNP Industries' downsizing the eastern division. This helped us put the change into perspective. It lessened the communication gap between the headquarters and the field branches. His actions let us employees know that he cared. We believed he was going to do everything he could to lessen the impact the changes were having on our jobs, our families, and our lives. We understood the direction the company was taking and knew our leader would continue to tell us the truth."

Put the experience into a larger context. Helping your employees work through their emotions makes it possible for them to begin to heal. This movement gives you an opportunity to rebuild communication trust and helps employees reframe their experience by discussing the bigger picture: the business reasons for change. Honestly acknowledge the changes the organization went through and why. In doing so, you must continue to acknowledge what people have experienced. Only then will employees be in a position to accept the new direction in which the organization is headed and to see their role in it.

The process of healing from betrayal is a process of inquiry. The questions that people ask will guide their journey.[2] Responding to their questions honestly will provide employees with understanding, awareness, truth, and renewed hope for a trusting relationship with you and the organization.

Help employees realize there are choices. Experiencing betrayal leaves employees feeling very vulnerable and at the mercy of the forces of change. They may need help seeing that they have choices regarding how they react to their circumstances. The more people are aware that they can choose their actions, the more they are able to take responsibility for those actions. Employees may need help examining their assumptions, breaking out of their self-limiting beliefs, and exploring options and possibilities.

Embrace mistakes. Some of the behaviors discussed that aid in healing may be new for you, and you may not trust your competence in exercising them. It may take some practice developing these skills and becoming comfortable using them. During this time, you may make some mistakes. That does not automatically make you a failure. Embrace these mistakes as opportunities for learning, thereby turning them to your own benefit. After all, they provide valuable feedback regarding what works and what does not.

Just as leaders must be sensitive to employees' needs, employees need to be sensitive to leaders' needs. This may mean having some patience and understanding that the leader is grappling with change as well. Therefore, if a leader makes a mistake, it is not necessarily evidence that the leader can't be trusted. It *is* evidence that the leader is stretching, growing, and learning. When someone is practicing new ways of relating, people need to be supportive and understanding of his or her learning.

To gain support and understanding, you might find it helpful to share with people that you are learning new skills. Sharing this aspect of yourself demonstrates your trust in them and further extends the invitation to rebuild your relationship with them.

It is possible that you as the leader feel betrayed as well. It is as important that your feelings of betrayal be acknowledged. It is important that you get support to help your people see that.

Step 5: Take Responsibility

*"Leaders need to take responsibility for how change was imple-
mented. The restructurings took people by surprise and left
departments with minimal coverage to do the work. Questions
were not answered and needs not addressed. It's difficult to imagine the distress this has caused. Employees were in great distress
and felt quite isolated."*

Take responsibility for your role in the process. It is not helpful to
try to spin the truth or cover mistakes. It does not serve you or the relationship. Something quite powerful occurs when we tell the impeccable
truth—with no exceptions, no justifications, no rationalizations. Telling
the truth is the fundamental basis for trust in workplace relationships. It
demonstrates one's trustworthiness. We take responsibility when we
acknowledge our mistakes. Three simple words, *I am sorry,* reflect taking
responsibility and go a long way to rebuilding trust.

Help others take responsibility for their part. When people are in
pain, they tend to blame their leaders and behave in ways that contribute
to betrayal. We support others in taking responsibility when we help them
see their role in creating the climate of betrayal. Employees may not have
control over change, but they do have control over how they choose to
respond. Even though people may feel betrayed, those feelings do not
make betraying in return acceptable.

Make amends and return with dividends. It is the leader's role to
break the chain of betrayal and reverse the spiral of distrust. Because
actions speak louder than words, it is important that you take the first step
in mending fences with your employees. Remember that rebuilding trust
does not simply mean giving back what was taken away. It means returning something in better shape than it was originally in. If you have lost
trust by taking valued responsibilities away, you can regain trust by granting people even more significant responsibilities.[3] You must not only
replace but also make things better. If this is not possible, be honest about
the realities of the situation and what you can do to make amends.

Manage expectations. The level of expectations is directly correlated
to the opportunity for betrayal. To safeguard yourself and your employ-

ees against future betrayals, keenly manage expectations. Employees want to know what is expected of them and what they can expect in return. Emphasize the need to negotiate with them when their expectations cannot be fulfilled. This strengthens contractual trust between you and your employees.

Keep your promises. Managing promises is important in relationships. Trust is the result of promises kept. Don't make promises you know you can't keep; that just sets up you and everyone with whom you have a relationship for a downfall. When you realize that you cannot keep promises, renegotiate them; don't break them.

Be careful of what you promise and what you appear to promise. When you are attempting to rebuild trust, it is essential that you not try to justify past actions and that you address the perceptions of those who feel betrayed. "It is enough for an employee to have believed that a promise was broken for trust to be violated."[1]

Step 6: Forgive

> *"Many employees feel that they have been intentionally misinformed and lied to. They do not trust management. It will take time for forgiveness to happen. We need to bring in support to help us understand the surrounding circumstances and allow us to say what needs to be said, to 'get this off our chests.' This will help us shift from blaming management to focusing on problemsolving the issues, so we can begin to forgive."*

Recognize that forgiveness is freedom. Forgiveness is a gift we give ourselves. It is about freeing ourselves and others from the anger, bitterness, and resentment that can deplete our individual and collective energy and spirit and interfere with relationships and performance. When we help people forgive others, we help them free themselves. With forgiveness, they heal for their future by changing their attitude about the past. We help them see new possibilities.

For most people, forgiveness takes time, and it happens a little at a time. Over time, your employees may be willing to forgive, but you cannot expect them to forget. You can help them heal from the pain they felt, but you cannot erase the events of the past. Occasionally, your employees may still be a bit angry after they forgive. It is natural that they may experience lingering feelings of anger for the perceived wrongs they experienced.

Occasionally, you as a leader may need to forgive yourself. You did the best you could, and for whatever reason, it still wasn't enough. Beating yourself up mentally and emotionally is worthless and self-defeating. Acknowledge for yourself what needs to be said or done to put your mind and this issue to rest. Then just do it! Be compassionate and cut yourself some slack during the healing process!

Shift from blaming to focusing on needs. Because forgiveness is a personal matter, it is difficult for people to forgive a system. However, leaders can work to cultivate a more personal and trusting climate where healing and forgiveness can take place. They can begin to do this by helping people shift from blaming the organization or its leaders to focusing on their personal needs as they relate to business needs.

It is important to address persistent resentment and blame in an organization, as they are toxic to the individuals involved and to the whole system. They undermine trust, morale, productivity, creativity, and innovation. People continue to blame when they perceive that those who are responsible have failed to take responsibility. People in return feel that they do not have to take action and are therefore not responsible. People also blame when they are carrying experiences of the past into the present.

It is essential that leaders help people shift from a blaming mode to a problem-solving focus. What do your employees need to resolve the issues, concerns, fears, and pain they are feeling? What conversations need to take place? What still needs to be said? What needs to happen for healing to occur? What will make a difference right now?

Step 7: Let Go and Move On

"Our leader brought in outside skilled facilitators to provide the needed support through the transition. During the small-group discussions, they were neutral and made sure we were all heard. They held a tough line, helping us see our leader's point of view. The facilitators really drove home the responsibility we all shared. We had painful but powerful discussions. What a relief it

*was when we were able to forgive ourselves, because we were no
angels. But things really shifted when we also forgave our leader.
Wow—we have moved on and are all on board with our organization's new direction."*

Accept what's so. Leaders can help their people accept what has
happened. Acceptance is not condoning what was done but experiencing
the reality of what happened without denying, disowning, or resenting it.
It is facing the truth without blame. It is helping employees separate
themselves from their preoccupation with the past and helping them
invest their emotional energies in the present and in creating a different
future.

Realize that you won't always accomplish your goal. Although you
may not always accomplish your goal, it is important that you make a
good-faith effort and that your intentions are honorable. It is quite acceptable for leaders to disagree with their employees or not support a particular cause. Effective leaders do so with honesty and integrity.

Take the time; make the commitment. Building trust takes time and
commitment. When trust is lost, it is regained only by a sincere dedication to the key behaviors and practices that earned it in the first place. The
road back is not easy. However, by listening, telling the truth, keeping
your promises, and backing your employees, you will play an instrumen-
tal role in assisting your employees and organization to heal from betrayal,
rebuild trust, and renew relationships.

Give support! Providing support is a sign of your dedication to the
healing and rebuilding process. The number one mistake leaders make is
expecting people to immediately move from step 1 (observing and
acknowledging what has happened) to step 7 (letting go and moving on)
without doing the necessary work of the other steps. We aren't built to
work this way. People in pain cannot simply move on. They need to fully
go through the healing process. When people are willing and able to do
the work, it will lead to renewal!

Remember, your commitment to practicing transactional trust and
the Seven Steps for Healing, and engaging your people in the same, will
lead to transformation. Imagine the possibilities!

TRUST BUILDING IN ACTION

Reflecting on Your Experience

Individually reflect on the following questions and be prepared to discuss your insights and observations with your teammates.

1. Think of a major organizational change that reduced the trust within an organization or even caused a sense of betrayal. What did leaders do that contributed to the betrayal?

2. In this betrayal situation, in what ways did leaders acknowledge, if at all, the emotional price paid by employees? How did the emotional side of this change affect productivity within the organization?

3. After the betrayal occurred, what steps, if any, did the leadership take to promote healing from the betrayal? What would you recommend leaders do to help themselves and their employees let go of the past and move forward?

4. During a major organizational change, what would you recommend leaders do to address the needs of employees? What would you recommend for managing the new expectations that are being created during this change process?

5. How could leaders reframe change in terms of a larger context that would make sense to employees?

Application Exercises

A. *Cultivating Trust in Your Organization: The Role of the Senior Management Team.* Senior management teams need to address the question, "How do we, as a senior management team, cultivate trust within our organization?" In doing so, they explore ways in which they can provide overarching structure and resources to support the work of the frontline managers and employees.

Instructions:

1. Allocate an uninterrupted block of time for the senior management team to explore the following systemic questions as they relate to their organization. (Offsite retreat settings are ideal for this kind of work.)

- What does a culture of trust look like within our organization?
- What and where are our critical trust-related issues?
- What are the biggest barriers to cultivating trust in our organization?
- What policies and procedures are detrimental to trust between departments and across the organization?
- What policies and procedures do we need to rethink, rework, or rewrite?
- What does each senior manager need in his or her respective division to support the people in the field serving customers?
- What are the three top needs in each department? What can the members of the senior management team collectively do to support each other in meeting those needs?

2. Designate a skilled facilitator to lead the discussion, making sure roles and working agreements are in place.

3. Capture key points regarding each question on a flipchart. Identify essential issues to work on.

4. Prioritize the top three issues and create an action plan to address them.

Addressing these questions collectively not only begins the process of building trust within the organizational system but also starts the process of building trust among individuals within the senior management team.

B. *Identifying Behaviors That Build or Break Trust.* A team or group may use this template to identify which behaviors support or build trust and which behaviors detract from and break trust within the organization. Suggested steps are as follows:

1. Draw a large *T* on a piece of flipchart paper, and label the top center "Trust Within Our Organization." Then label the left and right columns "Builds Trust" and "Breaks Trust," respectively.

2. Have the team identify the specific behaviors that build and break trust within the organization and list them in the appropriate column.

3. Rank and prioritize the behaviors under each column. Select the three behaviors that break trust the most.

4. Strategize ways to resolve these three troublesome behaviors.

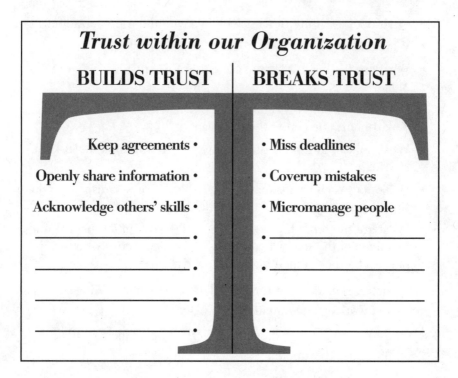

Trust Note

Organizations depend on relationships to get most work done and to coordinate the efforts of their workforces. Relationships depend on trust to succeed. When leaders lose sight of this and orchestrate change without sensitivity to and awareness of the people affected by the change, they betray themselves and their people.

Trust Tip

How leaders manage change affects whether their employees' trust will be built or broken and the desired outcomes of the change achieved.

12

STORIES FROM THE FIELD

EMPLOYEE SATISFACTION RENEWED

"Frank, you've got six months to improve these results, or you and your management team can forget your bonus for this year!" Cheryl said, with a little panic audible in her voice. "And I can forget mine too. How did this happen? Your division has the lowest employee satisfaction survey scores in the whole company. That means anywhere in the world!"

"I thought the numbers were going up," Frank offered defensively. "I don't know how they went down further."

"You're responsible for Learning Services. I don't have to tell you that your division is responsible for helping our business units and leaders throughout the world carry out their key strategic initiatives. And one of those initiatives is almost always employee satisfaction! And just how do you think we're going to sell our services to help them, when we

can't even help ourselves? Don't you think everyone in the company is
looking at these numbers? I know I look at everyone else's. They do, too."

Frank sat stiffly as he absorbed his boss's words. He had known all this before he entered the room, but he still did not have an answer. She was right and they both knew it, but she didn't have an answer either.

"Okay," Cheryl said after she had taken a couple of deep breaths. "My yelling at you is not going to solve this problem. We are out of time, out of ideas. We need help, and fast! I think I know where to go."

Later, Cheryl was able to reach Michelle Reina to ask for help. "We have to get those numbers up in six months," Cheryl said in a desperate voice. "I know that low satisfaction means that the employees probably aren't as involved in their work as they might be. They may even leave. After all, they do the things that anyone does when morale and commitment are low; they feel betrayed. That division is stretched superthin since the recent alignment that was centered on keeping just the people with core skills. I can't afford to lose any of them." Cheryl paused for a moment. "Can you help?"

"I hope so," answered Michelle. "We have to gather some information fast if we're going to have time to do anything to change those scores. I'm going to have to meet with your senior people and a number of others."

"Just let me know when you need them. I'll make sure they're there."

Over the next week, Michelle met individually with each member of the senior team and then leaders of other units that worked with this troubled division. She wanted to understand the history of the organization, the players, what their mission was, their strategies, their processes, and their desired outcomes. She asked each person, "What's going on here? Where are relationships damaged? How willing are you to participate in rebuilding these relationships?"

Once Michelle earned his trust, Frank confided in her how frustrated he felt. He had been hired from the outside a year earlier to take this division to new heights. "This job is not what I thought it was going to be. I inherited a mess. People are frustrated and angry about the restructurings that happened before I even got here. I can't get them to stop complaining. I'm sick and tired of hearing people whine about things that I had no part of and can't change. They're acting like spoiled kids who didn't get their way. And Cheryl doesn't want to hear about it anymore. She just wants people to move on. Well, I'd like that too, but they're so stuck in the past."

As Dave, one unit leader, put it, "Things have been bad for a long time. There are a lot of people around here in pain. Many are just not willing to do the top job they used to do."

There was no quick-fix answer, but some issues were surfacing that could lead to answers. Like a detective, Michelle needed more information and help, so she brought in Dennis Reina. For the next six weeks they created a safe environment for people to share their experiences and feelings. They conducted small focus groups and held one-on-one confidential conversations. By the end of the process, they had spoken with over 150 people. The Reinas listened to the employees' experiences (what had happened) and listened for what impact these experiences had on the employees and on others. These weren't pure "dumping sessions," though. The Reinas helped employees see what their options were as to how to behave.

Michelle stopped in Cheryl's office late one afternoon. Cheryl was hunched over her computer typing rapidly. Cheryl was so focused that a minute passed before she realized Michelle was there. "Sorry, Cheryl," interrupted Michelle, "I didn't want to disturb you, but if you could take a few moments to review what we have been learning, we've reached a critical stage in our process."

"Of course! Your work is a priority around here."

"Thank you. We're learning some important facts that have influenced your employee satisfaction scores. We are finding that many of your people were feeling like they were powerless victims. They didn't know how the leadership was evaluating them, and as shifts have happened, many employees are unsure of their roles and responsibilities, who their bosses were, or how these new jobs fit into the company's plans."

"How could they *not* know? We talk about those things all the time."

"I'm sure you do," Michelle responded, "but the messages are not getting through. Dennis and I have been working with them so they can see that they could do things differently. Sure, they couldn't control what had happened, but they can control how they respond. We've helped them map out their choices. We've also tried to help the employees understand why you, as leaders, have made the decisions you have."

Cheryl listened to Michelle's every word, but didn't say anything.

"We heard about how the Learning Services division has gone through two major restructurings in the last three years—that 30 percent of the division's workforce was downsized. People didn't understand where you and Frank planned to take the division in the future. Since they didn't know that, they couldn't see how they personally fit into the future here. They've spent a lot of energy wondering when the next restructuring would come and when they might lose their jobs.

"As you can see, those changes have not been accomplished as well as you thought. Employees found they were duplicating work being done elsewhere. Finger pointing and blaming are running rampant, as they often do when people are hurting, confused, and frustrated. A problem is everyone's fault, and no single person is responsible for fixing it. The rumor mill is alive and does not paint a pretty picture."

"This is hard to hear," Cheryl sighed. "But keep going. I need to hear it."

"People are struggling to balance their work and personal lives because of the expanded workload. They resent times when they have to choose between their family and work. They pay a big price regardless of their choice. Some comments we heard were, 'No matter how I use my time, I let someone down—either a team member because I didn't join that 9:00 P.M. conference with Asia or my family because I worked another Saturday morning.' 'We are constantly in a no-win situation. I either let my family or my team down.'

"This pressure has had a huge effect; many have felt they have lost their own lives. 'I've gained fifteen pounds in the last six months and have completely dropped out my exercise program. Who has time?!' 'I used to play racquetball on Saturday mornings with my buddies. I haven't seen them in three months.' 'I used to have my parents over for dinner on Sunday nights. Now I'm just too tired to cook, talk, or entertain. I know they love me no matter what and do understand, even though they are disappointed. But I feel lousy and miss seeing them.' 'I'm newly married. I want to be with my husband in the evenings and on weekends.' 'I honestly wonder how long I can keep this up. If I knew this was temporary, I'd grin and bear it, but I don't see it changing.' 'What am I doing here? Is it worth it? I don't see an end in sight.'

"The bottom line here is that everyone in your organization feels betrayed in a really major way," Michelle observed. "The betrayal continues to grow. These major trust issues are directly affecting employee satisfaction scores.

"I see the way trust was breached in so many ways. They thought they had an agreement with you and your leadership team that you would provide a structure to accomplish the goals of their division. Instead, they experienced what one person called 'structural roulette.' This person thought you just kept spinning the wheel when you didn't win immediately. They thought you didn't communicate clearly with them, so they didn't know what was expected of them, and you didn't appear to listen to them. Finally, when you kept changing people's responsibilities, they began to feel it was because you didn't have confidence in them. They experienced betrayals in all three types of what we call transactional trust: contractual, communication, and competence. Under these conditions, you can commend them for their loyalty that their satisfaction scores had not gone down sooner and further."

Cheryl looked as though a brick wall had fallen on her, just staring blankly at Michelle.

"That's the bad news," Michelle added. "Now for the good news. These people still believe in this company and want to be a part of it. We received commitments from every person we interviewed to do their part in rebuilding the relationships here. They want to heal from the betrayals. They want this organization to be successful and for them to share in it."

This latest news boosted Cheryl's spirits. "So you mean we have a chance to redeem this tough place we're in?"

"That's exactly what I mean. We challenged everyone else to take responsibility for their part in what has happened. I challenge you in the same way. Are you willing to make the changes necessary to heal, not only the betrayals experienced by your employees but also those betrayals you have felt from them?"

"Of course! I have to. What's it going to take?"

"We will need to spend time going over with you and Frank the specifics of what we've learned. We will talk much more about the nature of trust and betrayal and how to rebuild trust. We need to do this with the people in your immediate organization. They also need to learn more about how they must operate differently, so they don't just blame the two of you and the rest of the leadership team."

"Okay. Let's get started."

During the next several months, the Reinas helped everyone see how collaboration was breaking down due to poor communication. Individually and together, Cheryl and Frank were coached to understand what their people needed from them and to work through their own feelings of betrayal. They learned to trust others enough to share information with them. The division was behind on its deliverables (such as setting up a knowledge management system). They had not been honoring their commitments or delivering on time. Decisions were made by those involved on how to improve this.

Then the Reinas did some work on clarifying boundaries. They armed people with tools and skills to deal with difficult and ambiguous day-to-day situations. The Reinas helped them reframe their experiences and see them as opportunities that would strengthen them and the organization. They did this work through face-to-face meetings and global conference calls (Singapore, Germany, and elsewhere). The Reinas also provided coaching for many individuals throughout the division.

The leadership team received extra attention, which helped them clarify their roles, how trust had been lost, how they could rebuild it. Some of this was done as a group; much of it done as executive coaching. The focus made a difference.

Cheryl and Frank paid attention, they learned, and they changed their behavior. They earned the respect of their people. Relationships were rebuilt; a foundation of trust was created, and deliverables were getting back on track. Finger pointing gave way to collaboration, gossip to straight talk; expectations were clarified and roles and responsibilities negotiated; information sharing and open lines of communication allowed for greater life balance. As one employee put it, "I feel like I have returned to my family."

Sure, challenges continue, and people do have their share of "bad days." But they manage their tendencies to blame and react. They continue to share responsibility. "The model helps us maintain perspective. We understand we won't be successful and satisfied without trust. We are continuing to learn how to build trust, and we understand the steps to take when it is broken." "We count on our relationships with one another. We can actually focus on doing our work!"

At the end of the six months, Cheryl called Michelle. "I've got incredible news. You did it. No—I mean, *we* did it. Our employee satisfaction scores shot up. The jump was unprecedented. Being average never felt so good! We now have higher levels of employee collaboration and engagement, and less duplication of effort. We know we can take this even higher. Thank you so much for teaching us so much about ourselves. You have helped us learn more than we could have hoped for."

MANUFACTURING PLANT CLOSES WITH HEART AND HEALING

People were in shock! Some were in tears, others furious. Many were hurt and confused as the news spread across the shop floor: the plant was closing, and their jobs were being outsourced overseas.

"What's going on here?" questioned Stan Francis, production manager. "I thought we had an agreement that if we met our higher production quotas and contained our costs, the plant would remain open."

"We more than upheld our end of the bargain," said Steve Border, the shop steward. "It just didn't seem to make a difference."

The employees gathered around Stan felt hurt and were angry at management. But the manager could only shake his head. He was going to lose his job too.

Three years ago, the Donaldson Company manufacturing plant, located in a small midwestern city, was bought out by Thomas-Bingham Corporation (TBC). TBC had planned to announce the closing of this plant at the time it bought it, but the people at the plant challenged the company to give them a chance. The leaders and employees banded together to negotiate keeping the plant open. TBC management promised to keep the plant operating if the Donaldson facility reached the increased production quotas and contained costs. In the first year, Donaldson met the quotas, and in the next two years, it actually exceeded them.

In spite of the fact that the Donaldson employees and leadership more than kept their word, the TBC management reneged on their promise and decided to close the plant anyway. Everyone at Donaldson was devastated. They felt betrayed!

Accepting the inevitable, Donaldson leadership wanted to make the plant closing as painless as possible for everyone. They knew they needed help and decided to call a consultant known to work with employee morale issues. They chose Leslie Yerkes of Catalyst Consulting Group, author of two books on creating fun in the workplace, and asked her to help lighten the mood of everyone during this dark time, creating something "fun" before they all left. Leslie faced the leadership team after she heard the situation. "You can't sugarcoat the closing. It's just too serious, too painful. Be more respectful of your employees. A fun event wouldn't help your morale, would it?" There was quiet around the room and then hesitant voices saying no.

"It was all we could think of," responded Dave Smith, plant manager. "We wanted to do something to make people feel better."

"What can we do?" asked Stan.

Leslie paused for only a moment. Trained and certified in the use of the Reina Trust & Betrayal Model and approach, she named the situation. "The closing of the plant is a serious betrayal, and it hurts a lot of people. We need to handle the situation accordingly. I can help you!"

Leslie introduced the leadership team to the Reina Trust Model in a multiday trust-building workshop. She particularly focused their attention on the Seven Steps for Healing. Throughout the workshop, Leslie encouraged the leaders to deal with their own sense of betrayal. They realized that their desire to have a fun activity had come from their denial of their own feelings. Having made progress in working through their own pain, the leaders were in much better shape to start helping others in the plant. Leslie suggested that the leaders especially focus on using the seven steps as a framework to guide them and their employees through the process of closing the plant. She trained the leaders in the application of each of the seven steps to help them take care of the employees and do the right thing as leaders.

With Leslie's assistance each step of the way, the leaders first acknowledged to themselves and then to their employees the betrayal that had occurred and the impact that it had on each of them. The leaders wanted to fully understand the effect this plant closing had on their people, so they formally assessed the climate in their organization by using the Reina Organizational Trust Scale to measure the level of trust between management and employees. They wanted to know how much they were being blamed for TBC's decision. The plant leadership also took the time to hear people directly by walking around the plant and really listening to their employees—their concerns, anxieties, and frustrations. They talked with people at the water coolers, in the break rooms, out on the shop floor, in the hallways, before and after meetings. The leaders were creating a safe climate that allowed people to talk about what was happening.

"You need to give everyone a chance to share their feelings," guided Leslie. The leaders were very surprised at how quickly the employees started talking. Given permission to share, the employees talked about how their hearts were broken by the company's decision. Many had worked at the plant their whole adult lives. For more than a few, there had been more than one generation working at the plant. They had always been good workers but had committed to performing at an even higher level recently. They had been really proud of achieving the improvements demanded by TBC. Now they were going to be cut adrift.

"It helped a lot that Leslie prepared us and helped us structure the sessions," reflected Stan. "But when I was out there with a group of ten workers, I can tell you, some of this was really hard to hear. Most were feeling angry, some hurt, several talked about being sad, and a couple are definitely vindictive."

The plant leadership grasped how angry employees were about what had happened and how anxious they were about their futures. Employees recognized that they were losing not only their jobs but their livelihood, and they needed support! It turned out that the listening sessions provided some of the emotional support people needed and helped them turn elsewhere for more. At a leadership team meeting, Dave Smith had the first smile on his face that most could remember for months. "I just heard from TBC; they are going to provide the money we requested—demanded, really—so we can provide some skill retraining and job outplacement counseling." The whole team gave a collective sigh of relief. The plant leadership contacted plants in other industries in the region to advocate for their hiring Donaldson employees. From the Reina Trust & Betrayal Model, the plant leaders understood that giving support to their people was critical in order for them to effectively work through this situation and move on.

Leslie used the Reina Trust & Betrayal Model to help the plant leaders reframe the experience for themselves by considering the bigger picture. They had to admit that the marketplace was changing and that they wouldn't have been able to keep the plant going for long. At least at this point, there were some resources to help everyone make the transition. Realizing this, leaders were able to help their employees put the experience into a larger context and give their people the business reasons for the change.

"Just this morning I found myself talking to the image in my mirror," shared Stan. "You know, I still get so angry about this that I could explode." There were several nods of agreement around the table at the leadership team meeting. "I know many of the people on the plant floor still get upset so easily. There was nearly a fight yesterday, and when the foreman arrived, the two just walked away. They knew it didn't have anything to do with the other person."

"That is so true," said Dave. "Having a better understanding of why this change is happening certainly doesn't change the reality that they are going to be losing the jobs they had known, parting from coworkers, losing a part of their identity, maybe even having to move from their homes and leave their community."

The leaders worked hard at helping employees see they had a choice about whether to define themselves as victims. They helped employees explore different options, such as new jobs and new career paths.

In spite of their own feelings of being betrayed, the plant leaders accepted their part of the responsibility for what had happened. They had been too quick to accept TBC's promise to keep the plant operating and had not looked for any signs that the promise might not be kept. The leaders had learned an important lesson for their future. They had fought hard for the plant and the people who worked in it. These leaders felt a great deal of responsibility for the well-being of their employees. While acknowledging the pain everyone was experiencing, they also found ways to acknowledge the contributions, large and small, that employees were still making to the plant and to each other.

"You know," Stan suggested, "we need to recognize those workers who have been here for a long time. Each fall we have our tenure ceremony. We have to do it this year, even if it means we move it up five months so we can do it before the plant closes." The company leaders did hold a tenure ceremony to acknowledge the years of service and the contributions of each of their employees—many of whom had worked for the company since its inception twenty-seven years earlier.

Leslie reminded them, "Resentment, cynicism, and blame are normal reactions to betrayal. They won't go away by magic, but you are doing what you can to help everyone."

"It certainly will be better for employees," responded Stan, "if they work through those reactions while still at the plant so that they won't take them into a new job and organization. I think it will be a lot healthier." Using the trust model as the framework, they helped people shift from blaming leadership for their woes to creating the next steps in their careers. To be fully free from the power of the betrayal, leaders and employees had to choose to work through their pain. They didn't have to say it was okay that the closing happened, just that they could put it in their past. Some would blame their problems on this betrayal for the rest of their lives, but most were ready to move on.

After helping people through the final six months, leadership had to close the plant. *Now* it was time to throw a party. It was time for some fun! The employees planned the party, using money from the leaders. It was a plantwide bash to celebrate what they had been together and how much they had achieved. Because leadership went the extra mile to take care of their people, their employees wanted to acknowledge them, so the employees invited the plant leadership to attend the gathering. At the party, people read poems that they wrote about their work experience at the plant, sang songs, and played music. They laughed together and shed tears together. It was a passionate and powerful way to cap the transition and to help the employees let go and move on. Although the employees didn't condone what the management of TBC had done, they were able to accept their situation and move on without blaming the plant leadership.

Dave and Stan stood at the back of the room as the party wound down. "I think," reflected Stan, "everyone has done a lot of healing."

"Yeah, I do too," responded Dave. "Six months ago I never would have thought we'd be at this point now." They looked out over the dwindling crowd, knowing that in a few days these employees would go their own ways, many to work for other businesses and industries—but without the baggage of condemning their old company or their bosses. Leslie Yerkes had facilitated the leadership team in using the Reina Trust & Betrayal Model to help their people heal from betrayal and find their way through the inevitable changes they were facing. It was a learning process that built trust among the employees and the plant leadership alike, even though everyone at the plant lost their jobs. Dave looked at Stan with a smile and a handshake. "We did well. I'm proud of us all."

The employees and leaders lost their jobs, but what they learned about trust and betrayal will never be lost. They moved on with a depth of understanding about relationships and renewal that will be with them always.

Hospitality Organization Culture Turned Around

When Jack Knowles took the helm at QFS, he knew that he was now playing in the big leagues. As a part of BigCorp, QFS shared the larger corporation's reputation as a haven for the best and the brightest—a well-funded and highly respected organization that is highly decentralized, relationship based (as opposed to bottom-line based), and a standard setter in its field. Consistent financial growth was expected of all corporate units. Jack was excited, ambitious, and confident that this new job would be where he would make his mark.

The reality of QFS, however, was much as Jack had experienced at other firms in his early career. It was still the same old stuff in the trenches. Managers existed in a "netherworld" between frontline staff and directors. Directors mediated the "reality" of the organization with the strategic vision, planning, and sometimes myopia of the executives. Communication, process management, execution, reporting . . . it was all the same . . . confusing, contentious, and full of contradictions. The two things Jack now had were resources and a relatively forgiving decentralized structure within which he could really practice his leadership.

Jack knew that he needed more information about the dysfunctional dynamics of his senior leadership team and the organization as a whole. The more people he talked to, the more questions he asked and the more answers he heard, the more he knew something had to be done. He made a point of not just talking to his department heads. He wanted their perspective but also wanted the experiences of others more in the line of fire. To assist him during his transition into his leadership role, he hired Jan Sykes as director of HR.

Jan Sykes heard story after story from the staff about how people "done them wrong." You name it—they brought it to Jan. "People come to me and talk about betrayal, very personal stuff." She sees the staff as being in relationships, much as we have in our lives outside of work. "If I don't have trust in my boss or my coworkers, I can't function well; it's the same with my partner. You spend how many hours a day with each other at work?" From Jan's perspective, it wasn't so much that her job was a train wreck of betrayal and dysfunction. It was more like this: "To me trust is very personal. This is about a lifestyle thing. Trust is the foundation of relationships." She wanted everyone to grow and become whole. Jan believed that many people in her organization defaulted to behaviors that didn't build or promote trust. She felt that people have to do some "inner work" to get to the point of being sensitive to trust.

Jack agreed with Jan's statement that people within his organization defaulted to behaviors that didn't build trust. But it was in Bree Hardwick's story that Jack really experienced the pain. As a middle manager, she inherited a unit that had been devastated by betrayal. The previous manager was unreliable, vindictive, and petty. When Bree took over, "It was like working with forty-six abused children—they had all been betrayed. The betrayal was, as far as I could tell, both personal with the old manager and pragmatic in that this particular unit had failed at pulling off a grand opening of a new facility a couple of years ago. There was a lot of finger pointing."

As Jack learned this information, he took it very seriously. He realized that good relationships weren't just "feel-good" but necessary for an efficient organization. He knew that trust is an issue in every organization; some just deal with it better than others. From what he had learned about the interactions among employees throughout QFS, the company definitely could benefit from more trust. People in his organization had to be able to depend on each other if the company was to thrive. They had to do what they said they would do, communicate fully, and have the capability to do their jobs. Jack recognized these needs. Part of his recovery strategy was to hire Dennis and Michelle Reina and use their Reina Trust & Betrayal Model to assist him in building a foundation of trust within his organization.

One of Jack's initial moves was to hold a five-day retreat facilitated by the Reinas with seventy leaders throughout the organization. He wanted to get to know his people and to have his people get to know him. He also wanted them to understand that he had a plan and that the plan was going to revolutionize both the delivery of services and the culture of work at QFS.

Jack learned that building trust at QFS required a careful assessment of "where his people where at and how willing and able they were to change. The retreats and trust assessments provided by Chagnon & Reina Associates began to set the stage for a long-term and strategically crafted effort to build a new service model, better management skills, and, most important, a culture of trust.

Jan said, "Anyone who wants to understand themselves has to look at whatever they are doing in a systematic way." She put it very simply: "It is not about how others change, but about how I change. I start by looking within myself." Just as Jan learned, the others at QFS learned that one of the most significant features of the Trust & Betrayal Model is that "trust begins with *me*."

Bree began to use the Trust & Betrayal Model with the fifty employees in her service delivery group. She facilitated team-building exercises with her frontline staff, teaching them about the model through experiential exercises. "You can't really talk about it too much; the words just don't matter as much as what we *do*. You have to be a model. In our group, trust is so important because our jobs are fluid, almost chaotic. We don't feel we are in control of what we will be facing next. Things change minute to minute. We need to know we're supported, and I need to rely on my upper management in the same way!"

A big part of Bree's responsibility when she took on this new job was, as she put it, "to deal with the 'disaster' I inherited. The Seven Steps for Healing are always in the back of my head. I dealt with a lot of anger and a lot of grief, but we got through it. Now I believe that people here trust that others want to make everyone look good. There is much more of a sense that we are all in this together. It is refreshing to see people trust their colleagues; and know they are there to help them and assist them. I have seen how people have changed regarding the way they do things; they are much more devoted to the process and to each other."

"I feel vindicated," Jack Knowles said quietly. "I believed that the language of trust could help open communication in this company. I believed that if we all really bought into this process, we could grow and change as individuals and come together around this common theme. We could be happier and more productive. QFS is different now. It is a lot better place for all of us to work, and the people at BigCorp like the results we are achieving."

MILITARY BRANCH STRENGTHENS ITS SOLDIERS

"I hate this trust stuff! I'm only here because I was told to be here," John griped at the beginning of a six-day workshop on trust and betrayal. He then tried to disappear, keep silent, and hope he wouldn't be called on to volunteer anything about himself that really mattered. But at the end of a cycle of sharing, when everyone else had shared experiences of betrayal, the group turned their eyes to John. Trapped, he froze for a moment and then looked for an escape. Seeing none, he gritted his teeth and began to share some little pieces around the edges of his life. Once started, there was no stopping. Once he began

looking at the betrayals in his life, there was no turning back. During the course of the week, he came to understand how betrayal had formed his life, for the positive and not so positive.

He learned how betrayal had influenced his approach to life, in ways he was proud of and ways in which he was not so proud. He came to realize that although he knew, hands down, that people could trust him, he did not trust anyone. It just wasn't safe to. The deep wounds he carried remained unhealed. He was always looking over his shoulder. Through the workshop, John came to see choices he had that he had not seen previously. He gained a picture of another way to embrace relationships. It was an experience that changed his life.

John was one of nearly forty people from a major military organization who attended these workshops to learn about trust and betrayal. They were there because their commanding officer wanted to raise levels of authentic, courageous leadership. He knew trust was critical, particularly during a time of war. These forty were selected because they had the respect and credibility to then take trust building throughout this leader's command.

Some of John's colleagues were as reluctant as John, but they all attended because they were ordered to. Others had been deeply troubled by the lack of trust within their organization and hoped that this would be the start of something much better.

Cynicism, isolation, bitterness, and rejection—these feelings were all too common and had taken a toll on people and the ways they worked together. In an organization that prided itself on teamwork, honesty, and integrity, there was a shocking lack of these things. Yes, there were exceptions—people who continued to practice, foster support and reflected the values of the esprit de corps associated with our military. However, they experienced this negative behavior and unhealthy feelings as a daily struggle. Meanwhile, new members of the organization would come in full of enthusiasm and hope and, usually within three years, sink into the hole with most everyone else. People had questions about their supervisors, many feeling at risk during every interaction. Whether they were really being betrayed by their superiors could be debated, but many believed this notion to be true, especially as individuals sought promotions. The current work environment fostered what one member called "kiss up, kick down." Even friendships with peers had begun to erode, leaving individuals increasingly isolated at a time when more was expected of them.

Many worked even harder to get the work done. Others simply tried to hold on until they could get out. The turnover of these highly skilled and trained people was crippling the organization's ability to fulfill its mission. Something had to be done. In the military, all are there to serve the mission. That must not be compromised.

Leaders in the organization did not miss that there was a problem. They tried many things, some helping a little and some not at all. There was no magic bullet. As the pressure from outside the organization increased, especially multiple deployments to combat zones, the strain within the organization approached the breaking point.

As the leaders discussed the continuing problem, one officer observed that all their problems seemed to boil down to one source: there wasn't enough trust. They had been talking around this issue for years but had not addressed it directly. It was time to face it. The senior leaders became convinced and decided to spend some of their dwindling financial resources on seeing if trust work would make the difference they needed. They used a decision matrix to objectively evaluate the various approaches to trust. They wanted something based in research that had rigor, they wanted something behavioral and concrete, and they had to be able to measure their performance. They narrowed their choice to Drs. Dennis and Michelle Reina and their Reina Trust & Betrayal Model and approach, and selected people to learn how to use it.

The program had some simple but powerful expectations: support individuals' growth; help them become aware of how they trust; increase satisfaction at work; serve our country with pleasure; move beyond politeness; increase feelings of competence; improve their sense of being appreciated and valued. If these goals were achieved, the organization was expected to have improved retention and productivity.

Within months, the initial workshop was scheduled and planned. Representatives from throughout the organization from around the world were brought together to be trained and to take the trust building approach they learned back to their units, where they would teach others. The workshop was not a sit-in-class-and-take-notes type of experience. Participants had to face their own trust and betrayal experiences and explore how these experiences had affected their lives and their relationships. In short, they had to do "their work."

Several participants reported that this workshop was a life-changing event for them. It changed the ways they worked with others on the job, and they found they took the approach home. Marriages were revitalized as couples talked about how they trusted each other and had experienced betrayals. One officer reported that his relationship with his children changed as he came to recognize ways he had betrayed them and learned to make different choices. He realized they were paying attention when, on occasion, they used the trust language when talking with him. Consistently, participants shared stories of how the introduction of the language and concepts of trust and the bringing of awareness of trust into their lives changed their relationships with coworkers, superiors, and subordinates. As one person described it, "Trust is to relationships as blood is to the body. Without them, the other dies."

The participants left the workshops enthusiastic and ready to spread the word. One participant said, "I'm really proud of the organization for taking the gamble on hearing what is really going on and trying to do something about it." The kickoff to the trust work was a success. The challenge for these advocates was to share their experiences and the approaches they learned, without the support of the extensive workshop they had had. Returning to each of their bases, they had to decide how best to reach people. As is typical in such situations, each of the participants also went back to his or her regular responsibilities. They had to find ways to pack the trust building into an already full schedule. No matter how committed they were, their being pulled many directions made it harder to spread the word effectively—particularly during war.

Having a big block of several days means that participants can experience the impact that trust and betrayal have had in their lives. It is made "real." Once the workshop participants were leading their own programs, they found it impossible to have as much time for the hundreds of new participants as they had had for their own experience. But they took it one step at a time and gradually saw the difference the trust-building work made. They have seen the need people have to learn about trust and to tell their story. They have also seen the powerful impact they can have through modeling trust-building behavior in their daily actions.

More people are aware of how trust issues affect their individual and collective lives. With each new workshop, more people are learning the concepts, the language, and the behaviors that build trust. Pockets of trust are breaking out as people are actually using the model and accompanying tools. This is leading to growing hope for many people who had come to believe there was no hope for real change in the ways people in the organization interact with each other. Individuals are finding hope for themselves as they change their own lives.

Diving into trust and betrayal has caused participants to become reflective at times. As one person put it, "Trust work is messy! You have to deal with parts of your life that you don't want to deal with. But it's worth it." Many participants have come to see, time and again, that trust is an individual responsibility. Individuals have to choose when to trust, and they have to choose when to heal from betrayals. It does no good to wait for a betrayer to change before beginning to heal. The Seven Steps for Healing are steps in a process rather than a single event. They are an approach to life. For several participants, learning that they could not heal anyone else was a relief. Realizing they would have to heal themselves meant they could no longer blame others for their continuing pain. Only they could bring it to an end through forgiveness and healing. The choice was theirs.

One participant described dealing with unhealed pain from betrayal as being like trying to keep a beach ball under water. It takes a lot of energy and concentration to keep on top of the ball, and waves often knock a person off. Then it's a scramble to get back on top of it before it pops above the surface. The ball is so demanding that people can focus only on getting back up on top of it. Many don't think to just let the air out of it. Healing from betrayal is letting the air out. It brings hope.

The commanding officer heard the stories of the forty who had undergone the training. He heard their commitment to trust building and knew that although it was solid, he too had to do his part. He could not expect his people to engage in something in which he was not fully willing to participate. He knew that if he wanted to grow trust, he had to give it. For him, giving it meant getting directly involved.

He asked his entire organization, worldwide, to complete the Reina Organizational Trust Scale. He wanted to know how his people perceived the level of trust within his organization. The 93 percent rate of return told him he was asking the right questions. It became clear that trust was important not only to him but to the whole organization.

The commanding officer brought the results to his 350 senior leaders from around the globe. He showed them where they had a strong foundation of trust and where they had work to do. People in the organization trusted their leaders' competence to carry out important military functions, but they did not trust them to hear feedback, especially around tough issues. They experienced their leaders demanding support, pulling rank when necessary, but felt they received support only when it was convenient. The commanding officer asked them to pay attention to the results and to commit to taking action to further develop trust. He promised to keep asking important questions and to do his part.

At the time of the writing of this chapter, the commander was taking steps to engage his leadership team in an extensive trust-building process. They will measure the level of trust in their relationships with others to raise self-awareness. They will measure the level of trust in their leadership team and use the results to strengthen their own team's trust. They will learn and apply the Trust & Betrayal Model to anchor their trust building leadership roles. They will listen to the voices of people's experiences as they recorded them in the open-ended questions on the Organizational Trust Scale and take responsibility to address the issues and needs that the scale identified.

In the meantime, the forty people trained in the Trust & Betrayal Model continue to bring the work forward. Their commanding officer is equipping them with additional trust building materials, instruments, and tools to support them. In him, they have a leader who is on board, engaged, and following through. He is demonstrating the very thing he sought through trust building—authentic, courageous leadership.

Although the organization-wide trust building process is in its early stages, some report that there are already gains for the organization. They continue to remember that trust is built every day, step-by-step. And for many people within this military organization, their own raised awareness of trust, betrayal, healing, and renewal has changed their lives forever.

HOSPITAL BUILDS TRUST AFTER ACQUISITION

"We've got to do something!" exclaimed Karen Green vice president for regional services. "I thought morale at Willow Bay couldn't get worse, then it did. Nurses are almost tripping over each other to get out the door. I just heard today that more may resign. With all the blaming, gossiping, and undercutting going on there, I'm surprised we still have as many there as we do."

A year and a half earlier, Willow Bay Hospital had been acquired by Greenleaf Health Care Systems, a large conglomerate. Many had been proud of Willow Bay's solid reputation as one of the area's finest community hospitals. Losing their autonomy was a blow. Undercurrents of mistrust that had remained hidden before the acquisition bubbled into plain sight with the change. Willow Bay was one of several hospitals reporting to Karen.

She continued, "They are questioning any decision made by management, especially any that they attribute to Greenleaf. To them, every decision appears to be a bad one. When they are expected to do something differently, they challenge it rather than give it a chance. Any new directive becomes a fight. And they continue to question the capability of the other nurses. None seem to be as good as the standards they have set. I don't think even *they* measure up to the standards they use for everyone else. And I'm not sure how to turn this around."

"You're not the only person who needs to turn this around!" responded Monica, an internal consultant at Greenleaf. "The people of Willow Bay are the ones to address this with you. It's our job to help them."

"How do we do that?"

"Are these people heartless, vicious, totally self-centered people?"

"Of course not. They are dedicated health professionals giving some of the best care available."

"Do they want to work at a place where morale is bad and they don't trust their coworkers or the administration?"

"I don't think so. I assume that's why so many are leaving."

Monica, with a thoughtful look on her face, sat back. "Then we have a lot to work with. You know that we have been introducing the Reina Trust & Betrayal Model elsewhere in Greenleaf. I think it could help the people of Willow Bay turn things around. We've had good success with it in other areas of our system."

Monica went on, "It's obvious that people feel betrayed. I'd like to learn more about how people are feeling. I have some guesses, but it is important to hear it from them. And if morale is low, people are needing to talk. We need to give them a safe place to do just that, constructively. I'd also like to plan a way to introduce the concepts and language of trust to everyone at the hospital. I need to put them on the same page."

"You have my full support. What do I need to do?" inquired Karen.

"I'll need your help engaging others. The first person I want to talk with is Carol Simpson, your director of operations. I'd also like to meet with each member of the management team. I think it's best that I do that one-on-one. I will soon need their help to set up sessions to introduce the Trust & Betrayal Model with all members of the hospital."

Monica continued, "Karen, this is not going to be easy. But I have learned steps to rebuild trust. They will help us find our way. It will take time. And we'll get there. We have to trust the process!"

Karen experienced the first sense of hope about Willow Bay that she had felt in months. This would be such a relief if it actually worked. It would be great to be able to deal with all the other fires that were coming her way.

On a Thursday morning, Karen and Monica settled into Carol's office. Karen began, "We've talked this morale problem into the ground over the past year and have tried different strategies. Despite our best efforts, morale just keeps getting worse. I began to realize that we were trying to do too much on our own and weren't taking advantage of other resources within Greenleaf. I know that you met Monica before. I asked for her help, and she's here for us."

"Monica, I'm glad you're here. I don't know where to go with this to make it better."

Monica responded, "Let's see if working together we can change that. And I do emphasize working together, not only the three of us but everyone at Willow Bay. Let's start by your telling me your take on what is happening here."

"It seems that it's quite acceptable here to blame anything that appears to go wrong on Greenleaf. There are complaints every day about how doing things the 'Greenleaf way' is screwing things up. Gossiping and rumors are getting out of hand. Some of it is really vicious, tearing down fellow workers. As you know, one of the results of this kind of environment is that we are losing nurses, physicians, and some of the support staff. We are becoming dependent on registry nurses to cover our shifts. Should this continue, we will have a serious problem with continuity of care. I'm really concerned that it could put the quality of our care at risk."

Carol paused and looked at the other two for a moment before continuing. "Yesterday I talked with my long-term nursing supervisor, Toni. I think you need to talk with her directly. Hopefully it won't be an exit interview, since she told me she was thinking about leaving. There is a physician who was formerly here who is recruiting nurses for his new hospital. She is one of my best, the staff love her, and she may be resigning. We can't afford such losses."

The conversation went on for another hour as Karen and Monica asked questions and Carol answered. It was clear that Carol was well informed and emotionally spent. The job was taking a serious toll on her. Karen was beginning to realize that the problem was even bigger than she had thought.

Monica worked with Carol to plan a series of workshops to introduce the topic of trust using the Reina Trust & Betrayal Model. Carol confided in Monica how worn down she had become. The stress was having a major impact on her life. She had a received a call from another hospital; they would be extending her an offer, and it would be tempting.

The atmosphere of the early introductory workshops on trust was highly emotional. People began to become comfortable as they told their stories and worked through some of the issues between them. They put sensitive subjects on the table, trusting that Monica would help them. They talked about how they felt let down by leadership and belittled by Greenleaf.

It was important for Karen to know that the staff felt disappointed by her. Monica, with care, gave Karen the feedback she needed to hear. "Karen, I have learned that the staff doesn't really understand you. They feel you have let them down. Are you willing to hear their views?"

Monica continued, "I'm finding that they are thinking of you as a ghost who floats in, almost never seen but pulling strings in the background. They know you are an important player. But for many of them, you represent the evil Greenleaf empire. They don't think that you've tried to come to know them or to learn how they have done things. They feel that you have 'come in' and simply asked them to change before you really understood their ways. I know how much you care about them and how much you respect their work and how much you want to support them. The challenge is that right now they don't know that. We have to find a way to help them hear you and for you to hear them. It is only then that healing and rebuilding will begin."

Karen hired a professional coach, Dr. Michelle Reina, someone who really understood issues surrounding trust. This coach helped Karen understand people's concerns and vulnerabilities. Most important, the coach helped Karen understand what her people needed from her as a leader and as a person. With her coach, Karen administered The Reina Leadership Trust Scale (a 360-degree survey) that helped her understand trust in her relationships.

Karen grew to understand how people behaved when they were disappointed and betrayed. She dug deep into herself to renew her role as a leader and her convictions about health care, caring for sick children, and supporting families. This was not just a job for her; this was her passion. She wanted to make a difference in people's lives.

Coaching helped her find the courage to do what she knew was most important—talk with the staff. Karen began communication sessions so that she could speak to everyone on the staff. She acknowledged how she had overlooked and failed to understand their needs, how they felt betrayed. She described her own experience of feeling overwhelmed at times and her own disappointment at seeing the way people treated one another and her.

The staff knew that Karen was skillful and had depth of knowledge. During these sessions they saw a side they had not seen before—her heart and humanness. Karen acknowledged that rebuilding had to occur. She told the truth: "I can't do it alone," and she asked them if they would be willing to work with her. This was a major turning point in letting them know that Greenleaf in general and Karen in particular were for real. She asked them to do their part. Reframing and taking responsibility began to take place. They could see that she cared, that she was serious and on their side. This was a time for healing.

Karen felt it was important that they have some baseline measurements of trust. Although Monica's introduction to trust was helping, they needed to know where they still had work to do. She also wanted them to measure improvements. They drew upon the Reina Organizational Trust Scale to measure the level of trust in employees' and management's behaviors. The results showed that employees' perceptions of management's behaviors were particularly negative, as were their perceptions of themselves. Gossip was a major problem, as were channels of communication, information sharing, and people backing one another up. An "us against them" dynamic was common. Karen sighed when she saw the numbers: "At least we have some room for improvement!"

Eventually Carol decided to accept another offer. Ironically, Toni was still there, reporting she hadn't quite made up her mind yet. Carol's departure set off a wave of antiadministration feelings and more rumors. Carol was replaced by Cynthia, who was sent by Greenleaf. Karen had thought Cynthia would be okay, but Cynthia made it clear she was unhappy being there; of course, that contributed to more feelings about the administration at both the hospital and Greenleaf. Within a few months, Kevin was appointed as the permanent director of operations for the hospital. Karen and Monica welcomed stability in this position!

Kevin proved to be very capable and quite an advocate for the trust work. He was familiar with it from other assignments for Greenleaf. He stepped in and began to use the trust model to support the rebuilding and healing process.

"I talked with Toni the other day," offered Kevin, "and she told me that she had decided to stay. I thought it would be good for you two to hear why she made that decision, so I asked her to stop by now." As he said this, he got up and opened the door so that Toni could come in. She greeted everyone and sat down. Kevin said, "Toni, I'm so glad you decided to stay. Would you tell Karen and Monica what led you to this decision?"

"Of course, I've been up and down with this. I had a physician say that she needed me. She told me how much she depended on me. She said my experience was vital. I've been told many times that I'm important here, but at that moment I really heard that I was valued. I don't need to hear that on a daily basis. I just need to know it and feel it inside. It helped me remember how important this place is and how important what we do is to me. I don't want to lose that.

"Also, attending Monica's session on trust and betrayal helped me see things differently. At first I didn't want to go. I thought they would be trying to convince me that I was seeing things all wrong and should put on a 'happy face.' But they didn't. They were talking about the same things that caused me to think about leaving. I didn't feel blamed; that made a difference. The discussions around trust and betrayal helped me see that I do have some choices. They also helped the others in the room see that we're all a part of what has been so frustrating to us. I believe that we can shift that and create the kind of environment we want.

"So, I thought it might be good to also have a one-on-one discussion with Monica. She helped me see my role in supporting the rebuilding of trust. After talking with her, I really 'bought into it.' It was that one-on-one that did it for me. I decided to stay."

Karen reached out and shook Toni's hand. "I want to thank you for staying. You are an important part of this hospital, and we need you. We're all learning how to be more trusting and trustworthy. I hope we can learn a lot more about it together."

"I do too," Toni replied and left to go back to work.

"An experience like that is just part of the evidence that this process is making a difference," began Karen. "Yet we can see that some of these problems are deep and involve the whole hospital. Addressing them is going to take more than an introduction to trust in occasional discussion. We need to find some way of going deeper with everyone at the hospital."

"I agree," stated Kevin, "but I don't know how to do that. I just can't take people off the floor; it's impossible."

Monica saw her chance. "I would like to make another suggestion. I learned of a tool called Reina Trust Building On-Line. It is a way to engage people over time, in depth, in the Trust & Betrayal Model and help them actually put those behaviors into practice every day. I think it would be a good fit for us since it would allow us to involve everyone at different times of the day and night and at an affordable price."

Monica made arrangements to engage everyone in the Trust Building On-Line. It provided the solution that allowed everyone to become more aware of trust and to learn trust-building skills and behaviors. Participants learned about how they trust, how others trusted, and how they could use trust-building behaviors to do their jobs. Because it was impossible for people to take much time away from patient care, learning modules were designed to be completed on-line in fifteen to twenty minutes. People engaged in the Trust Building On-Line process in learning clusters. Each cluster communicated with one another via a designated on-line community dialogue space. Monica and other trained facilitators helped keep the groups moving, on track, and involved. This approach gave the people in the hospital a chance to really engage with one another on a regular basis. Employees participated in the process every week over a four- to five-month period. Over the course of a year, everyone participated. Relationships formed and deepened; trust grew.

And people were using what they learned. Kevin reported at one of their update meetings with Karen and Monica how he had talked with a nurse in the emergency department. "He was amazed at the way people were now talking. They did it first on-line and then started talking more on the job. They were definitely taking it seriously."

Karen, Monica, and Kevin continued to look at their progress. "I believe we have made a real difference," Karen began. "I know that I have learned so much about trust and betrayal, especially how I was committing trust-breaking behaviors all the time without knowing it. I can also see that the pattern of blaming Greenleaf for every little problem has faded away. As people deal more directly, they don't need a scapegoat. Now when someone says they have an issue with Greenleaf, we pay more attention to it."

"I like what is happening with the Willow Bay Council," reported Kevin. "It really helped that they already had the role in advising the leadership team. We got them involved, and the council helped drive the model through the organization. They built collaboration, and as a result they even became more effective as a council."

"I've got something to add, too," said Monica with excitement in her voice. "We have the results of the latest Organizational Trust Scale that everyone took. I'm sure the two of you will like what I have to say. Changes in perceptions about management in the past year have continued to improve. There is a 12 percent increase in staff perceptions of management's trust-building behaviors and a 23 percent reduction in their perception of management's trust-breaking behaviors. The level of trust in employees' behaviors went up across the board. The open-ended responses show that employees resist jumping to conclusions and talk directly with one another about problems rather than gossip; they respect personal needs and organizational policies; and they collaborate more freely and share accomplishments. They report that they address operational needs, more readily hold themselves accountable, and keep agreements. Doesn't that look a lot brighter than when we started this process?", Monica exclaimed.

We are practicing transactional trust behaviors more consistently.

"I am really gratified," said Karen, "and I know those at Greenleaf are too. Facing our trust issues has improved communication and how we deal with our challenges as well."

Kevin offered, "I am going to put metrics in place that help us more tangibly measure the positive impact this has had on our business performance. I know it is there; I want to demonstrate it. And, on a more personal note, I have seen some numbers that are important to me. They convince me that we have turned the corner. Our turnover has returned to the levels prior to the merger. I'm really glad that Toni and others like her have seen that this would be a good place for them to stay and work. We now have what was missing: a strong foundation of trust.

A LEADERSHIP TEAM TRANSFORMS

"For such a competent group of people, we sure had problems working with each other!" exclaimed Candace, department director. "When I look back over the past three years, it is amazing how it has worked out. We had issues about trust in nearly all of our interactions with each other and couldn't even acknowledge them. No wonder all the different things we had done to improve our communication and

cooperation hadn't made a real difference. Of course, things would get better for a while after each program or consultant, but then we would slip back into our old ways. We just hadn't addressed the issues deeply enough to really make things better. Now that we have faced ourselves and looked at the ways we broke trust with each other, we are making progress that is going to stick."

Candace paused to look at the others in the room. The leadership team members were gathered for their semiannual review of their progress on their many trust-building tasks. They had made enough progress that they could reminisce about their experiences.

"I remember," said Bart, a unit manager, "when some of us finally were willing to admit that we had problems trusting each other. Wow! That was tough to do. We knew we needed help, especially from someone who really understood how to fix trust problems. I'm so glad we contacted the Reinas. It was almost serendipity, when we suddenly had that opening time slot for the agency conference. Michelle Reina's activities and talk got our attention. We could move from just talking with them about trust to actually beginning the work."

"We just didn't know how much work it was going to be," added Bonnie, another manager. "I remember when we were asked to participate in the Organizational Trust Scale survey as preparation for that presentation. I asked, 'What's this?' But I filled it out and was amazed at the results. Michelle Reina interpreted the information we gave on that instrument. When she talked about trust in her presentation, she talked about how we trusted, or, as the case was, didn't trust."

"Yeah," replied Bart, "like how we wouldn't talk much with each other. I left you to do your job, and you let me do mine. At least after hearing the results of the scale, I knew we had a lot of competence trust in each other. I knew everyone in this room could do a good job. I just didn't want to be a part of what you were doing. Now it seems really weird; I usually think of being isolated when we are dealing with people we don't see very often. We were isolated, and we saw each other all the time."

"We have learned a lot," observed Candace with a slow look around the room to catch the eye of each person. "I know that I have been healing so many of my wounds, and I hear from each of you that you are healing, too."

"I heard the rumors of my staff talking to Candace about their complaints about me," offered Bonnie. "But Candace, you didn't talk to me about it. I was left wondering what people were saying and what impression of me you were forming in your mind. It was getting strange, but I kept trying to do my job. I had to wonder, though. Candace, you seemed to be watching what I was doing and telling me how to do some of the details of my job. I definitely felt you *micromanaging* me, and I resented it. I'd go home after work and scream at my dog—I was that frustrated!"

"I don't think we'll ever forget those feelings of being micromanaged," reflected Bart. "I always felt like I was being kept on a short leash. That was the strange part. I assumed I was hired to do this job because I was qualified to do it. I had done it elsewhere. I knew I could do it here. Yet I kept having the feeling that Candace didn't really believe I could do it without her keeping track of almost everything I was doing. Candace, I kept wishing you would let me do my job and focus on doing yours."

"Aren't we ever going to let that go?" replied Candace with a sad tone in her voice.

Not knowing what to say, everyone sat looking at Candace. Finally Bonnie broke the silence. "Candace, we *have* let it go, at least as much as we can. I know my feelings about it were very intense. We just touched them again. I also know things are changing. Candace, I see you changing, and I see all of us changing too. We are slowly but surely putting those things behind us."

"I want to come back to what I think got us moving," suggested Bart. "As part of that agency conference, we participated in taking the Organizational Trust Scale. I remember not thinking much of it when I started completing my form before the conference. By the time I'd reached the end of the form, I found I was really thinking about the answers. I even went back and thought more about some of my earlier responses. I remember laughing to myself when I wondered whether my answers would really be tabulated in confidence. I was laughing because it was funny to think about not trusting the process of handling a trust survey. When I finished my instrument on-line, I was still feeling a little cautious. Then I waited to see what the results would be.

"I remember seeing the results just before the conference. They seemed pretty positive. I began to wonder if I was the only one who wasn't trusting. But, of course, I wasn't going to talk to anyone else about their assessment of it. I was a little relieved when Michelle Reina gently, but firmly, said that the results showed some things we needed to look at. But it was obvious that we didn't want to. I know now that I wasn't the only one wanting to avoid dumping that can of worms out on the table and watching those slimy parts of us spreading out where everyone could see them."

"That conference was a hit," added Bonnie. "I really liked what Michelle added to it. Not surprisingly, after the conference there was a burst of better communication, and I heard everyone feeling more hopeful. And then there was that slip back to the old behavior, just as had happened before."

Candace shook her head as she remembered those times. "Not again! Seeing what was happening really upset me. I kept thinking, 'We can do better than this.' I knew we had to do something different or we would just keep sliding backwards. But what? There was something about Michelle that gave me confidence. I think it was the way she could tell it to me straight and leave me feeling hopeful rather than beaten down. I knew we were going to need all the straight talking we could handle. When Michelle came back, she really helped us zero in on what was happening on this leadership team. I agreed that we should administer the Team Trust Scale as preparation for further work.

"Remember that follow-up workshop for just our leadership team? I didn't really know what was going to happen, but I had the sense that we were rolling in the right direction. Michelle helped us craft a vision of how we wanted to operate with each other. It was a feel-good exercise. We all could feel good about it, but it also felt a little fantasy-like. Then Michelle calmly, but effectively, hit us right between the eyes. She reported back to us what we had said on the Team Trust Scale. In our own words and ratings, we had described how, in many ways, we didn't trust each other. We squirmed and danced as we listened, but we couldn't avoid our own assessment. Michelle kept coming back to what we had said we wanted, pointing out the statement we had just created. And she reminded us again of what we said on the Team Trust Scale. She kept after us until we began to face the issues we had identified. It was a hard time for all of us. The critical thing we needed to learn was that this was about *what we were doing*. We had the power to do something about the situation, and it was going to take a while, perhaps a long time, to really make the changes we wanted."

"I'm glad we formed that bond with Michelle," reported Bart. "We needed that because we then went into dealing with some really tough issues. Using words like *trust* and *betrayal* was really hard at first. We were much better at dancing around issues. I think we had a conspiracy never to talk about anything that would have an emotional impact on another person. I don't think it would be possible to use the word *betrayal* without affecting the other person. So we just let things ride. We were trying to 'be nice.' We thought we could fool ourselves that being nice would keep the whole thing from having any emotional impact."

"I think that workshop exposed the illusions we had about how we were relating to each other," added Bonnie. "But in spite of the commitments we made to keep working on these issues, there was a big part of me, and I think of everyone else in this room, that just did not want to keep digging into these long-held wounds. You know, I'm feeling a little bit of that right now."

"That's so true, then and now," reflected Candace. "Michelle kept talking about how we each had to own our part in what was happening. I'll admit that there was part of me that wanted everyone else to change so the situation would be better. When I realized that I would have to change too, it really scared me. I didn't know how to make this kind of change. That's when I asked Michelle to be my coach."

"Wasn't that when we introduced Trust Building On-Line?" interjected Bart.

"It was. Michelle talked about the importance of expanding the trust and betrayal work beyond the leadership team. Having everyone in the agency, no matter where they were located, learn the same language and concepts at their own pace and then discuss it all with their on-line groups was such a boost to our process. And we didn't even have to pay for travel to get them together. And those professional moderators certainly kept the groups on task."

"I think," added Bart, "that having everyone working on their trust and betrayal issues really helped change the climate. I know having my team members talking about it meant there wasn't any opportunity to slide. After all, I was supposed to be more experienced in this than they were."

"With all the emotions around here, it was good to fall back on the Trust & Betrayal Model, Bonnie added to Bart's comment. We used the model to align people to the work and to hold them accountable. There have to be accountability and consequences to drive high performance."

"I remember," continued Bart, "Michelle saying time and time again, 'It starts with *you*.' It took me a while to realize that the 'you' was *me*. I had to take time to look at my own beliefs. It takes each and everyone of us looking at ourselves because trust is built on the group experience. *Trust* is such a loaded word because it means different things to different people."

"Well," said Donna in an intense voice that instantly got everyone's attention. "The big moment for me was when my beliefs changed a little over a year ago. Candace had us sitting in this very room, and I thought my world was coming to an end. I don't think I have ever seen Candace get so upset as she was when she came into the room and couldn't even sit down. Candace, you just paced back and forth for what seemed like an eternity before you started talking. And when you did start talking, I didn't like what I was hearing. I can still hear it in my head as though you were saying it today.

"You told us that you had had it with being the scapegoat—that everything going wrong in this agency was your fault. You were willing to take responsibility for your share, but everyone in this room was going to have to take their share too. I remember how frustrated you were that a year before that meeting you thought everyone in the room had committed to working on their own trust and betrayal stuff. You asked each of us to commit to telling you when we thought you were doing something that was hurting trust. I remember each of us made that commitment to you. You also made a commitment to us. You got yourself a coach, and I could tell you were dealing with some very heavy stuff. I saw you make changes. I saw you loosen the reins some, letting us work without your watching so closely. I saw and heard you invite and expect us to demonstrate communication trust with you and each other.

"But one year later we were back in the same room, and you were furious. The results of the latest Team Trust Scale had just come in, and it was obvious that there were people on this team who were saying things on the form that they wouldn't say to your face. You told us, in no uncertain terms, that you felt betrayed, that everyone had a contract with you and that contracts had been broken. I felt like I had kept my commitment, but I was still shaking. *Had I said everything directly that I had felt and had reported on the instrument?* I asked myself.

"Well, you didn't call any of us out individually on this. You did demand that each of us get a coach and start facing our own issues around how we were working and communicating with you and each other. You said we would be responsible for getting our own coaches, at agency expense, but you would be willing to help make some connections if that would help. So we all left that meeting, and within a few weeks, all of us had coaches. I know that my coach made a difference for me."

The room was silent. Everyone either looked down or continued to look at Donna. The emotions of everyone's experiences were flooding over them.

"That meeting," said Candace quietly, "was one of the hardest times in my life. I was so hurt and angry. I did feel betrayed . . . and right in the middle of your doing this work on trust and betrayal. There was part of me in complete disbelief. It was also a time when, I now know, I came to trust each of you in a much deeper way. Before then, I hadn't trusted you enough to confront you. When I did, you came through. You got your coaches, you did some great work, and we are at a different place this year. The fact that we were recently rated by the Gallup organization as having 'best practices' for our teams says something very good about what we're doing. On top of that, I just got the results of the latest Team Trust Scale from Michelle. By the way, I am really glad we're administering the scale and the Organizational Trust Scale every six months. It's much harder to slip back when movement is measured. Oh yes—the results. Here are the numbers. You can see that we have reached a very different and higher place than we were a year ago. Congratulations to all of us."

The mood in the room became quite a bit lighter with that news. Immediately there were smiles and little side conversations.

"I do want to say a few more things about our trust work," said Candace. "We have done a lot of healing. Three years ago, there was so much pain everywhere we turned. We felt it, our coworkers felt it, and everyone else in the agency felt it. We have come to live the Seven Steps for Healing. It has made a huge difference. We have practiced the four characteristics of transformative trust. We have had the *courage* to face this pain and its causes and then keep facing it. We have demonstrated that we have the *conviction* to make this a very different place in which to work. We continue to hold to the course. We have expressed *compassion* for each other rather than assume the worst. In being compassionate, we have invited compassion in return. And, one of the real blessings of this work, we have created a true *community*. I know that for me, this feels very different, very good. I am very proud and pleased to be a part of this whole experience."

9/11

This story was told to our colleague Dick Weaver on this unforgettable day.

The double doors of the training room burst open. "Hey! I've got something to tell you immediately," interrupted Bill with a quivering voice. "A plane has just struck the World Trade Center in New York, and the building is on fire. I have to go now. My family lives in Manhattan. I don't know what other crazy people are out there. I have to take care of my family. You decide what you need to do."

Gathered in the meeting room of the Vermont lodge, nearly a dozen people had just finished their breakfast and were getting ready for today's training. They were enjoying the peaceful setting as they munched on their morning rolls and drank their coffee. Bill had been a part of a lighthearted conversation just before he stepped away from the group when his wife opened the meeting room door and signaled for him to step out. He was gone only a minute; his face was full of fear when he returned. It had taken a moment before he had gotten people's attention, but now everyone sat in shocked silence. "What did he just say? What's going on? A plane crashed into a building? It couldn't be true." All of them kept going over and over Bill's few words in their minds. It couldn't be real!

September 11, 2001. We all remember where we were and what we were doing when we got word of the tragedy that morning. Now all it

takes are the numbers 9/11 to bring it all back. This small group, gathered
in a lodge deep in the woods of Vermont, was just getting started on the
third day of their certification training in the Reina Trust & Betrayal
Model. Interestingly enough, they were about to spend their morning
exploring the nature and power of betrayal. Instead of having to remember betrayals from their pasts, these group members were facing what one
participant called "the ultimate betrayal." This betrayal would change
their lives and the lives of everyone else in the country.

Dennis and Michelle Reina were just as stunned as everyone else
when Bill made his announcement, and quickly left the room. They too
had family and friends who might be at risk. Michelle's family lived down
the street from the Pentagon. Dennis had relatives in New York and New
Jersey. They also had responsibilities as the workshop leaders. "Obviously
we are going to have to change our plans for this workshop," said
Michelle. "We have to decide whether it is even appropriate to continue.
We need to find out more about what is going on. Sounds like we also
need to contact our families. Then we can decide together what we'll do
next. Let's come back together in an hour." There were nods of agreement
around the table and then everyone went quietly back to their rooms.

In each of the rooms, TVs were quickly turned on and soon filled
with images of the second plane crashing into the WTC's south tower and
then the video of the smoke rising from the Pentagon. People attempted
to call home but most often heard only busy signals because of jammed
circuits. They kept calling, with an increased sense of desperation. They
had to talk with their families, especially their young children. There was
such relief when they finally got through. Debbie's five-year-old daughter
was crying, very confused. "Mommy, the planes hit the buildings. Why did
they do that?" There were no answers that day. There were only feelings
of anger and a sense of being betrayed. Innocence was lost; the world was
suddenly a different place.

The workshop participants all saw the animated maps showing the
locations of planes still in the air. Once all planes were ordered to land, it
did not take long for the maps to start clearing. Because everyone had
flown in to the workshop, no one was going to be able to get home any
time soon. Their freedom to move about the country was gone. One more
blow was added to the overwhelming experience of betrayal.

The hour passed quickly, but people returned to the meeting room before the time was up, one by one sliding into the big easy chairs that formed their working circle. They were deflated, all the air and energy punched out of them by the combination of hits they had absorbed. Michelle looked around the room. "In the face of what has happened, we have some choices to make. We can bring this program to a close, and each of you can try to find ways of getting home to your families. We can stay together as a group and keep an eye on what is happening in New York and Washington. Or we can spend some time dealing with what just happened and then continue the workshop. The choice is yours to make, as a group."

Roused to action, they did a quick check-in to make sure everyone had reached their loved ones. They had. Then the group became animated as they talked about their choices. Don had been quiet, but when he cleared his throat, everybody turned to him. "I want us to stay together. I'm not ready to make a choice about whether to continue the workshop, but I am ready to try to make some sense of what is happening. Can't we do that together?"

"We can," Dennis responded, "if that's what everyone wants. What would the rest of you like?" There was swift agreement. "Okay, let's gather up some blankets, some water, and a little food. We can take a walk in the woods. I know just the right place for us to deal with something this upsetting." The group quickly moved to the tasks without any further direction. Ten minutes later, they were all gathered again, this time with their arms full. Dennis led the way out of the lodge and down a narrow path into the woods. The day was just warming up, so the air still had a bit of fall crispness. The light feeling of the bright blue sky and early fall colors in the trees were very different from the heaviness they all were feeling. There was little talking as they walked. Most of the time there were only the sounds of their footsteps and a few bird songs. Later, some would describe it as a walk, others a hike, but all agreed that they entered a dimension where time and distance had little meaning.

They had just passed through a dense stand of maple trees when they entered the clearing of an open field and knew immediately that it was the right place for them to gather. Surrounded by pines, maples, and aspen, they could look up and see the deep blue sky. The sun had not yet reached the floor of the clearing. They spread blankets around in a circle and lit a candle in the middle. To help settle people, Dennis led the group in a short meditation. When they were finished, the group was ready. "Let's start with our talking about what has happened." Immediately, those around the circle shared what information they had learned from the TV and conversations with others. As they shared, they got the sense that they had all the facts there were to know at that time. The discussion then moved to larger issues and the meaning of what happened. Debbie spoke up: "I don't know if anyone else is feeling this, but I'm feeling really off balance, talking about such a horrendous event while we are in such a peaceful setting. I feel guilty to be in such a beautiful, peaceful setting with such loss in our country at this time. It feels more like we're talking about some really bad movie plot, not this kind of tragedy."

"We know this really happened," responded James. "We all have the images seared in our minds. But we don't have to keep our focus totally on these details. How will we ever move on from this?"

"Your question is true for any betrayal. At some point, we have to step back and get a new perspective on it," Dennis chimed in. That exchange helped the whole group take their sense of what happened to a much deeper level.

Everyone shared their fears and their anger, a particularly natural thing to do given the circumstances. Most were more concerned about the impact on their family and friends than on themselves. Dennis brought the conversation back to those in the circle. One by one, people reached deep inside themselves and talked about their own fears and anger. They also talked about what was most important to them in life: their families, friends, and loved ones; doing meaningful work and making a difference. They talked about higher purpose, both their own and that of such a tragedy.

As each one talked, the group listened and gave encouragement. They were learning more fully of one another. Don noticed how the sun spread across the floor of the clearing. He felt it was a gift of light to them. After the final person talked, the group explored how they would provide support to each other for the rest of the week and beyond, as well as how each person would get and give support among family and friends.

The group was learning more about betrayal and healing with each passing minute. They shared their reflections.

"It is often helpful, when we feel betrayed, to think about it in more than one way," Michelle guided. "I suggest looking at what purpose this might have had in our own lives. What are the messages we need to hear? And how do we understand ourselves better because of this?" Those questions really made people think. Some of them needed solitude, and they got up and found small paths into the dense forest. A couple of people took a walk together, talking softly, while the rest of the group remained on their blankets in the clearing. After a little more quiet time, Joe spoke up. "Those are hard questions! I will live with them for a long time. Right now, I really know that I'm angry. My head says it would be good for me to answer them, but my heart wants to hurt the people who did this." Michelle looked at him thoughtfully and replied, "I really get that. It's going to take some time before you are ready to look at these questions. Answering them at some point, when it is right for you, will be important to moving on." The others drifted back, and many of them shared the beginnings of their thinking about Michelle's questions.

Dennis noticed that there was energy coming back into the group. "I want to remind us all, Michelle and I included, that we will need to take responsibility for our own reactions, attitudes, and behaviors in response to this devastating event. This is a huge betrayal, one we and the world will never forget. Let us consider what a temptation it is just to stay angry. We will eventually need to consider what else we're going to do to help ourselves and others heal from this."

Chris encouraged people to look at the other side of what had happened: "What kind of anger, especially from betrayal, must the hijackers have had that would have led them to this act?" Joe and Debbie looked startled at Chris's last question.

Joe said, "I hadn't thought about the hijackers at all, just about what they had done. They were just faceless terrorists until you asked that."

"Yeah," added Debbie. "I can see that I won't be able to let go of this thing until I try to understand where they are coming from." The others slowly joined this conversation. It was obviously a stretch for all of them, but they were thinking hard about this.

Evening began to come, and people prepared to leave the woods. Dennis paused and looked into each face. "I want to remind all of us that we are trying to heal from a huge betrayal. The healing process means we can release the power of the event over our lives. Simply put, it's forgiveness. That doesn't mean we say it was okay; it certainly was not. It also doesn't mean we put our heads in the sand. It means we remain open to look for what we might learn from this betrayal. Forgiveness means we don't let it control our lives. This is too big a betrayal for any of us to be healed at this moment. It is something we can work to create in our lives. I appreciate how engaged everyone is at this time here in the clearing. Let's have a closing meditation."

As the meditation was concluded, the candle was blown out. The participants began to gather the blankets and other things they had carried to this special place. As Joe and Michelle shook the pine needles from a blanket, he was taken back to times when he had shaken blankets as a child while camping. In the midst of all the pain of the present moment, that visit to the past gave him great comfort.

There was little conversation as they walked back to the lodge, each person deep in thought. Once back in their meeting room, they returned to their usual chairs. After checking in with one another, they agreed they were ready to continue the workshop. Joe spoke for the group: "I believe that an important reason this terrible thing happened is that there is not enough trust. I don't think it is a coincidence that we are here on this day, working on trust, learning about betrayal. Dennis and Michelle live this stuff. They used it today, and it made a difference for me. I feel an obligation to learn all I can about trust and take it into the world. It is the most powerful thing I can do to help us never repeat the horror that has happened today!"

The group spent the next four days together. Together they learned about trust, betrayal, and healing. They learned that when people are in pain, confused and distracted as they are, you cannot just expect them to move on. People need to be supported to acknowledge what has happened, how it is affecting them. They need support to be ready to move on.

The people together on that day have moved on to teach the very principles they came to understand that week. Their support of one another and the depth of their understanding of trust and betrayal have helped them touch and make a difference in the lives of thousands . . . building trust, healing from betrayal, and discovering renewal.

REFERENCES

CHAPTER 5

1. E. Erikson, *Childhood and Society* (New York: Norton, 1950).
2. Ibid., p. 6.

CHAPTER 6

1. D. Brothers, *Falling Backwards: An Exploration of Trust and Self-Experience* (New York: Norton, 1995).
2. Ibid.
3. Ibid.

CHAPTER 7

1. B. Hedva, *Journey from Betrayal to Trust: A Universal Rite of Passage* (Berkeley, Calif.: Celestial Arts, 1992), p. 7.

CHAPTER 8

1. E. Kübler-Ross, *Death: The Final Stage of Growth* (Upper Saddle River, N.J.: Prentice Hall, 1975).
2. L. B. Smedes, *Forgive and Forget: Healing the Hurts We Don't Deserve* (San Francisco: HarperSanFrancisco, 1996).
3. Ibid.

CHAPTER 9

1. B. Hedva, *Journey from Betrayal to Trust: A Universal Rite of Passage* (Berkeley, Calif.: Celestial Arts, 1992), p. 5.
2. L. B. Smedes, *Forgive and Forget: Healing the Hurts We Don't Deserve* (San Francisco: HarperSanFrancisco, 1996), p. 224.

CHAPTER 10

1. Adapted from R. Napier and M. Gershenfeld, *Groups: Theory and Experience,* 5th ed. (Boston: Houghton Mifflin, 1993).
2. R. W. Rogers, *The Psychological Contract of Trust: Trust Development in the '90s Workplace* (Pittsburgh, Pa.: Developent Dimensions International, 1994), pp. 41-42.

CHAPTER 11

1. F. J. Navran, *Truth and Trust: The First Two Victims of Downsizing* (Alberta, Canada: Athabasca Educational University Enterprises, 1995), p. 134.
2. B. Hedva, *Journey from Betrayal to Trust: A Universal Rite of Passage* (Berkeley, Calif.: Celestial Arts, 1992), p. 16.
3. Ibid, p. 132.

INDEX

ABOUT THE AUTHORS

Dennis and Michelle Reina have devoted the last fifteen years of their professional lives to developing a comprehensive trust building approach that helps people renew relationships, transform cultures, and improve performance. They are passionate about making a contribution to trust building and healing in people's lives—at work and at home. They are co-founders of The Reina Trust Building Institute, the nationally recognized trust building experts firm. With the help of their Reina Trust Building Institute team, Dennis and Michelle have facilitated expansive consulting initiatives and developed trust building measurement tools, training programs, and workshops; an online trust building community; action-learning experiential exercise tools; and learning aids. They each hold master's degrees in organizational development and doctorates in human and organizational systems from Fielding Graduate University. Together and independently, they are sought-after consultants, keynote speakers, and executive coaches.

Dennis grew up on the Jersey Shore. As a former rock climber and cross-country ski instructor, he has a love for nature that takes him on wilderness treks throughout the country. Dennis earned his bachelor's degree in marketing from the University of Maryland and holds a master's in holistic health education. When he developed the Seven Steps for Healing (discussed in this book) with Michelle, he did not anticipate that the seven steps would be the tool that helped him recover from two bouts of cancer. However, the steps powerfully guided his healing—of body, mind, and soul—and led him to a deeper understanding and appreciation of life and relationships. As a result of a lifetime of healing experiences, Dennis has developed a keen sense of resilience and renewal, topics of his workshops and next book. Today he remains cancer free.

Michelle grew up as an army brat living a life of change and transition. She earned her bachelor's in business administration from St. Mary's University. After business trips, she enjoys returning to her nest in the mountains of Vermont, where she makes her home with Dennis. Michelle has identified a unique need women have to step into trust building in each other's presence. She offers workshops and retreats to support that need and is in the process of writing a book for women about lifetime relationships. The process of doing so nurtures her heart and soul.

Dennis and Michelle met in graduate school and fell in love on the dance floor. They relish their time together, walking along Caribbean beaches, hiking, canoeing, skiing, picnicking, and always, always dancing. They find great joy being with their two sons—Patrick, an aspiring actor, and Will, a college student—and their two school-age godchildren, Timothy and Julia.

WORKING WITH THE AUTHORS

Speaking Engagements

For the last fifteen years, Dennis Reina and Michelle Reina have shared their leading-edge trust building work with thousands of people. Their informative, engaging message helps people learn concrete strategies to build and maintain trust in their relationships in order to transform cultures and renew relationships. Dennis and Michelle, together and independently, are available for keynotes, conferences, and seminars anywhere in the world.

Consulting

Dennis and Michelle are co-founders of The Reina Trust Building Institute, a consulting and organizational research and development firm, and are recognized as trust building experts worldwide. Dennis and Michelle have devoted a combined thirty years to researching and developing the Trust & Betrayal Model and a comprehensive yet practical approach to trust building. Their company partners with leaders who want to build trust, renew relationships, and transform their cultures. The firm provides practical and measurable trust building strategies and programs that integrate trust-building behaviors and methods into business initiatives and human performance that drive business results. The Reinas have linked trust building strategies to such initiatives as employee engagement and satisfaction, change and transition, team and leadership development, innovation, creativity, risk taking, and collaboration. The Reina Trust Building Institute uses a variety of modalities, including workshops facilitated face-to-face, and/or online, learning experiences that transform cultures and lives. A partial list of organizations the firm has worked with includes American Express, Ben & Jerry's, the Boeing Company, Children's Hospital of Milwaukee, Dartmouth-Hitchcock Medical Center, Eastman Kodak, Harvard University, Johns Hopkins Medical Center, Johnson & Johnson, Kimberly- Clark Corporation, Nokia, Norwich University, Standard Life Canada, U.S. Army Chaplaincy Corps, U.S. Army Corps of Engineers, U.S. Treasury Office of the Comptroller of the Currency, and Yale University, and Walt Disney World.

Trust Building® Training Programs

The Reinas, through their firm, The Reina Trust Building Institute, provide training programs that put the principles and trust building tools discussed in this book into action. The programs include a core Trust Building® program, an executive briefing, a women leaders program and a certification program.

Coaching

If you would like to work directly with Dennis or Michelle, they offer Transformative Trust-Based Coaching. Through a process of inquiry, reflection, and discussion, you can learn how to use the Reina's trust building and healing approach to transform your relationships at work and in life.

TRUST BUILDING® RESOURCES

Trust Building® Measurement Tools

Dennis and Michelle Reina have developed researched-based, statistically valid and reliable web-based tools to measure trust and benchmark your trust building progress at the organization, team, individual, leader, customer, and patient levels.

Trust Building® On-Line

This powerful community building tool creates a 24/7 asynchronous (not-at-the-same-time) self-paced or facilitator-led web-based learning environment that supports sustainable trust building that is integrated with business desired outcomes.

The Trust & Betrayal Model®

Desktop quick reference guides and wall charts of the Trust & Betrayal Model® illustrated throughout this book are available. They are great tools to support discussion and to maintain awareness and practice of trust-building behaviors.

The Trust Building® in the Workplace Learning Guide

The Learning Guide is loaded with activities to help you practice the behaviors of trust building and put the principles into action. This provides an excellent complement to this book and the model.

Trust Building® Action Learning Equipment

The most powerful way to learn about trust is through experience. We have developed trust building action-learning equipment that provides participants with shared experiences of trust that help them put the principles into action. These stimulating experiences create the "safe container" to have trust-related discussions with the people with whom you work. These fun, engaging tools may be used with a group as small as six or with hundreds.

Contact Information

If you would like to book Dr. Dennis Reina or Dr. Michelle Reina for a speaking event, consultation, training, or coaching; to find out about their trust building tools, programs, and workshops; or to register for their newsletter, please go to their company website:

www.ReinaTrustBuilding.com

or contact their office at:

The Reina Trust Building Institute
560 Black Bear Run
Stowe, VT 05672
Phone: 802-253-8808
Fax: 802-253-8818
E-mail: info@reinatrustbuilding.com

ABOUT BERRETT-KOEHLER PUBLISHERS

Berrett-Koehler is an independent publisher dedicated to an ambitious mission: Creating a World that Works for All.

We believe that to truly create a better world, action is needed at all levels—individual, organizational, and societal. At the individual level, our publications help people align their lives and work with their deepest values. At the organizational level, our publications promote progressive leadership and management practices, socially responsible approaches to business, and humane and effective organizations. At the societal level, our publications advance social and economic justice, shared prosperity, sustainable development, and new solutions to national and global issues.

We publish groundbreaking books focused on each of these levels. To further advance our commitment to positive change at the societal level, we have recently expanded our line of books in this area and are calling this expanded line "BK Currents."

A major theme of our publications is "Opening Up New Space." They challenge conventional thinking, introduce new points of view, and offer new alternatives for change. Their common quest is changing the underlying beliefs, mindsets, institutions, and structures that keep generating the same cycles of problems, no matter who our leaders are or what improvement programs we adopt.

We strive to practice what we preach—to operate our publishing company in line with the ideas in our books. At the core of our approach is *stewardship*, which we define as a deep sense of responsibility to administer the company for the benefit of all of our "stakeholder" groups: authors, customers, employees, investors, service providers, and the communities and environment around us. We seek to establish a partnering relationship with each stakeholder that is open, equitable, and collaborative.

We are gratified that thousands of readers, authors, and other friends of the company consider themselves to be part of the "BK Community." We hope that you, too, will join our community and connect with us through the ways described on our website at www.bkconnection.com.

BE CONNECTED

Visit Our Website

Go to www.bkconnection.com to read exclusive previews and excerpts of new books, find detailed information on all Berrett-Koehler titles and authors, browse subject-area libraries of books, and get special discounts.

Subscribe to Our Free E-Newsletter

Be the first to hear about new publications, special discount offers, exclusive articles, news about bestsellers, and more! Get on the list for our free e-newsletter by going to www.bkconnection.com.

Participate in the Discussion

To see what others are saying about our books and post your own thoughts, check out our blogs at www.bkblogs.com.

Get Quantity Discounts

Berrett-Koehler books are available at quantity discounts for orders of ten or more copies. Please call us toll-free at (800) 929-2929 or email us at bkp.orders@aidcvt.com.

Host a Reading Group

For tips on how to form and carry on a book reading group in your workplace or community, see our website at www.bkconnection.com.

Join the BK Community

Thousands of readers of our books have become part of the "BK Community" by participating in events featuring our authors, reviewing draft manuscripts of forthcoming books, spreading the word about their favorite books, and supporting our publishing program in other ways. If you would like to join the BK Community, please contact us at bkcommunity@bkpub.com.